William Gallogly Moorhead

Outline Studies in the Books of the Old Testament

William Gallogly Moorhead

Outline Studies in the Books of the Old Testament

ISBN/EAN: 9783337312442

Printed in Europe, USA, Canada, Australia, Japan

Cover: Foto ©Lupo / pixelio.de

More available books at **www.hansebooks.com**

Outline Studies
In the Old Testament

OUTLINE STUDIES IN THE BOOKS OF THE OLD TESTAMENT.

W. G. MOOREHEAD, D.D.
Prof. of New Testament Exegesis in United Presbyterian Theological Seminary.

New York : Chicago : Toronto
Fleming H. Revell Company
London and Edinburgh

Entered according to Act of Congress, in the year 1893, by Fleming H. Revell Company, in the office of the Librarian of congress at Washington. All rights reserved.

PREFACE.

A survey of the Bible, however cursory and partial, cannot but prove helpful; for the book is a great light-center, and no one can wander into its neighborhood without catching some of its beams. These Outline Studies in the books of the Old Testament pretend to be no more than helps in the reading of the Scriptures—than to catch a few of the beams that radiate from that fountain of light. How imperfect they are no one can so fully realize as the author. They are neither critical nor expository. They are designed for beginners in Bible study. The one aim has been to furnish for Young People an analysis of the contents of each book, and some of the more prominent features.

In the preparation of the Outlines all available aid has been freely employed, more especially Fraser's Synoptical Lectures, Horne's Introduction, Smith's Dictionary of the Bible, Stanley's Lectures, Edersheim's Temple Service, and various Commentaries.

If these Studies serve to deepen in any one the conviction that the Scriptures are the very Word of God, and that the entrance of their inspired words "giveth light," none will so rejoice as the author.

W. G. MOOREHEAD.

Xenia, Ohio.

PREFACE TO THE SECOND EDITION.

To the great surprise of the author who anticipated no such fortune for his book, a second edition of these Outline Studies seems to be called for. Candor prompts him to say that the surprise is a grateful one. Many needed corrections have been made for this edition, though perhaps not all the mistakes have been detected.

W. G. MOOREHEAD.

XENIA, O., April, 1894.

CONTENTS.

	PAGE		PAGE
Bible Study	5	Song	197
Scrip. Types	12	Prophecy	206
Genesis	18	Isaiah	218
Exodus	26	Jeremiah	240
Leviticus	37	Lamentations	256
Numbers	49	Ezekiel	260
Deut	56	Daniel	275
Joshua	62	The Minor Prophets	297
Judges	70	Hosea	300
Ruth	80	Joel	307
I Sam'l	88	Amos	313
II Sam'l	97	Obadiah	320
I and II Kings	105	Jonah	323
I aud II Chron	113	Micah	332
Ezra	121	Nahum	338
Nehemiah	127	Habakkuk	343
Esther	132	Zephaniah	345
Job	140	Haggai	348
Psalms	157	Zechariah	352
Proverbs	182	Malachi	361
Ecclesiastes	190		

BIBLE STUDY.

The object of the following pages is to furnish the student of Scripture with the outlines of the Old Testament books. The design, analysis and principal subjects of each book are given as fully as the prescribed limits will permit.

But before we enter upon these studies some preliminary matters require brief mention.

First: The temper of mind with which Scripture should be studied. In its origin and contents the Bible differs from other books. It comes to us with divine sanction. It claims to be the word of the living God. It asserts that God has attested the validity of its claims by signs and wonders and mighty deeds. Assuming its plenary inspiration, it follows obviously that the Bible should not be taken up in the spirit in which we approach other books. How shall we read it?

1. The Bible should be studied with the profound conviction that it is the word of God; that it contains a revelation from Him, a revelation of Him, and a revelation of ourselves likewise, 2 Tim. iii:16; Heb. i:1, 2; 2 Peter i:20, 21, etc. We want to settle it definitely with ourselves that this book primarily is not made up of the words of the various writers whose names it records—not of the words of Moses, David, John and Paul—but of the words of God. The inspired writers affirm that these are not their

utterances, that they are not the originators of the messages they deliver. Thus the apostle Peter writes: "Knowing this first, that no prophecy of the Scripture is of any private interpretation," 2 Pet. i:20. By this is meant that it did not originate with the prophet himself, nor is it tied up to the times of the prophets, 1 Pet. i:10, 11. Of course, there is a human element in the Bible. Its language is human, else there would be no revelation at all. Its truth enters into the realm of human reason and intelligence. Nevertheless, let the conviction take firm hold on us when we open the Bible, that God is here speaking to us.

2. In our study of the Book its unity should not be overlooked. The Author of the New Testament is also the Author of the Old. One mind pervades them both, the mind of God. The Epistle to the Hebrews opens with this sublime announcement: "God who at sundry times and in divers manners spake in time past unto the fathers by the prophets hath in these last days spoken unto us by his Son"—in each case, whether by the prophets or by the Son, the Speaker was God. The Old Testament is the promise and prophecy of the New, and the New is the promise and prophecy of glory. The great subjects of the one are identical with those of the other. What lies in the one as buds, blooms into mature foliage and fruit in the other. As an ancient Latin father has well said: "The New Testament lies concealed in the Old, and the Old stands revealed in the New."

3. Christ is the center of Scripture, its one preeminent theme, John v:39; Luke xxiv:27, 44; Acts xxviii:23, etc. The Book had a great variety of

penmen, and these differed from each other very widely as to gifts, natural and acquired. They range all the way from the highest poet and thinker like Moses, David, Isaiah, Paul down to the humblest artisan and rustic, as were Amos, Matthew, Mark and Peter. It stretches over a period of some 1600 years in its composition. And yet it is a book essentially of one idea—one majestic thought runs through it all from first to last, binding together its diversified parts into a single and harmonious whole. Jesus Christ, in His person and work, in His mission and offices, in His first and His second advents, is the one glorious topic of the Bible, its sum. Toward Him all its lines converge; in Him all its strange voices harmonize and blend; in Him its promises and predictions have their fulfillment. If we fail to find Him in the Old Testament, it will become a meaningless and wearisome book to us; for it is a sort of skillfully arranged lattice-work through which the devout reader may always see the Redeemer in His wondrous ways with His people.

4. We should come to the Bible remembering the functions it fulfills in our redemption. Most conspicuous is the place it holds in the salvation of men. By it, as the means in the hands of the Spirit, regeneration is effected, Jas. i:18; 1 Pet. i:23. By it faith is nourished, Rom. x:14, 17; Jno. v:24. By hearing the words of Satan man was lost; by hearing the words of God men are saved; "He that heareth my words and believeth him that sent me hath everlasting life." By the testimony of Scripture we are justified. Rom. iv:3; "Abraham believed God and it was counted unto him for righteousness."

We also believe the same divine testimony as to the righteousness of God in Christ, and are justified. By it we are sanctified. Jno. xvii:17; 2 Thess. ii:13. By it we grow. 1 Pet. ii:1-3. It is the sure remedy for sins. Ps. cxix:11. But why continue the recital? There is no stage in our career, there is no circumstance, or condition, or relation possible to us, but some word of God is exactly adapted thereto; and the chief aim of Bible study is to lead us into so large and accurate acquaintance with the Scriptures as that we shall know how to use them for our guidance and growth.

5. Recognition of the doctrine of progress in the revelation contained in the Bible is another requisite to a right study of the Word. The Book is one of growth. Not all the truth was given at once. Gradually God communicated His mind to men, Heb. i:1. Genesis contains in germ all that the books which follow unfold; the Pentateuch holds in latency all the prophetic writings. Thus the Bible becomes a living organism. Men build their systems much as they build a house, laying beam on beam. God constructs His revelation as He does the oak of the forest. He plants the germinal seed amid the clods of a wasted Eden and it grows and expands parallel with the development of the race. We see the progress referred to in the revelation of the law of love, man's first duty to man. What progress there is from Genesis to 1 Cor. xiii; and yet the love so wonderfully opened in this chapter lies in germ in the oldest records of the Bible. The same truth is seen likewise as to the doctrine of the Godhead, the divine Unity being first insisted on, and then the later revelation of the Trinity. In

fact, progress touches every doctrine and duty of which the Scriptures treat.

6. Another thing to be borne in mind is the supreme authority of the Bible. God has spoken in His word, now speaks. Our duty is to hear and obey. The Bible is not simply a book of opinions; it is not only true, it is the truth, absolute and final. Nothing is to usurp its functions or authority; nothing must be suffered to become its rival. Man's reason and word lead to darkness and infidelity. Man's word mixed with God's is superstition; God's word alone is the exact truth, from which there is no appeal. Whatever this Book repudiates is heresy; whatever it condemns is sin; whatever it is silent on is not essential to salvation. Of all preached from the pulpit, spoken from the platform, read from the press, the prescription is "Take heed what ye hear." Of all spoken by the Lord, recorded by the Spirit, written in the Bible, the injunction is, "Take heed how ye hear." The first may be truth mingled with error, and the duty is to sift it, and to separate what is precious from what is vicious. The last is the pure truth, and the duty lies not in discriminating where there is nothing to discriminate, but in the posture of mind we maintain toward it.

To allow the Book to have supreme sway over us is a vital point. Obedience to the Word as we come to know the Word is an essential element in Bible study. "If any man will do his will he shall know of the doctrine whether it be of God, or whether I speak of myself," Jno. vii:17. This "obedience is the organ of spiritual knowledge." Singleness of heart to please God is the grand inlet for further knowledge. He that honestly uses the light he has shall have more light, and still more. "Then shall we know if we follow on to know the Lord." He who refuses to do God's will, as he comes to know that will, need not be surprised if in process of time the Bible becomes to him a sealed book, and the light that was in him becomes darkness.

Second: The names of God in the Old Testament. His name is that whereby He makes Himself known. His name is a revelation of Himself.

God (Elohim), the first divine name we encounter in the Bible, Gen. i:1, the most comprehensive, perhaps, of all. It is God who creates, who judges, delivers, and executes punishment on evil-doers.

God Almighty (El Shaddai), the all-sufficient One, the infinitely Able One. It expresses a double idea, viz: God's almightiness, His power to fulfill every promise He has made His people; and His faithfulness in performing every word He has spoken, Gen. xvii:1, 2; xlviii:3, 4; xlix:25, etc.

LORD (Jehovah), a name expressive of covenant relationship, Ex. iii:14, 16; iii:4; Lev. xvi; Isa. liii: etc. The LORD is the Self-existent and unchangeable One who enters into covenant engagement with those who are the objects of His pity and love. Perhaps it is not too much to say that Jehovah is God entering into history in His redemptive relations with His people.

Lord (Adonai), Master, Owner, Gen. xv:2-8; Mal. iii:1, etc. In Ezek, xvi:8, 14, 19, 23, 30, we find the two names, Jehovah and Lord, united together, and they appear to denote God as the Master and Husband of His people Israel. The attentive reader of the Bible will easily distinguish between the two names last mentioned by noting that Jehovah is always printed in the best copies of the Bible in small capitals, thus: LORD, whilst the other (Adonai) is printed Lord.

All these great titles of God, and others, are given us in the Old Testament as revelations and manifestations of Him whom to know is eternal life. They designate God's various relations to men. The same thing obtains among us. My father is a man; he is likewise a citizen, an office-bearer, and a man of affairs. But he is especially my father, without ceasing to maintain his other relations. God is the Creator, Sovereign and Judge; but He is the Father of believers without ceasing to be all that is implied in the other titles he takes.

SCRIPTURE TYPES.

Another matter which seems to require mention is, the Typology of the Bible. Inadequate and erroneous views alike are entertained on the subject. Some find types everywhere in the Old Testament, specially in the Pentateuch, others next to none. It is firmly believed that the teaching of Scripture on the subject is neither meagre nor obscure. Only briefest notes are subjoined.

That there are types in the Old Testament no one would venture to deny. The New Testament justifies the assertion. It takes up a large number of persons and events of former dispensations, and treats them as being prefigurations and prophecies of the future. One who has not looked with some care into the subject will be astonished to discover how largely the New Testament writers find pre-intimations and adumbrations of Christ in the Scriptures of the Old. Care must be had, however, in the pursuit of such a study, for we are not inspired. Let this two-fold caution be our guide: (1) Not to seek for types everywhere; (2) never to press the typical teaching to such an extent as to imperil the historical character of the Bible. Let it be remembered that exposition is not imposition, nor is it interpretation to draw out what *we* have first read in.

Our word *type* is derived from the Greek term *tupos*, which occurs sixteen times in the New Testament. It is variously translated, e. g., twice *print*, John xx:25; twice *figure*, Acts vii:43; Rom. v:14; once *fashion*, Acts vii:44; once *manner*, Acts xxiii:25; once *form*, Rom. vi:17; twice *pattern*, Titus ii:7; Heb. viii:5; and seven times *example*, 1 Cor. x:6, 11; Phil. iii:17; 1 Thess. i:7; 2 Thess. iii:9; 1 Tim. iv:12; 1 Pet. v:3. It is clear from these texts that the inspired writers use the word type with some degree of latitude of application. Nevertheless, we observe that one general idea is common to them all, one thought predominates; viz, *likeness*. A person, event, or thing is so appointed or fashioned as that it resembles another: the one is made to answer to the other in some essential particulars; the one matches the other in some prominent feature. The two things thus related receive the names of *type* and *anti-type;* and the link which binds them together is this correspondence, or resemblance, of the one with the other.

Types are a set of pictures, or object-lessons by which God would teach His people about His grace and saving power. The Mosaic system was a sort of kindergarten school; and yet some of the deepest things of revelation are found in these ancient types. An old writer has said, "God in the types of the last dispensation was teaching His children their letters. In this dispensation He is teaching them to put these letters together, and they find that the letters, arrange them as they will, spell Christ, and nothing but Christ."

In creation God uses one thing for many purposes One simple instrument meets many ends. For how many ends does water serve! And the atmosphere: —it supplies the lungs, supports fire, conveys sound, diffuses odors, gives rain, wafts ships, fulfills besides one does not know how many other purposes. And God's Word is like His work, *is* His work, and like creation, it, too, is inexhaustible. How large a place the ark of the covenant filled in Israel! It was the central piece of the tabernacle; at it God gave communications to His servants; at it propitiation was made or completed; it led the people; it parted the waters of the Jordan; and yet what a type of good things to come the ark was. So also was the high priest, who, notwithstanding the varied service he rendered the people, was, in all that he did and in his very office and dress, an eminent type of Christ. Whatever God touches, be it a mighty sun or an insect's wing, a great prophecy or a little type, He perfects, for the place and the end for which He designed it.

I. What are the distinctive features of types? A type to be such must possess three qualities. 1. It must be a true picture of the thing it represents or typifies. Hence a type is a draft or image of some great feature of redemption. 2. The type must be of divine appointment. The type is designed in its original institution to resemble its antitype. Both are pre-ordained as constituent parts of the scheme of redemption. As centuries often lie between the type and its accomplishment in the antitype, of course infinite wisdom alone could institute and ordain the one to be the picture of the other. Only God can make types. 3. A type always prefigures something future. In all Scripture types there is prophecy. Prediction and type differ in form rather than in nature. This fact distinguishes between a symbol and a type: a symbol may represent a thing of the present or past as well as one of the future—e. g., the symbols in the Lord's supper. A type always looks toward the future. Another thing in the study of types should be borne in mind, viz., that a thing in itself evil, can never be the type of good.

II. *Classification of types.* They may be distributed under three heads: 1. Personal types; by which are meant those personages of Scripture whose lives illustrate some truth or principle of redemption. Such are Adam, Melchizedek, Abraham, Moses, Jonah, etc. 2. Historical: in which are included the great historical events that under the guidance of Providence became striking foreshadowings of good things to come: e. g., the deliverance from Egypt, wilderness journey, conflict for Canaan, etc. 3. Ritual: such as the altar, sacrifices, priesthood, tabernacle, etc. There are typical persons, places, times, things, actions, in the Old Testament Scriptures, and a reverent study of them leads into acquaintance with the fullness and blessedness of the Word.

III. Characteristic differences in the types of certain books of the Bible. 1. Those of Genesis are mainly personal and historical. It is the book of beginnings—of sin and judgment; of mercy and forgiveness. Accordingly, here are types which connect with the person and work of the Deliverer: *e. g.* Adam, Melchizedek, Abraham, Joseph (see Rom. v:14; Rom. iv:1-25; Gal. iii:6-14; Heb. vii:7). 2. The types of Exodus have other features. They bring out more especially the precious doctrine of redemption by blood, and its blessed consequences. The passover, appointment of the priesthood, and the tabernacle, are the proof of it. The blood of the paschal lamb lay at the foundation of Israel's relation with God, and it prefigured, at the same time, that great redemption which Christ in due time was to accomplish: Ex. xv:13, 16, 17; 1 Cor. v:7. 3. Those of Leviticus differ from the preceding. Here we find types that contemplate access to God; restoration to the divine favor when sin has come in to interrupt communion, and holiness of person and walk. Of course, the ritual of Leviticus has to do with sin, but it is the sin of a people who have been redeemed from bondage, and separated unto God; and this fact invests the types of the book with a peculiar character. 4. Those of Numbers are suggestive of the wilderness life and pilgrim journey of the people of God. 5. In the types of Joshua we encounter another phase of the general subject. These relate to the possession of the promised inheritance, and the soldier life, as we may call it, of the saints. Joshua should be studied in connection with the Epistle to the Ephesians. The two books match each other as type and antitype. Furthermore, the types of Genesis are mainly intended for the instruction of the individual believer; while those of the books that follow contemplate a corporate body of worshipers.

IV. How much of the Old Testament is to be regarded as typical? Two extremes are to be avoided. First, the extravagance of the Church Fathers, as Origen, Jerome and Ambrose (revived in our day by Andrew Jukes). They sought for types in every incident and transaction recorded in Scripture. Even the most simple circumstance was believed to hide in itself the most recondite truth. Mystery and mysticism were seen everywhere, in the cords and pegs of the Tabernacle, in the fruits of the field, in the yield of herds, in the death of one, and marriage of another. The serious objection to this system is, that it wrests Scripture out of the sphere of the natural and locates it in that of the arbitrary and fanciful: it ignores the historical facts and tends to destroy the validity of the record. Second, the undue contraction of the typical element. Prof. Moses Stuart expresses the view as follows: "Just so much of the Old Testament is to be accounted typical as the New Testament affirms to be so, and no more." This opinion assumes that the New Testament writers have exhausted the types of the Old, whereas these examples of the typical bearing of the Old Testament are obviously but samples taken from the storehouse where many more are found. If they are not, then nothing is more arbitrary than the New Testament use of types. For there is nothing to distinguish these from a multitude of others in the Old Testament to which the typical element so manifestly belongs. The view assumes that divine authority alone can determine the reality and import of types—a view that applies with equal force against prophecy. Besides, it unwarrantably separates the two Testaments, and discards a large portion of the Old. Wherever the three characteristic features already mentioned are found in any event, transaction or person of the Old Testament there is a type.

GENESIS.

The title of the first book of the Bible is of very ancient date, and is well chosen. *Genesis* means the source or primal cause of things; and this book relates the beginning or origination of the earth and all that it contains. Genesis also is the beginning of the revelation of God to man, the Bible. Here are the germs, the deeply fastened roots of all that follows after. Here are the beginnings of the human race, the family, the community and the nation, of sin and sacrifice, of promise and prophecy, of language, of arts, civilization and history.

Broadly, the first five books of Scripture may be described thus: Genesis records the introduction of sin into the world, and its consequences; Exodus teaches the doctrine of redemption by blood; Leviticus, access to God, worship, holiness; Numbers, the pilgrim life of God's people; Deuteronomy, obedience, the blessedness of obeying God, the misery attending disobedience.

Genesis falls naturally into two parts: Part I., chapters i-xi, which contain a very brief but very comprehensive history of the world from the creation to the confusion of tongues; Part II., chapters xii-l, which narrate the history of Abraham and his family to the death of his great grandson Joseph. By far the larger portion of the book, it is thus seen, is occupied with the story of the chosen people, Abraham and his descendants; and from this twelfth chapter of Genesis to the close of the Old Testament, the Bible is devoted to Israel and to God's ways with that favored but disobedient race.

The principal topics of the book are the following:

1. *Creation*, Gen. i. All readers must admire the simple majesty of this remarkable chapter. Three times the word "create" is used in it, verses 1, 21, 27, and each time it marks an epoch or era in the sublime process of the Almighty's work. Some timid Christians have been not a little disturbed by alleged scientific discoveries which appeared to antagonize if not demolish this Mosaic account of creation. They were needlessly alarmed. As time goes on and thoughtful men come to know more about the truth of this marvelous universe in which we dwell, they approach closer and closer to Moses' record. Never, perhaps, in the history of scientific investigation, did Gen. i. stand so solidly and triumphantly as now! "In the year 1806, the French Institute enumerated not less than eighty geological theories which were hostile to the Scriptures; but not one of those theories is held today" (Prof. Lyell, cited by Dr. Townsend). If the Bible is God's book, we may settle it definitely in our minds that it will come forth out of the smoke of battle with a lustre all the brighter for the conflict. This account of creation reveals the unity, power and personality of God. It denies polytheism—one God creates. It denies the eternity of matter—"in the beginning" God made it. It denies pantheism—God is before all things, and apart from them. It

denies fatalism—God here as everywhere acts in the freedom of His eternal Being (Murphy).

2. *The Fall*, chapter iii. "The story of the fall, like that of creation, has wandered over the world. Heathen nations have transplanted and mixed it up with their geography, their history, their mythology, although it has never so completely changed form and color and spirit that you cannot recognize it" (Delitzsch).

One of the strange proofs of the truthfulness of this account, if proof were needed, is found in the universal presence of *serpent worship* in the olden times. It was practiced in China, India, Palestine, Greece, Ireland, Italy, Africa—in short, all over the world. No other religious form was more common, save sun-worship, with which this was usually associated. Our own continent bears testimony to its presence in some of the ancient remains. In southern Ohio there exists a huge snake made out of earth and stones, a thousand feet long or more, and which was once an object of homage on the part of the aborigines. The savage of Louisiana carried a serpent and sun, the symbols of his religion, and tattooed them on his skin. In Mexico the serpent is found in the rude pictures of that strange people, the Aztecs, entwined with their most sacred symbols. The main elements of serpent-worship were, a tree, a woman, and a serpent. George Smith in his "Chaldean Account of Genesis" presents his readers with a fac-simile of a drawing found in the excavations about Babylon which has two figures sitting on either side of a tree, holding out their hands toward the fruit, while back of one of them is stretched a serpent. Singular that rational beings should pay their highest honors to a repulsive snake!

It was one aim of the old Serpent, the Devil, in the temptation of our first parents, to put himself in the place of God as an object of worship. How well he succeeded, the universality of this form of idolatry attests.

3. *The Flood*, chapters vi-viii. There are three supreme tragedies connected with the history of our race; the fall, the flood and the cross. The flood was God's judgment on the guilty world; Calvary was His judgment on the sins of His people in the person of their blessed Substitute, Christ.

The sin which called down the judgment of heaven on the apostate race is referred to in Gen. xi:1-8. It was the intermarriage of the sons of God with the daughters of men. Who are meant by the "sons of God?" Many interpreters think the angels. There are very strong objections to this view. Good angels would not commit this sin: bad angels are not called "sons of God." The statement in Jude 6, 7, may mean that the sin of the fallen angels was spiritually what that of Sodom was carnally. Besides, the offspring of these unholy alliances are called men, which they could not be if the product of demons and women, Gen. vi:4, 5. It seems more natural and Scriptural to regard the "sons of God" as the pious Sethites. Already the separation of the godly from the wicked had taken place, Gen. iv:26. The former called themselves by the name of the Lord. Their sin was their breaking through the barrier, ignoring their call and character, and their going over into the ranks of the wicked and contracting evil alliances with them. It was deliberate and universal apostasy from God.

4. *Origin of languages and nationalities*, chapters x, xi. The tenth chapter anticipates the disaster recorded in the eleventh. The division of one race into tribes and nations was necessitated by the confusion of tongues. Sixty-nine are mentioned, of whom sixteen are independent and the rest affiliated nations.

This is another fruit of sin, the first sin. What a prolific thing sin is! Good may have arisen from the formation of separate nations and the partition of the earth among them; but how much evil likewise. How these nations have trampled each other out in the rage of their huge passions.

Tongues originated in judgment, the gift of tongues in grace. When God gave the law telling what man ought to be, He spoke in one language. When He told at Pentecost what He is, He spoke in many tongues. What a barrier difference of language is to intercourse among the peoples of the earth; what an obstacle to the progress of missions, and even to a full knowledge of the inspired word! No wonder John Trapp wrote (1660) this about it: "This great labor hath God laid upon the sons of men, that a great part of our best time is spent about the shell (in learning of language) before we can come at the kernel of true wisdom, especially Scripture wisdom." In the last book of the Bible, Babel, Shinar, tribes, nations and tongues are all gone; and paradise lost is succeeded by paradise regained.

5. *The Chosen People,* xii-l. This part of Genesis relates to the origin of the Hebrews and their history from Abraham to the emigrations into

Egypt. In it we have (1) Abraham's call, xii. His ancestors were idolators, Josh. xxiv:2. As a solemn protest against that system, as also the forming of the new stock from which the Messiah was to spring was Abraham led away from his country and friends. There seem to be two stages in his call. The first, when he left Ur and settled at Haran, Acts vii:3; Gen. xi:29-32. The second, when he departed from Haran and dwelt in Canaan, Gen. xi:1-6. He was 60 when he departed from Ur, and 75 when he went forth from Haran. He went out blindfold, but the God of glory led him by the hand, Heb. xi: 8. (2) God's covenant with Abraham, xv. The parties are, God and the patriarch—but God does all, pledges all, promises all; and it is all of grace, there being no conditions to be fulfilled by Abraham. (3) Ratification of the covenant, xvii. Circumcision, its sign and seal added. (4) The covenant attested by God's oath, xxii. (5) The history of Isaac, xxiv-xxvi. Twice was the covenant ratified to Isaac; once at Gerar, then at Beersheba, xxvi. (6) The history of Jacob, xxvii-xxxv. The covenant was confirmed to Jacob at Bethel, xxviii (first time); at Bethel, xxxv (second time); at Beersheba, xlvi; when on the way to Egypt. These three patriarchs are the covenant-heads of Israel—and the enactment and ratification of the covenant are the prominent features of their lives. After the descent into Egypt by Jacob and his household, no more mention of it is made till the Exodus. (7) The history of Joseph, xxxvii-l.

6. *Chronology.* The dates here given are only approximate. The chronology of the Bible is difficult to unravel.

From Adam to the flood, 1656 years.

From flood to call of Abraham, 367, or 427, if born at 130 of Terah's age.

From call of Abraham to Jacob's migration into Egypt, 215.

Sojourn in Egypt, 430.

Abraham was about 100 years old when Isaac was born. Isaac was 59 and Abraham 159 when Jacob was born. Jacob's life overlaped Abraham's sixteen years. Jacob was 130 when he migrated to Egypt. Rawlinson is of opinion his "household" numbered at that time 3,400 souls, ("Moses," p. 2). Joseph was 39 when his father went down to him, and he survived Jacob about fifty-four years.

Transmission of the ancient traditions. Noah could receive from his father Lamech what he had received direct from Adam: Shem could transmit it to Abraham, and he to Jacob. So that the account of the Creation, the Fall, the Flood, and Abraham's call could pass through only five hands between Adam and Jacob.

7. A prominent fact that Genesis teaches is the connection between sin and suffering. These two have been named the "Twin Serpents," and the name is well chosen. Sin, suffering; the one follows the other as certainly as night the day. It is a fixed and imperative law. Expulsion from Eden follows the transgression of our first parents. Expulsion from the presence of the Lord was Cain's punishment. The flood was the necessary issue of the admixture of the "sons of God" with the "daughters of men," Gen. vi:2, 3. It is always so; it is the history of man. He that sins must suffer. He that is profligate in his youth must have rotten-

ness in his bones, a worm that never dies, and a tongue that no drop can cool, if he repent not. "Be not deceived; God is not mocked; whatsoever a man soweth, that shall he also reap," Gal. vi:7, 8. *That!* Not another kind of harvest, but *that*—the product of the seed sown.

8. Another great truth taught in this earliest record of human things is *separation*. No sooner had sin entered into the world than God began to call out His own servants and people from among the ungodly. From the beginning He drew the line of separation between His own and the wicked broad and deep. When His people crossed the line, went over into the camp of the enemy, corruption ensued, and judgment fell on the guilty world. This principle holds still: "Come out from among them, and be ye separate, saith the Lord, 2 Cor. vi:17, 18.

9. *Dangerous Confederacies.* We have an example of such danger in the oldest Union of which history speaks, that of Babel, and its huge tower. The annals of the race are full of the like disastrous efforts of men to unite in compact bodies independent of God, and in hostility to His will. The business of a Christian is to keep clear of all entangling alliances. "Shouldest thou help the ungodly, and love them that hate the Lord?" 2 Chron. xix:2.

EXODUS.

The second book of Scripture is closely connected with the first. *Now* might be read *And;* for the first verse of Exodus is a repetition of Gen. xlvi:8. The whole law is a conjunction, the schoolmen used to say. Exodus continues the story of the chosen people. The theme of the book is the deliverance of Israel from the oppression of Egypt, and their separation to God. The key-verse is Exodus xii:13; the key-word, *blood*.

The chief figure is Moses, whose life is divided into three periods of forty years each, forty years' training in the learning of Egypt; forty years' training in God's school in the desert, Ex. iii;1; and forty years as the leader and law-giver of Israel.

The book may be divided into three parts:

I. Bondage of Egypt, chaps. i-v.

II. God's intervention for Israel's deliverance, vi-xviii.

III. The Law at Sinai; The Theocracy constituted, xix-xl.

Exodus has three principal topics, viz.: the passover, the law, and the tabernacle; i. e., redemption, obedience, worship; life, loyalty, love.

1. *The Oppression*, chapters i, ii. How long it continued before God interfered on behalf of His suffering people, is not known. Probably it culmi-

nated under the long reign of the great monarch Rameses II, "Child of the Sun," "whose proud and scornful face with its curling nostril and peculiar fall of the lower lip, with its long profile so majestic and beautiful, is seen on the monuments of Egypt to this day" (Stanley). It was this man, no doubt, to whom it was pretended the gods gave the falchion of destruction with the command, "Slay, and slay, and slay," who caused the Israelites to serve with rigor, and who made their lives bitter. God saw their affliction, and came down for their deliverance. "When the tale of bricks is doubled then comes Moses." This is the proverb which has sustained the Jews through many a long oppression.

2. *The Judgments on Egypt*, chapters vii-xi. As we read the description of the ten plagues, we discover that each of them is aimed at some idolatrous practice, or at some despotic feature of the government of the Egyptians. It was not an ordinary river whose waters were turned into blood, but the sacred Nile, to which religious honors were paid. It was not the common cattle that died in the fields, but the calf of Heliopolis, the bull of Memphis, to both of which worship was given. It was a nation that worshipped the sun, that called its king "the Child of the Sun," which sat in darkness for three days. It was the governing class, the haughty men who wielded the absolute power of death, the proud and stubborn nation, whose first born were smitten with death. What God did in Egypt was for a *sign* to men. He poured shame and ruin on the beast-worship, water-worship, sun-worship, and tyranny of the land.

3. *The Passover*, chapters xii, xiii. This is the

prominent feature of Exodus, and one of the most significant ordinances of Israel's after-history. The fundamental doctrine of atonement, revealed in Genesis, speaks forth in this second book in unmistakable terms. Israel was sheltered by the blood on the night when the angel-destroyer passed through the land. God's word about the blood was, "When I see the blood I will pass over you." They were a poor, enslaved, ignorant people, despised by their masters, degraded in their own eyes. But with the blood-sign of atonement upon them, they were "comely" in God's sight. "Thou seest no iniquity in Jacob nor perverseness in thine Israel," was Balaam's testimony not long after. Blood redeemed, sanctified, and delivered them.

The exodus marked a new era in the history of the chosen people. The month of deliverance became the first of their calendar ever after. It was pre-eminently Israel's redemption whereby they were brought into new and more intimate relations with God, just as the death of Christ who "is our passover, sacrificed for us," is the eternal salvation of all believers.

4. *Sinai and the Law*, chapters xix-xxiv. Save Calvary, no other spot is hallowed with such stupendous scenes as Sinai. Everything around tended to make the occasion a most impressive one. The massive grandeur of those rocky heights, the frowning peaks in all directions encircling the mount, with every outward form of animal and vegetable life withdrawn; the thunders and the lightnings; the voice of the trumpet, the descent of the darkness on the summit, all combined to render the revelation there given the most solemn and imposing.

The law given at Sinai consists of two parts: the decalogue, and the secondary laws which flow from it. Lying at the base of all other legislation of the Jewish dispensation are the ten commandments. These "Ten Words," as they are called, constitute the very essence of the covenant with Israel. Considered as a religious and ethical code, the decalogue sums up in the tersest form all human duties, whether toward God or man.

The secondary laws are those which springing out of the decalogue, were more particularly intended to regulate the conduct of the people in their relations with one another, chapters xxi-xxiii. They may be thus grouped: Laws connected with the rights of persons, of property, the Sabbath and festivals. They are civil, criminal and ceremonial laws. Israel constituted a theocracy. God was the Head and Sovereign; the people were to be a nation of priests unto Him; therefore holy, upright, pure and honest.

5. *The place of worship, the tabernacle*, chapters xxv-xl. It was the Lord's dwelling-place among His people, xxv. It is commonly called "the tabernacle of the congregation," as if it were the meeting-place of the tribes. But this is not all the meaning of the phrase. The revision of the Old Testament has done good service in the cause of truth in rendering it uniformly, "the tent of the meeting," for it was here that God and His people met together; here that He gave forth His oracles for their guidance and instruction. It is quite suggestive that He chose a *tent* for His dwelling. It denotes how completely and graciously He identified Himself with His own. If they dwell in tents,

so will He. If they journey, He will also Where they go He goes. "In all their affliction He was afflicted."

The tabernacle had two compartments, the first called the Holy Place in which were the golden Candlestick, the Table of Shew-bread, and the Altar of incense—i. e., light, food, communion; the second, the Most Holy Place which contained the Ark of the Covenant, with its Mercy-seat or Propitiatory, and overshadowing cherubim—the Throne of the Lord, that symbolized the Throne of Grace, Heb. iv:16. The compartments were separated by a strongly woven veil, four fingers in thickness, the Rabbins say, with its three colors, blue, purple, and scarlet, in-wrought with symbolic figures. The Most Holy Place was shrouded in darkness, and was inaccessible save to the High Priest who entered it but once a year. A court surrounded the Tabernacle within which were placed the Altar of Sacrifice and the Lavar, and the Priests and Levites lodged. Kitto's estimate of the cost of the Holy Tent is $1,250,000; William Brown's, $1,500,000.

That the Tabernacle was designed to embody vital truth and teach it to God's people is certain. In Heb. ix:9 we are told it was "a parable for the time then present"—an object-lesson to faith. What did it teach? (1) It symbolized God's presence with His people, Ex. xxv:8, "That I may dwell among them, Ex. xxix:44-46. Cf. 2 Cor. vi:16. (2) It taught the necessity of holiness. God's dwelling with His people in the Tabernacle demanded holiness on their part, Lev. xx:26; xxi:8; Num. v:3, etc. It was His presence with them that made them what they were. He identifies Himself with

His children now more intimately than then, Jno. xiv:23; Eph. ii:20-22; I Jno. iv:16, etc. Once He dwelt *among* His people, now He dwells *in* them. By and by there will be a more glorious and ineffable tabernacling with the redeemed, Rev. xxi: 3, 4. (3) It was a figure of God's plan of bringing sinners to Himself, Heb. ix:23. By means of the blood of beasts the people were made ceremonially clean, and relationship with God was maintained. By the blood of Christ we are brought into eternal fellowship with Him. The altar of sacrifice set forth the truth about pardon, justification: the laver, cleansing, or sanctification. In short, the rites of the Tabernacle were a type of God's method of salvation. (4) It was a symbol of the incarnation of the Son of God, Jno. i:14; "and the word was made flesh, and dwelt (tabernacled) among us." The Lord dwelt with His people according to His promise, Lev. xxvi:11, 12, in the Sanctuary. But now He has come to take up His permanent abode with them by "wedding Himself forever to their flesh." We note a sort of progress in the manifestation of God to men—first, His presence in the Tabernacle. Second, the Incarnation. Third, the indwelling of the Holy Spirit. Fourth, the descent of the New Jerusalem, the Heavenly Tabernacle, into the glorified earth.

6. For the service of the Tabernacle Aaron and his sons were set apart as priests, together with the Tribe of Levi who were to execute the duties assigned them under the direction of the priests, Ex. xxviii; Num. iv.

7. *The pillar of cloud and of fire*, Ex. xiii:21, 22. Its first appearance was at Etham, "in the edge of

the wilderness." This fact is very suggestive. Just when all roads and canals, cities and villages are left behind, and an untried and trackless wilderness lies before the people, then God provides for them the mysterious cloud which never leaves them till the long journey is over, and guidance is no longer required.

(1) The cloud symbolized God's presence with His people, Ex. xiv:19, 24, 25; xxxiii:9, 10.

(2) The cloud served as a guide for the people, Ex. xiii:21; Num. ix:17, 18; Ps. lxxviii:14; Neh. ix: 19, etc. They were incompetent to be their own guides. He alone who had brought them into "the great and terrible wilderness" was able to conduct them through it. Hobab's "eyes" would not do, Num. x:31; only Jehovah was sufficient.

(3) It adapted itself to their necessity, Neh. ix: 19. It was a leader by day, a pillar of fire by night.

(4) It was a shelter for the people, Num. x:34; Ps. cv:39.

(5) It was a defense, Ex. xiv:19; Deut. i:30. In all the various offices and movements of the cloud, that which most impresses the reader is this, the minuteness of God's care for His people, His personal interest in them. Nothing is too small for Him to do for them, nothing too great. He studies their comfort, attends to every detail of their lives and their happiness. He is just as mindful of His children now. "But the very hairs of your head are numbered," Matt. x:30; "casting all your care upon Him for He careth for you," 1 Pet. v:7. Over us also He throws the great ægis of His protecting care, and beneath His wings how safe we are!

8. Israel's sojourn in Egypt. Is it possible to

ascertain its duration? Can we reconcile the apparently discrepant statements of Scripture with respect to it?

In Gen. xv:13 God announced to Abraham that his seed would be a stranger in a land not theirs, and be afflicted 400 years. Stephen in his defence before the Sanhedrin quoted this prediction, and identified it with the oppression of Egypt, Acts vii:6-19. One land is denoted, not two countries. This is clear from the promise contained in the prediction, "But in the fourth generation they shall come hither again," Gen. xv:16. The affliction, obviously, was to be outside of Canaan, for at its termination Abraham's seed was to be restored to their own land. It is generally held that the term "generation" is equivalent to a period of one hundred years. In Ex. xii:40, 41, it is expressly stated that the duration of the sojourn in Egypt was 430 years. The Septuagint Version has a various reading—"Now the sojourning of the children of Israel which they sojourned in Egypt *and in Canaan* was four hundred and thirty years." But those ancient translators certainly knew the meaning of the expression, "children of Israel," i. e. sons of Jacob. They would hardly be guilty of writing such nonsense as that Abraham, Isaac and Jacob were the children of themselves.

The genealogy recorded in Ex. vi, Num. iii, etc., of the family of Moses and Aaron (Levi) appears to reduce the length of the sojourn to 215 years. But if no omission of links in this table be allowed, a very serious difficulty confronts us. The line runs thus: Jacob, Levi, Kohath, Amram, Moses. Kohath, Moses' grandfather, according to Ex. vi, had four sons, Amram, Izhar, Hebron, and Uzziel. The male descendants of these four men numbered at the time of the Exodus, 8,600, Num. iii:28. If we assign one-fourth of this number to Amram, Moses father, we have over 2,000 males belonging to his family; and the number must be doubled to include the females—4,000 and more in that one household. I Chron. vii:23-27 contains another genealogy covering the same period as that of Ex. vi. According to this table there are at least ten generations between Jacob and Joshua the son of Nun, whereas in Ex. vi there are but five between Jacob and Moses. Moreover, Joshua seems to have been grown at the time of the Exodus. How are we to reconcile this apparent discrepancy between the genealogies of Exodus and I Chron.? Thus: the list of names given in Ex. vi is not complete; some of the generations lying between Jacob and Moses are dropped out. It is not uncommon to find such omissions in genealogical tables of Scripture. In the most important of all, that of Christ in Matt. i, three successive generations are thrown out, viz: the immediate descendants of Athaliah. If we allow for such omissions in Ex. vi, the difficulties are cleared away.

If now we conclude that the sojourn was of 430 years' duration what are we to do with Paul's statement in Gal. iii:17, to-wit: "And this I say, that the covenant that was confirmed before of God (in Christ), the law which was four hundred and thirty years after, cannot disannul, that it should make the covenant of none effect"? If we understand the apostle as dating from the original enactment of the covenant with Abraham (Gen. xv), then he is in conflict with Moses and Stephen whose chronology makes the period between that transaction and the Exodus to be about 645 years. If they are right, or rather, if our interpretation of them be right, then is Paul's date wrong to the extent of two hundred years and more. Is it credible that the man who wrote 2 Tim. iii:16, "All Scripture is given by inspiration of God," and who claimed for his own teaching an authority identical with that of Jesus Christ Himself (1 Cor. vii), should have blundered two hundred years and more in a date with which he was perfectly familiar?

We believe the key to the difficulty, and the solution of the entire question, lies in the apostle's use of the word "confirm before," or confirmed forth, as the original may mean. This word (*prokuroo*) is never employed in the New Testament, nor so far as we have discovered, in the Greek version of the Old, to designate the institution of a thing, a first transaction; it signifies to ratify, or confirm a thing already in existence.

A single instance of its use may be given. In Gen. xxiii we read that Abraham bought a field of Ephron, paying the stipulated price for it in the presence of witnesses, and it "was made sure unto Abraham," verse 17 (Sept. "Establish"). Afterward, Abraham buried Sarah in Machpelah, and so the field with the cave in it "was made sure unto Abraham," verse 20. In this case the word in the Sept. is Paul's "confirm." Nothing can be plainer than this. The burial of Sarah ratified the transaction which had been previously concluded between the two men.

The original institution of the covenant is recorded in Gen. xv, and was accompanied by a solemn sacrifice, the voice of God, and a supernatural darkness. But this covenant was afterward confirmed, as in Gen. xvii, when its sign and seal, circumcision, was added to it. It was again confirmed when Abraham offered Isaac, Gen. xxii. Nor was this all. It was confirmed to Isaac, Gen. xxvi: and to Jacob at Bethel and Beersheba, Gen. xxviii, xxxv, xlvi. The last confirmation was to Jacob when he was on the way to Egypt in the wagons which Joseph had sent to convey him thither. No otherwise can we understand the repeated declarations of Scripture that Isaac and Jacob were associated with Abraham as the divinely chosen heads of the covenant, cf. Ex. ii:24; vi:4-8; xxxii:13; Lev. xxvi:42; 1 Chron. xvi: 16, 17, etc. These three men, these and no others, are the covenant men. But how could Isaac and Jacob be united with Abraham in it? Certainly not in the institution of the covenant, for in that Abraham stood alone. They could only be in the subsequent acts in which God renewed and amplified its terms, and in which He made these two men parties to it with Abraham. And these subsequent acts are precisely the confirmations and ratifications to which Paul alludes in Gal. iii:17.

The last confirmation, in conjunction with the visible manifestation of God, transpired at Beersheba when Jacob was on the way to Egypt, Gen. xlvi:2-4. It is believed that Paul dates his 430 years from this point, and this was precisely 430 years before the exodus, Ex. xii:40, 41. Therefore, Paul perfectly harmonizes in chronology with Moses and Stephen.

LEVITICUS.

The chief design of this third book of Moses is indicated by its title. It is the hand-book of the priests—their guide-book. Naturally it follows Exodus. The tabernacle having been set up, and its services arranged, the duties of its ministers would next be defined. Like Exodus, Leviticus has three main topics: Sacrifice, priesthood, feast. Holiness is the key-word; xvii:11; xx:7, are the key-verses.

Leviticus falls into two general parts:
I. Access to God, chapters i-xvi
II. Sanctification of the people, xvii-xxvii.

There are five sections in the book: 1. Offerings, i-vii. 2. Consecration and investiture of the Priests, viii-x. 3. Holiness both of person and life, xi-xv. 4. Atonement and righteousness, xvi-xxii. 5. Feasts, xxiii-xxvii.

That which strikes the reader of this book is the predominance of sin. The Levitical legislation is mainly occupied with it. Sin, man's sin, sin before and after justification, is the secret of Judaism and the secret of the gospel: Face to face with the Mosaic ritual we are face to face with sin. God's holiness is another prominent feature of this book. He must punish sin; for His righteousness demands reparation for human guilt. In the sacrificing priest and in the blood that streams from the victim, in the fire that consumes it, in the ashes, in the water, in the incense and the prayer, in the distance between Himself and the people, in the darkness and loneliness of the Most Holy Place, His dwelling, we see the solemn portraiture of God's holiness, and His purpose to deal with sin according to its deserts. The multiplicity of the rites with which this book is filled is proof of the insufficiency of such a system to take away sin. The continued round of sacrifices, the altar always wet with blood, brought sin to remembrance rather than judged and removed it, Heb. x:3. But we shall not forget that this book is largely prophetic. Its wondrous, complex typology announces the coming of One by whom all here prefigured shall have its complete fulfillment. Christ is the supreme center about which these ordinances turn; and they are luminous to us now because of the light He sheds upon them.

1. *The Sacrifices of Leviticus*, chapters i-vii. They are pictures of the one offering of Christ. He is the sum of them. As no one of them was a perfect representation of Him and His work, five were instituted in order to set forth something of the perfection of His sacrifice. There are three parties to a sacrifice: the offerer, the priest and the offering. The priest acts as mediator. The priest and priestly action imply God and the sinner who are to be brought together in peace. The offering points unmistakably to sin done, and to the absolute need of expiation. The offerer is the offender who is regarded as identified with His sacrifice.

The main features of the sacrifices are *substitution, imputation, death*. By substitution is meant that the life of the victim is given for that of the offender. In imputation the punishment due the guilty party is charged or imputed to his sacrifice. This transference was symbolized by laying of the hands of the offerer on the head of the victim. And death was the execution of the penalty incurred by the offender.

In the application of sacrificial types we see all the elements just mentioned combined in the person and work of the Lord Jesus. He is at once the Priest, the Offerer, and the Victim. In His death there is priestly action, Heb. ix:14; Jno. x:17, 18. His offering is Himself, Heb. x:10. He and those for whom He acts, are identified, Jno. x:11; Gal. ii:20.

The offerings of Leviticus are divided into two classes, viz: "Sweet savour," which are three—burnt, meat, and peace offerings. The other classes were for expiation, viz: Sin and trespass offerings.

The burnt offering (Lev. 1) heads the list because it had some of the distinctive features of all the others, and was the morning and evening sacrifice to Jehovah, Ex. xxix:42. It was for acceptance and atonement, vss. 3, 4. It was wholly given to Him, and in it He had His satisfaction. It sets forth the devotedness of Jesus, His complete self-surrender to God, Eph. v:2. Its application to believers is in Rom. xii:1, 2. The meat-offering, which was vegetable, was the complement of the burnt offering (Lev. 2), and seems never to have been presented alone save in the case of Cain. It followed a bloody sacrifice; it could not be accepted of itself. Cain came to the Lord with the fruits of the ground. He stood in nature. He refused to acknowledge himself a sinner needing atonement. Abel came as one under condemnation, but as one who knew of the provisions made for pardon. Abel came with blood. "Without shedding of blood there is no remission," Heb. ix:22. Christ is the fulfilment of the meat-offering—the holy, spotless One. But it is only as He is apprehended as the sacrifice for sins that He becomes the food of the soul. Without passing through death He could not have been the meat-offering, Jno. xii:24. The peace-offering, (Lev. 3) was a communion feast; the Lord, the priest, and the offerer had each his portion. The sin and trespass offerings (Lev. 5) contemplated expiation. The bodies of the victims were burned without the camp, as if charged with sin and so judged and consumed, Heb. xiii:11, 12. It was the blood of the sin offering alone which was brought into the Most Holy Place, and sprinkled on the mercy seat, Lev. xvi:14. Having made a perfect offering for sin Christ appears in the presence of God for us, Heb. ix:11, 12, 24.

The sweet savour and the sin offerings are alike in this, that *blood* is the foundation of all right relationship with God. In both kinds the offerer and the victim are identified. They differ in this; the sweet savour were for acceptance and worship. In them what was presented unto God was grateful to Him, and on the ground of it He and the worhiper communed together. In them sin is not the predominant idea. It is in the sin-sacrifice. The essential feature in this last is propitiation. He who came with it came not so much a worshiper as a sinner—not for communion, but for pardon. He came to receive in the person of his substitute, the victim, the punishment due to his sin.

In the sin-offering the *penalty* is prominent: in the trespass offering *ransom*. In the first, expiation is prominent; in the second, satisfaction. Both are fulfilled in Christ who was made sin for us, and who gave His life a ransom for many.

2. *Consecration of Aaron and his sons*, Lev. viii. This ancient ceremony is full of significance. The high priest and his sons were alike washed with water, vs. 6. Aaron was then anointed with the holy oil, the sons were not, vs. 12. (Oil is the emblem of the Spirit, 1 Jno. ii:27; 2 Cor. i:21, 22.) The sin-offering was then slain and the blood sprinkled, vs. 15. Then the blood and the oil mingled were put on Aaron and the sons. Eminent type! Jesus was anointed with the Spirit before His sacrifice, the disciples not. After His death and resurrection, the Spirit was shed forth upon them, Acts ii; Jno. vii:39; xvi:7.

3. *Laws respecting food, etc.*, chapter xi. Why should the great God occupy Himself with such matters? (1) He is concerned in the physical wellbeing of His people. He has redeemed their bodies, and these are objects of His regard as well as the soul. Here is the best system of dietetics ever appointed. (2) In their food and dress the Jews were to be a separate and "peculiar" people. (3) They were to be holy. All the animals they were permitted to eat are of cleanly habits. Israel was taught holiness to the Lord in all things.

4. *Uncleanness, leprosy, etc.*, chapters xii-xv. These laws touch some delicate matters; but studied in a devout and reverent spirit they yield immense profit to the soul. Ruskin tells that his mother compelled

him when a youth to read right through the Bible, even the difficult chapters of Leviticus; these especially held him in greatest restraint, and most influenced his life. The underlying truth in all is sin, its transmission, defilement, incurableness by man, and God's provision for its removal.

5. *Feasts*, chapters xxiii-xxv:19. There are eight of them (if we include the Day of Atonement), and they were designed to remind the people that they were God's tenants-at-will; that the land was not their's, but His; that their time was not their's, but His; that their persons were not their own, but His. Moreover, in the great jubilee, which was the fiftieth year, the sublime doctrine of earth's final redemption, and its restoration to God, and its deliverance from the curse of sin, was constantly taught. What a blessed day that will be when all the people of God even as to their bodies shall be delivered, when the lost inheritance shall be restored, and nature shall sing her glad song of redemption!

6. *Doctrine of the Redeemer*, chapter xxv:24-55. This is a precious section of our book, for it is strikingly illustrative of the work of Christ as the Redeemer. (1) The redeemer in Israel was to be one near of kin with him who was to be redeemed, vss. 25, 48. So Jesus, Heb. ii:14-18. (2) He was to redeem the person, 47-50; Ruth iv:4,5. So Jesus has bought His people, 1 Cor. vi:19, 20. (3) He was to redeem the property that had been disponed away, vss. 25, 29. So, too, Christ hath redeemed for us our lost inheritance, 1 Pet. i:3-5. (4) He was to avenge the brother on his enemies, Num. xxxv:12. The "avenger of blood" seems to have been a near kinsman of the one injured. And Christ will in due

time take vengeance on the enemies of His people, Deut. xxxii:43; 2 Thess. i:6-8.

7. *Obedience, and disobedience, and their consequences,* chapters xxvi, xxvii. The blessedness of obedience is first mentioned and commended, xxvi:1-13. Disobedience and its sure punishment is next painted in the darkest hues, xxvi:14-39; but on repentance God will have pity and restore, xxvi:40-46. In this last section of the chapter there is a distinct prophecy of Israel's final restoration and blessing,—"I am the Lord." Leviticus teaches the great doctrines of purity, separation, sanctification, obedience, service. May it be ours to learn the priceless lesson!

Any study of Leviticus which omits the sixteenth chapter would be defective and unsatisfactory. Accordingly some brief notes are devoted to this very suggestive subject—the day of atonement in Israel. In each of the first four books of the Bible there is one chapter which comes to us with peculiar force, to which we turn almost instinctively for typical instruction. Genesis xxii, which records that strange and impressive scene, the offering of Isaac by his own father, is the first: Exodus xii, which contains the supreme doctrine of redemption by blood, is the second: Leviticus xvi, the atonement chapter, is the third: Numbers xiv, the chapter which narrates Israel's unbelief and failure, is the fourth.

1. Lev. xvi stands alone. No mention is made elsewhere of what took place on that solemn day. It seems to be closely connected with the death of Nadab and Abihu, vs. 1. These two young men had died because of their disobedience and presumption. The priesthood had failed. The insuf-

ficiency of all that had been hitherto appointed was thus made manifest. And so the day of atonement was established as a still deeper display of God's grace and love, and of the inadequacy of Mosaic rites to take away sin.

2. It was observed on the seventh day of the tenth month, and was to be a day of humiliation, vss. 29, 31. Affliction of soul answers to a contrition of heart. The people laid aside all secular employment. The sense of sin was to be deepened to its utmost intensity in the national mind and exhibited in appropriate forms of penitential grief. It was a day of godly sorrow working repentance.

3. It occurred but once a year. As seven is the perfect number, so a year is a full and complete period. There is no time that does not fall within the year. It was *the day* of the Mosaic economy. It pointed to the supreme fact:—"Christ was once offered to bear the sins of many," Heb. ix:28 (the word for "once" is strong—*once for all*). There is no repetition of His sacrificial work. In the whole year of time there is but one atonement day, Rom. vi:9, 10; Heb. ix:26.

4. The high priest. The day imposed upon him the most weighty duties. We are told that one week before the day came he left his own house and dwelt in the sanctuary. During the night preceding it he was denied sleep, and on the day itself he fasted until evening. His dress was not that of "beauty and glory" which on other great festival occasions he wore, but one of pure linen, vs. 4. No gold glittered on his brow, nor tinkled in his steps, nor mingled its brilliancy with the royal colors of his robe. All was laid aside. One cannot but think

of the inspired description of the high priest's great anti-type, the Lord Jesus, Phil. ii:6-11. He humbled Himself, put off His robes of glory when He came down into this world to offer Himself a sacrifice for sin. It was an earth-like garment He wore while He was here, though ever and anon He let it swing open for a little that the star of royalty over His heart might be seen!

It would seem, from vs. 17, that in the immediate acts of expiation Aaron was alone. He was neither to be accompanied nor assisted by any one. Striking type of Him who accomplished expiation for the sins of believers: "Be not far from me, for trouble is near; for there is none to help," Ps. xxii: 11; "Reproach hath broken my heart, and I am full of heaviness; and I looked for some to take pity, but there was none; and for comforters, but I found none," Ps. lxix:20. On the day of atonement in Israel, Aaron was alone, unassisted. On the day of Calvary Jesus was alone. All alone He wrestled in the garden; all alone He hung on the cross. Lover and friend were put far from Him: even the Father hid His face from His suffering Son. *By Himself* He made purification of sins, Heb. i:3.

5. The offerings of the day: First, there was the sacrifice for the sins of the priestly family, vss. 6, 7, 11. The high priest could do nothing in the work of this great day until propitiation for himself and his house had been made, Heb. v:3; ix:7.

Next, the sin-offering for the people which consisted of the two goats, and constituted the main features of the day. They were designed by lot, the one "for Jehovah," the other "for Azazel," the scape-goat. The goat for Jehovah was slain; the sins of the congregation were symbolically transferred from the people to the goat "for Azazel," and solemnly put upon its head, after which it was led into the wilderness, and let go. Mindful of the variety of opinion that prevails as to the meaning of the expression "for Azazel," the writer does not hesitate to express the belief that it signifies "for removal," "for the complete bearing away."

The two goats form but one offering. In vs. 15 the slain goat is described as a "sin-offering for the people." Both animals were charged with the sins of the congregation; and the reason for the use of two instead of one, as in the ordinary sacrifice, is probably that given by Keil, viz., the physical impossibility of combining all the features that had to be set forth in the sin-offering in one animal. The cognate truths of atonement and remission are vividly taught in this sacrifice. The slain goat symbolizes the doctrine of atonement or covering of sins; the scape-goat their removal. God has His claims upon the sinner which must be met—the punishment of his guilt. The sinner has his needs likewise, viz., the putting away of his sin, its complete removal; and this is wrought for him ceremonially by the dismissal of the goat into the wilderness, bearing the load of sins upon him. The punishment of sin, the pardon of sin—these are the truths taught by the two goats. That it all has its fulfillment in Christ needs hardly to be said. The language of this chapter is carried over into later Scripture and applied to Him, Isa. liii:6, 12; Jno. i: 29; 2 Cor. v:21; 1 Pet. ii:24, etc.

6. Entrance of the high priest into the most holy place. Three times on this eventful day he passed

through the veil into the Divine Presence, the Shekinah. The first was with the holy incense and the censer. The sacred room was clouded with the smoke from the burning incense. The smoke served as a thin veil between himself and the presence, "that he die not," vss. 12, 13.

The second entrance was with the blood of his own sacrifice which he sprinkled seven times on and before the mercy-seat. Atonement was thus made for his own sins and those of his house—their trespasses were "covered" from the presence of the Lord. For the holy priesthood was involved in sin, was polluted and defiled, and nothing but the blood could cover the guilt.

The third entrance was with the blood of the slain goat, which was also sprinkled at the mercy-seat; and when this third entrance had been made the priest returned to the holy place and sprinkled the united blood of the two sacrifices at the veil, and put of it on the horns of the golden altar, Ex. xxx:10.

It was for the rebellions against the government of God, for resistance to His grace, the transgressions, the iniquities, and the unknown sins that had brought the holy house into such a state of moral pollution, which made expiation a necessity. Atonement was made for the holy of holies, for the holy place, for the veil, for the golden altar, and for the brazen altar in the court. There was a call for blood everywhere in the sanctuary, and for all its parts, else the throne of God could not abide in Israel. What a picture all this is of God's estimate of sin, and of atonement for it! "Without shedding of blood there is no remission." If God taught

His people of the olden time the great doctrine of atonement by such a vivid object-lesson as this, how is it possible, now that the true sacrifice has been offered for sin, how is it possible for a man, for any man, ever to be saved but by the blood?

7. No blood went into the presence of God into the most holy place but that of the sin-sacrifice; none other touched the mercy-seat save this. Listen to that awful, tremendous word written by the inspired Paul: "He hath made him to be sin for us who knew no sin, that we might be made the righteousness of God in him"—made sin! Not only a sin-offering, as some would have it; but *sin!* Montanus in his Latin translation renders vs. 9 thus: "And Aaron shall bring the goat upon which the Lord's lot fell, and *shall make it sin.*" If this be the real meaning of the verse, then we know something more of what Paul meant in 2 Cor. v:21. With His own blood Jesus has passed into heaven itself, now to appear in the presence of God for us, Heb. ix:12, 24, etc. "As far as east is from the west, so far hath He removed our transgressions from us," Ps. ciii:12. The one perfect offering has been made. The account of sin is canceled. The cry of wrath is hushed. Believe!

NUMBERS.

The title of this fourth book of the Bible is probably derived from the numbering of Israel of which we have the record in the opening chapters. But it hardly indicates the object of the book, for the census forms but a small portion of it. The book contains much important matter both of a historical and legislative character. The key-word is pilgrimage; the key-verse, Num. x:29: "We are journeying unto the place of which the Lord said, I will give it you; come thou with us, and we will do thee good; for the Lord hath spoken good concerning Israel."

Numbers falls into three clearly marked parts: First, the departure from Sinai, the account of the organization of the tribes, incidents by the way, and arrival at Kadesh-barnea, chapters i-xii. Second, unbelief and rebellion upon the report of the spies, chapters xiii-xix. For thirty-eight years thereafter the people marched and counter marched in the wilderness until the generation which came out of Egypt was dead, except Caleb and Joshua. The period is passed over in almost total silence. The nation was under the divine rebuke, and is treated as if its relations with God were suspended. Third, the second arrival at Kadesh, chapters xx-xxxvi. This portion of the book is crowded with great events, the death of Miriam, and Aaron, Balak and

Balaam; the refusal of Edom to allow a passage through his territory, and the wearisome journey around Edom, and the final appearing of Israel in the plains of Moab opposite Jericho. Among the principal topics the following may be mentioned:

1. *Census of the army, and the probable number of Israel.* The quota raised from each of the tribes included all the able-bodied males from twenty years old and upward. It was an army which, in the condition specified, was a universal conscription. Altogether it amounted to 603,550 men. The same number is given in Ex. xxxviii:26. Some are disposed to estimate three non-combatants for each soldier, others four; in which cases the whole host of Israel would consist of about 1,810,000, or about 2,414,000. Others still reduce the number to one million and a half. But at any rate, a vast host was that which wandered here and there in the peninsula of Sinai for forty years. Skepticism interposes a grave objection to the inspiration of this record. After swelling the numbers of Israel to the uttermost, and after exaggerating the sterility of the wilderness, and the scanty supplies to be had from any quarter in the whole region of territory, it asks: How could such a multitude in such a place for so long a time be maintained in life? Leave God out of the account, and the difficulty is insoluble. Arithmetic triumphs. Bring Him into it and all is plain. Reflect whether that Infinite Being who swings the world upon His arm and feeds the creatures thereof with His hand could not support twice the number for twice the time. The question resolves itself into this: Was God with His people or not?

2. *Organization of Israel*, chapters ii-iv. The no-

tion might be entertained from a hasty reading of this history, that the journeys of the wilderness were marked by confusion and disorder. No mistake could be greater. God was their Leader, and He is the Author of order, not of confusion. There was an appointed place of worship; an appointed ministry of worship; appointed seasons of worship. The civil and military arrangements in Israel were as complete as the religious. Scarcely had the redeemed people put the Red sea between them and the land of their bondage when they were thoroughly organized. The army was divided into four grand sections or corps, with three tribes to each division, and with a commander for each. Each grand division had its standard, each tribe its ensign. It is not possible to determine what these standards were. Tradition has it that they represented the cherubim—the lion, the ox, the man, the eagle. In the encampment they formed a sort of hollow square, with three tribes lying on each side of the square. The tabernacle was in the center of the square. On the march, six tribes were in the van, and six in the rear, with the tabernacle in the center between these two great divisions. The position of the sanctuary was thus a central one, always central. God was in the midst of His people, their Protector and Helper, Ps. xlvi:5. The Levites were organized into three divisions corresponding with the three sons of Levi, Gershom, Kohath, and Merari, and their special duties assigned them. Thus order reigned throughout the entire multitude.

3. *Laws of Numbers.* A few as specimens are here given. (1) Laws touching personal habits, and conduct or deportment toward one another, chapter

v. Here are very wise sanitary regulations which municipal governments would do well to imitate. England for many years struggled to destroy leprosy among its people, and succeeded only when it completely isolated all lepers. Moses enacted such a law three thousand years before England. No wonder Israelites who observe Moses' law as to personal habits are the healthiest of people. (2) Law of the Nazarite, chapter vi. The Nazarite was not an order, monastic or otherwise; but he was one who took a vow in order to a more complete consecration to God. The vow was voluntary, and limited as to time. Three things the Nazarite practiced: abstinence from wine, i. e., renunciation of the enjoyments of life; unshorn hair, i. e., subjection (1 Cor. xi:10); keeping himself undefiled from contact with a dead body, i. e., renunciation for the time of the obligations arising from natural relations. "The Nazarite was to be a living type and image of holiness." (3) The ordinance of the red heifer, chapter xix. Out of the ashes of this sacrifice the water of purification was prepared. It is alluded to in Heb. ix:13. Throughout the book there is no mention of the laver. The water of purification appears to have taken the place of the laver in some measure during the pilgrim journey of Israel.

4. *Israel's unbelief and failure*, chapters xiii, xiv. In about two years after quitting Egypt they were at Kadesh, on the borders of the promised land. The report of a majority of the scouts created consternation among the people. Giants held the land; the cities were walled and very great, and the inhabitants strong. Thus ran the report. Panic-stricken, their first thought was to march straight

back to Egypt; their next, to stone Moses and Aaron, Caleb and Joshua, the men of faith. Want of courage, downright cowardice, one would say, was the reason of their conduct. But in Heb. iii:19 it is very differently interpreted. "So we see that they could not enter in because of unbelief." And this their unbelief struck at all God had declared Himself to be, and promised to do for them. (1) It was an impeachment of His *word*. He had said He would bring them into the land and give it them for an inheritance. He even had taken an oath to Abraham that He would do so. And they by unbelief said He would not. God said "yes;" they "no." God said, "I will, I surely will;" they said, "Thou wilt not." (2) It was an impeachment of His *power*. Were the Anakin stronger than the army of Egypt? Were cities and walls mightier than the Red sea? They had seen the display of His power. Could they not rely on Him for even greater displays of it? (3) It was an impeachment of His *goodness*. In manifold ways had He showed His love for them. He had delivered them from Egypt; been their Guide through the wilderness journey, had fed them by the way. And now in full view of Canaan, could His mercy fail? Unbelief, "It ties up the hand of God." Twice Jesus marvelled; once at *faith*, Lu. vii:9; at unbelief, Mark vi:6. Luther said, "Nothing damns but unbelief."

5. *The sin of Moses and Aaron*, chapter xx:1-13. It has been said that God's people fail in that for which they are noted. Job's patience gave way; Abraham's faith wavered; Moses' humility broke down. At first sight it might seem a small matter for which these two eminent servants of God, Moses

and Aaron, should be excluded from the land of promise. But if the reader will ponder the narrative of their trespass, and the passages which elsewhere refer to it, he will find that their's was a most serious offence. Petulance amounting to unjustifiable anger was one element in it, Ps. cvi:32, 33. The patience which had distinguished his course for so long a period suddenly failed, and he "spake unadvisedly with his lips." Disobedience was another element. God had commanded him to "speak" to the rock; whereas Moses struck it twice with the rod. Unbelief was also in the sin. This appears in his action and his words. He called the people "rebels," and yet he was himself at that moment in rebellion, Num. xxvii:14; "For ye rebelled against my commandment." "Must we fetch you water out of this rock?" His vexation and anger carried him into such lengths of unbelief and sin! Furthermore, the "rock" was a type of Christ, 1 Cor. x:4. Once already it had been "smitten" by the divine command, Ex. xvii;6, 7. To smite it a second time was to destroy the type; for Christ the antitype dieth but once; death hath no more power over Him. Taking all the circumstances into account, the sin was heinous, for it was rebellion against God. The punishment seems severe, but it was not disproportionate to the sin.

6. *The brazen serpent*, chapters xxi:5-9; Jno. iii:14, 15. *Evil and its remedy.* Many and striking are the analogies between the brazen serpent and the Saviour. A few may be pointed out. (1) Poison of the reptiles, sin. (2) The remedy, serpent of brass; Christ made in the likeness of sinful flesh and for sin. (3) The remedy lifted up, Christ lifted up.

(4) Healed by looking, faith in Christ, saved by a look.

7. *Balaam and Balak*, chapters xxii-xxiv. Balaam's history is one of the strangest of the Bible. A most gifted man, he was utterly without principle, was the slave of the lowest and most despicable of passions—greed. Three inspired writers (2 Pet. ii: 15, 16; Jude 11; Rev. ii:14) stamp his character with unqualified condemnation. There was in him perversion of splendid endowments, perversion of conscience, total selfishness. Unable to curse Israel and so gain Balak's reward, he insidiously counselled their corruption by unholy alliances with the Moabitish women, and by the licentious rites of idolatry. His evil counsel worked only too well to Israel's sorrow and hurt. But the avaricious prophet paid dearly for his reward; he fell by the spears of the people he sought to ruin, and died, not as the righteous, but as the fool.

8. *Aaron's death*, chapter xx:23-29. Before his death Aaron, by command of the Lord, was stripped of his priestly robes, which were put upon his son and successor, Eleazar. His priesthood could not pass into the heavens; it would continue only on earth. There is but one priest who has carried His priesthood with Him into the glory—the Lord Jesus Christ, Heb. iv:14.

DEUTERONOMY.

The name Deuteronomy means *second law*. It suggests or may suggest that the book contains a second code of laws, or a recapitulation of laws already given. It is rather a summary of what it most concerned the people to keep in mind, both of the Lord's doings on their behalf, and of what they should do when settled in Canaan. The key-word is obedience; key-verse, chapter iv:1. The contents of the book are distributed into four parts: (1) The discourses of Moses, chapters i-xxx. In the discourses Moses gives a brief summary of the events that had taken place during the past forty years, chapters i-iv; next he recapitulates the law of Sinai, with modifications, and more specific directions as to various ordinances, chapters v-xxvi; and then he shows the advantage of obedience, and the awful punishment for the neglect of the law, chapters xxvii-xxx. (2) Committal of the book to the custody of the Levites, and a charge to the people to hear it read once every seven years, chapter xxxi. (3) The song of Moses, and the blessing of the twelve tribes, chapters xxxii, xxxiii. (4) Moses' death and burial, chapter xxxiv.

From chapter i:3 we learn that it was at the end of the forty years' wandering, and just one month and seven days before the passage of the Jordan.

that Moses pronounced the discourses contained in this book. It is believed that it took seven days to deliver the discourses and farewell. The old generation that came out of Egypt, with very few exceptions, was sleeping in the wilderness. Another generation had arisen during the forty years, and trained to hardness by the wilderness discipline, it was to make the conquest of Canaan. They were now stationed in the plains of Moab. The good land of which they had heard so much was parted from them only by the Jordan. They seemed to have been eager, hopeful, resolute; and just such counsel, warning, and promises as Moses gives them were what they needed. How solemnly did the accents of the well-known voice fall on their ears— how impressive was the majestic presence of that extraordinary man, whose age was now one hundred and twenty years, and yet without a trace of physical decline or mental decay—for they knew it was for the last time they should see and hear him.

The circumstances under which the discourses of the book were delivered, explain largely its peculiarities. A certain "school" of interpreters is quite sure that Deuteronomy was not written by Moses, that it is of much later date. Various considerations are put forward in support of this view. Now it is immensely significant that this book is quoted often in the New Testament, and its authority recognized as fully as that of any other. Ninety times it is quoted and alluded to by the Saviour and the apostles. The threefold use of the word by our Lord to repel the assault of the tempter, exhibits His confidence in the Scriptures; but the texts He uses are all from Deuteronomy. Is it credible that the Son of God would quote from a spurious document? Besides, the writing of this book is directly ascribed to Moses, Deu. xxxi:24, 25; and if it was not, then it is forgery, which none but an infidel would dare allege. If we keep in mind that Moses here addresses a new generation of his people, that the time is at the close of his own life, and just as the people were about to cross the Jordan and enter upon their inheritance, that they required such instruction and warning as is here given them, we shall find the key to all the difficulties that have been raised against its genuineness.

1. *Deuteronomy is in great part prophetic.* It has Canaan in immediate prospect. Modifications of laws and ordinances are made to suit the changed conditions of the Israelites. Moses is fully conscious of his own prophetic standing. He designates himself as the representative of that other Prophet in due time to be raised up for Israel, chapter xviii:15-19. The hope of Israel as to the fulfilment of the promise of the Messiah, rested mainly on this prediction of Moses, Jno. i:45; vi:14; Acts iii:22, 23. The intimations of Israel's future, with which Leviticus closes, are drawn out more at length in this book, chapters xxvii-xxxiii. It is evident to the seer (chapter xxviii) that the warnings and awful curses pronounced against disobedience would prove ineffectual, and the result would be followed by a dispersion of his people among the nations of the earth. And yet their continued existence is prophetically secured. They were not to become extinct, in spite of their frightful trials and age-long persecutions and tribulations; they were to abide, until God's purpose in their sufferings should be ac-

complished, and then restoration, blessing, and peace, never again to be taken away, were to be their portion, chapters xxx, xxxii.

2. *Blessings and curses of the two Mounts*, chapter xxvii. When the land had become theirs, the people were to set up great stones and plaster them with plaster. Upon this smooth surface they were then to inscribe the law. The law contained the conditions on which the land was to be enjoyed. Strict observance of it alone guaranteed continued possession. Then the people were to divide into two companies. Six tribes were to stand on Mt. Gerizim to bless, and six on Mt. Ebal to curse. The blessings are not here recorded, although from Josh. viii:34 it may be inferred they were. The curses are written out in full, and are twelve, to correspond with the twelve tribes, it is thought. It is noteworthy that both the law and the curses are found together on the same mount, viz., Ebal. Law and the curse going together! Most suggestive. "As many as are of the works of the law, are under the curse: for it is written, Cursed is every one that continueth not in all things written in the book of the law to do them," Gal. iii:10; Deu. xxvii:26. The dreadful list closes with this sweeping imprecation. No blessing here; only appalling maledictions on the disobedient! Hopeless is the case of him who is under law for righteousness for it is written, "By the deeds of the law there shall no flesh be justified in his sight: for by the law is the knowledge of sin," Rom. iii:20.

3. *A gracious promise*, chapter xxxiii:25. "And as thy days, so shall thy strength be." There are many "great and precious promises" in the book,

and even in this chapter, but this exceeds. What a *general* promise it is. Our days, all our days, till life shall end. What a *particular* promise it is; for it takes up our days, each day, and day by day to the end. What a *varying* promise it is; for it adapts itself to each day, and every kind of day, black or bright, prosperous or adverse, happy or miserable. Surely it is a glorious promise! But there is more in it. When one read to "Uncle Tom" the words of the Lord Jesus, "Come unto me all ye that labor and are heavy laden," the poor slave said, "Them's good words, but who says 'em?" These, too, are good words, but it is all important to know *who says them*. One who knows our days, Ps. cxxxix:1-6. One who orders all our days, Ps. xxxvii:23. One who measures our days, Ps. xxxi:15. One who loves His people through all the days, Jer. xxxi:3. One who will be with His people through all the days, Matt. xxviii:20. "And, lo, I am with you all the days, even unto the end of the world."

4. *Moses' death and burial*, chapter xxxiv. It was the belief of the ancient Jews that Joshua wrote the account of Moses' death, contained in this chapter. However that may be, evidently it was long ago added to the book. The end of the great leader and law-giver was at length come. It might still have seemed a triumphant close was in store for the aged prophet. "His eye was not dim, nor his natural force abated." No look of a dying man had he, as he climbed to the top of Pisgah. It was a deliberate march to death and burial. From the summit he saw the goodly land—he "saw it with his eyes, but he was not to go over thither." It was his last view. From that height he came down no

more. Josephus' pathetic description of Moses' end may be here inserted: "Amidst the tears of the people, the women beating their breasts and the children giving way to uncontrolled wailing, Moses withdrew. At a certain point in the ascent he made a sign to the weeping multitude to advance no further, taking with him only the elders, the high priest Eleazer, and the general Joshua. At the top of the mountain he dismissed the elders, and then, as he was embracing Eleazer and Joshua, and still speaking to them, a cloud suddenly stood over him, and he vanished in a deep valley." In that strange land, the land of Moab, Moses, the servant of the Lord, died, "And he buried him in a valley," "And no man knoweth of his sepulchre unto this day." On the grave of the law-giver in the mountains of Moab, on the grave of an infinitely greater than Moses, the Lord Christ, the darkness settled. **No** one knows of either with any certainty.

JOSHUA.

The book of Joshua is the record of the conquest of Canaan and its partition amongst the chosen people. Moses, the representative of the law, could bring Israel to the borders of the inheritance, but he could not lead them into it. Joshua (Je-hoshua, Jehovah the Saviour) alone could. "The law was our schoolmaster to bring us unto Christ, that we might be justified by faith," Gal. iii:24.

The book is divided into two parts: Part I., chapters i-xii, the conquest; part II., chapters xiii-xxiv, distribution of the land among the various tribes. The key-word is possession; the key-verses are, Josh. i:2, 3.

The history of Israel continues through this and the following books. The historical portions of the Old Testament are devoted to the subject of the theocracy, its practical working, and the failures of the chosen people to attain that for which more especially they were called of God. Joshua was written not long after the events it narrates. We can not enter now into the proof of it. But let the reader ponder chapters v:1, 6; vi:25; xxiv:26, etc. If, as Lias and others hold, it was written not later than fifty years after the events recorded in it, then Deuteronomy was in existence at that remote period; cf. chapter viii:30-34; Deu. xxvii:2-8.

1. *A lesson in courage*, i:2-9; v:13-15. Joshua was Moses' successor as the leader of Israel, Num. xxvii: 18; Deu. xxxiv:9. To him was given the supreme task of leading the people into the inheritance and conquering it for them. What he needed was *faith*, assured confidence in God who had promised to give them the land, and *courage* to execute his commission; and these he had in an eminent degree. It is remarkable how large a place courage has in the Bible. Count its "fear nots" if you can. "Add to your faith virtue," i. e., courage, 2 Pet. i:5. Boldness is an essential element in courage, to do and to dare. All successful workers for God have it. Paul had it but longed for more of it, Eph. vi:18-20. (See Acts iv:13, 29, 31, etc.). Courage has its root in faith, and faith its root in the Word of God. See what wonderful use Joshua's faith makes of God's promise after the perilous defeat at Ai, vii:9: "And what wilt thou do unto thy great name?" What a mighty plea that is! As if his defeat were God's defeat! This is faith and courage combined. A fearful man, a discouraged man, never accomplishes much in this world. "They were afraid to confess him." "I was afraid and went and hid thy talent in the earth." Fear is a failure. "Be strong and of a good courage." Read and study Heb. xi.

2. *The passage of the Jordan*, chapters iii, iv. It was a memorable event, this transit across the ancient river, one to be perpetuated forever, iv:1-3, 20-24. The passage of the Jordan meant for Israel the exchange of the wandering, nomad life, for one of settled habits and permanent abode. It meant the organization of the Hebrews into a nation, and

the development of their national life; the preservation of the knowledge and truth of God, and the custody of the revelation which was now being given. The conquest of the little strip of territory called Palestine, where God was to make Himself known as no where else in all the world, where in due time His own Son, the Lord Jesus Christ, was to appear, was an era in the world's history. Let us note some things respecting it.

(1) The order of the passage, iii:6. The ark of the covenant of the Lord, borne by the priests, was to lead the march. The reason is assigned in iii:10. It was to strengthen the faith and courage of the people. If God open the river for them to pass over, is it not a token and a pledge that He will do for them all He has promised as to the possession of the land? God goes before them, for the ark was His throne; there His presence was displayed, Ex. xxv:22. A mighty struggle confronted them; a task so great, an enterprise so difficult, that human sagacity and prowess were no match for it. God goes before, to encounter, Himself, the difficulties and the dangers, and to open for His people a way which they could not open for themselves. See Jno. x:3, 4. Jesus is our Leader. (2) The time of the passage, iii:15. The barley-harvest occurred about the end of March or in early April. (See ii:6, a proof of the exact knowledge of the writer of Joshua of the time and circumstances.) The river was at its flood, bank-full, from the melting of the snows in the Lebanon. At such times, travelers tell us, it rushes on like a "mill-race." From its rise at the foot of the Lebanon to its grave in the Dead Sea, the Jordan has a fall of 3,000 feet—more than fifteen

feet to the mile. It is likely the two spies swam it; and it may be they were selected for this reason; but it was simply impossible that the mixed multitude of men, women, children, and flocks and herds should do so. God chose this season that His power might be manifested. It was nothing for Him to arrest the swift volume of water which that day was pouring down to the Dead Sea; for at His bidding once before, the waters of the earth had found their proper beds and settled there, Gen. i:9. Thus the passage of the Jordan was an additional proof and pledge of His love and care for them, and therefore they could enter on the conquest of their inheritance with confidence and courage.

3. *Capture of Jericho*, chapter vi. Jericho was the key to the land. It was immensely important that a signal victory should be achieved at this point. If the invaders failed here all was lost. But they could not fail, for God marched at the head of their column. What an extraordinary assault it was, to be sure, if such it can be called. A procession round the walls for seven days; not a word spoken nor a sound heard, save the blowing on seven horns by seven priests, until the seventh day arrives, when they were to make the circuit seven times and the army was to "shout" at the close of the seventh round. Nothing more! Think of General Grant trying to take Vicksburg with bands of music, or Von Moltke the great fortress of Metz with its splendid French army by drum and fife! Could anything be more absurd? Bishop Hall thinks the soldiers and people of Jericho made themselves merry with the spectacle of those solemn processions round their city. No doubt the

Jews heard many a bitter gibe at the stupendous military skill of their General Joshua. But if so, their pleasantry was not for long. The "shout" brought down the walls.

(1) Obviously, there is not the slightest connection between the means and the end. No sword drawn; no engine planted; no sappers and miners to undermine the walls; no assault made. They were to go round the city day after day, and then go into camp at the close of each investment. Nothing more.

(2) It was a sublime lesson in faith, Heb. xi:30, "By faith the walls of Jericho fell down, after they were compassed about seven days." Faith appears in their obedience to the divine directions. They believed God. The Jews knew quite well that the means were not adequate to the end. But God had spoken; this was enough for them. It was not something which faith did or to which faith prompted, but something God had promised, and faith acted on the ground of the promise. Faith can dare anything where God leads the way. Faith removes mountains.

(3) The miracle was calculated to inspire the Jews with confidence and enthusiasm. They were invading Canaan. They were to encounter immense difficulties and obstructions in the execution of their divinely appointed mission. They saw these huge walls tumble down by a "shout" of their army; and they could not but see how strong and mighty the God is who marched at the head of their forces. How the event must have filled and thrilled their hearts with courage and confidence! Ps. xliv:1-3.

(4) It was intended to strike terror to the hearts

ot the Canaanites. We know from the record that it had this effect. The hearts of the idolaters melted within them, and they fought for a cause already lost.

4. *The extermination of the Canaanites*, Deu. vii:1-6; Josh. vi:17-21. This is a serious topic; for it involves the justice and holiness of God, and our sense of right. Of course, in a brief paper such as this, it is impossible to discuss it as it should be. However, some things must be set down which may tend to help the reverent student of the Bible to a correct view. God gave this commandment. Why?

(1) Palestine was Israel's by gift and grant of God, Gen. xii:7; xiii:15; xxvi:3, 4, etc. The Jews, therefore, were conquering their own territory. Their right to dispossess the Canaanites is based upon the right of God to govern this world, and to dispose of any portion of it according to His sovereign pleasure.

(2) The Canaanite probation, Gen. xv:16. For four hundred years at least God had borne with them. Ample opportunity they had to amend their ways, and obey God. They blindly refused, held steadily to their evil pursuits, and sank deeper in sin, and at length judgment broke down upon them in appalling severity.

(3) Their moral character, Lev. xviii:21-25, 27-30; xx:1-24; Deu. xii:29-32, etc. What is told us of them in the Bible, presents them in the darkest possible terms. Their wickedness was something colossal. Profane history gives them the like character. (The reader is referred to any competent writer on the Phoenicians, who formed part of the original inhabitants of Palestine.) They were fallen into total

apostasy; into immoralities the most revolting Human sacrifices, licentious orgies, worship of demons, practices which cannot even be alluded to were common. Cruelty the most atrocious, crimes the most unnatural and defiling were a part of their religion. It was simply a question whether Israel should be kept pure by their extermination, or all knowledge and truth of God be swamped. The two peoples could not live together.

(4) God punishes nations for their sins in time, for nations have no existence as such in the life beyond. Israel was expelled from the same land for their apostasy from God, and their rejection of the Messiah.

(5) It was terrible surgery this; but it was surgery, and not murder: the excision of the cancer, that the healthy part may remain. The words of Carlyle touching Cromwell's work in Ireland, fit this case: "An armed soldier, solemnly conscious to himself that he is the soldier of God the Just,—a consciousness which it well beseems all soldiers and all men to have always—armed soldier, terrible as death, relentless as doom; doing God's judgments on the enemies of God! It is a phenomenon not of joyful nature; no, but of awful, to be looked at with pious terror and awe."

5. *Defeat at Ai*, chapters vii, viii. It was caused by the disobedience of Achan. Achan's sin sprang from covetousness, vii:21. This is the root of sin; Gen. iii:6; Jas. i:15. (1) Sin robs God. All the metals were to be brought into the treasury, vi:19 (2) Sin delights in what God abominates, vii:11 "The accursed thing" refers probably to the Babylonish garment Achan stole. (3) Sin breaks cov-

enant with God, vii:11, 15. All believers are in covenant relation with Him. (4) Sin involves others as well as the sinner himself. The crime of Achan was imputed to all Israel. vii:11. Sin never stops short with the transgressor. (5) Sin brings defeat, shame and death.

6. *Battle of Beth-horon*, chapter x. A word as to the disputed point in this record touching the "sun standing still." The writer does not accept the view that this is *poetry*, vs. 13, and no miracle was wrought. He believes that God interposed to grant what His servant had asked. A miracle should not be magnified beyond the purpose for which it was wrought. God observes a kind of parsimony in His supernatural operations. What Joshua really asked for was, prolongation of light, as the astronomer Kepler has said. And it is believed that light was supernaturally given him in answer to his prayer. He who gave the Hebrews light in Egypt while their neighbors, the Egyptians, sat in darkness, could easily give light over the restricted region.

7. *Partition of the land*, chapters xiii-xxi. By this division every family of Israel had its homestead. On the basis of it, restoration of alienated property was made at the year of jubilee. When the Jews are restored to their own land again they will settle there according to this ancient distribution. The land is God's, Lev. xxv:23. It can never be disponed away finally.

Joshua's farewell to Israel is mingled with warning and pathos. There is in his words the entreaty of the father, and the command of the soldier. Let his noble resolve be that of us all: "But as for me and my house, we will serve the Lord."

JUDGES.

The book of Judges occupies a special place in the canon of Scripture. It describes the condition of Israel during the interval between the conquest of Palestine and the time of Samuel. It is the record of a remote and turbulent age. "In those days there was no king in Israel, but every man did that which was right in his own eyes." This sentence, so often repeated in the book, expresses the freedom and independence, the license and disorder, of the time.

It is difficult, perhaps impossible, to fix the chronology of the Judges. Paul's word in Acts xiii:20 (A. V.), does not settle the disputed points. I Kings vi:1 must stand until more light is had than we now possess to justify its rejection. The Revision of Acts xiii:20 affords no help: "He gave them their land for an inheritance, for about 450 years, and after these things, he gave them Judges until Samuel the prophet." According to this, the 450 years run out at the allotment of the inheritance by Joshua, and do not cover the time of the Judges. The most satisfactory explanation of the period of the Judges is that the years of Israel's oppression by their heathen neighbors are not reckoned in the 480 years of I Kings vi:1. The structure of the book is peculiar. The historical succession of events is regular till the close of Samson's judgeship (i-xvi), where it is broken off abruptly, and then follows the theft of Micah, the raid of the Danites, and the war between Benjamin and the other tribes, xvii-xxi. The history reopens with First Samuel. The book, accordingly, is divided into two parts: Part I., chapters i-xvi; part II., xvii-xxi. The keyword is disobedience; the key-verses, ii:11, 12, 15, 16. Why does this sacred writer drop the story of the Judges with xvi, and turn his attention to the robbery of Micah and the wickedness of the men of Gibeah? These chapters (xvii-xxi) are not a mere appendix. They form an essential part of the design of the Spirit in this Scripture. In part I. (i-xvi) we have the disastrous consequences of Israel's disloyalty to Jehovah as to the corrupt heathen in the land. They departed from God, and practiced idolatry. God's protection was then withdrawn from them, and they fell under the power of their heathen neighbors, whom, in violation of an expressed command, they not only tolerated, but formed alliances with. Then they cried to the Lord, and He sent the Judges for their deliverance. Apostasy, punishment, repentance, mercy and deliverance; this was the round Israel went for centuries. In the second part (xvii-xxi) the internal consequences of unfaithfulness are portrayed; the degradation, the savage cruelty, the lawlessness and profound immorality of the people. Interspersed with this mournful account is the beautiful story of Ruth, which chronologically belongs to the time of the war with Benjamin, Ruth i:1. Dark as the general record is, it is a joy to find it relieved by examples of faith and self-sacrifice, such as the book of Ruth discloses.

1. *Character of the Jews at the death of Joshua*, Jud.

i; ii:6-10; cf. Josh. xxiv:31. The men of the conquest were distinguished for faith and courage. They were free in great measure from the unbelief and pusillanimity which dishonored their fathers of the wilderness. The generation that took Canaan was one of the noblest that Israel ever had. They were so because of their training in the wilderness, and the splendid qualities and example of their great leader, Joshua.—Note: (1) One devoted and faithful man may induce his followers to serve the Lord: Joshua did so. (2) But a man to do this must himself be a true servant of the Lord: Joshua was such. (3) The removal of great leaders is often followed by a falling back from the vantage gained. It was so in this case. Israel did not long remain in the place where God under Joshua had set them.

2. *Apostasy of the succeeding generation*, ii:11-23. There is something startling in the swiftness with which the Israelites degenerated, iii:9. (Caleb's nephew was raised up for their deliverance.) The declension began among the children of the first occupiers of the land. Singular that those who must have remembered God's mighty deeds at the Jordan, at Jericho, and Beth-horon, should so soon forget their Deliverer and King, ignore the covenant so solemnly made at Joshua's death, and shut their eyes to the stone witness under the oak, Josh. xxiv:26. Surprising as it is, it is, alas! perfectly human. Men naturally gravitate toward evil. Placed in a position of responsibility, they always fail. The history of the race is a series of falls and recoveries.

Seven times, it is recorded, they "did evil in the

sight of the Lord," iii:7, 12; iv:1; vi:1; viii:33-35; x:6; xiii:1. Seven apostasies, seven servitudes to the seven heathen nations, seven deliverances! The most wonderful thing is sin—except God's infinite patience and mercy.

Note: Mercies despised, pledges to God broken, become the foundation for towering iniquity. "The depth of a man's fall is in proportion to the momentum acquired in bursting the bonds which held him." The children of godly parents, the children of prayers and holy teaching, who despise their birthright, become the Esaus of the world. Nothing is more fatal to the Christian calling than alliance with the wicked. He who makes the experiment of such entangling alliances, will speedily discover that his power is lost; that what he builds with the one hand, he pulls down with the other. *Separation*, this is God's call, 2 Cor. vi:17, 18.

3. *Israel's enemies*, iii:1-6. Besides the remnant of the Canaanite nations, whom the Jews failed or refused to expel from the inheritance, and who now sore vexed them, a new and formidable enemy appears in the history—the Philistines. Like Israel, they seem to have entered Palestine at a comparatively late date; so their name would indicate "strangers" or "aliens." They oppressed the Hebrews longer than any of the other heathen nations, viz., forty years, xiii:1. They were distinguised for the strength and the variety of their armor. The most complete vocabulary of arms in the Old Testament is taken from the panoply of a Philistine warrior, 1 Sam. xvii:5-7. They seem to have amalgamated with the remnant of the giants—at any rate, men of gigantic stature and strength were found

among them. Their chief deity was the grotesque idol Dagon, which had the trunk fashioned as a fish, and the hands and head of a man. No believing reader of the book can question the hand of a wise and just God in the troubles Israel endured at the hands of the Philistines. These enemies were used as a scourge of Israel. The chosen people found, as all backsliders must find, that God is as true to His threatenings as He is to His promises. They deserted the arm of strength; of necessity their arms became powerless. God's justice could not tolerate their sin; His love would not cast them off entirely. "Thou wast a God that forgavest them, though thou tookest vengeance of their doings," Ps. xcix:8.

4. *The Judges*, iii-xvi. Fifteen different persons, including Deborah, acted in this capacity during the period of the book. These officers are not to be confounded with the ordinary judges of the Theocracy, cf. Ex. xviii:21-26. They were men raised up for a specific purpose and endowed with extraordinary powers. Their duties were political rather than judicial. Most of them were military leaders, who rescued the people from the oppression of the heathen. They were not a regular succession of governors, but extraordinary officers who were roused by the inward impulse of God's Spirit to deliver their countrymen from the thraldom of their enemies. The judge had no power to make laws, for these were given by God; nor to explain them, for that was the province of the priest; they were upholders of the law, defenders of religion, avengers of crimes, particularly of idolatry and its attendant vices. They governed Israel as the subordinate

agents of Him who was the supreme Ruler of the people, by whom also they were called to their high office. The most prominent of the judges were Othniel, iii:9; Deborah and Barak, iv; Gideon, vi; Jephthah, xi; Samson, xiii:25.

5. *Moral features of this period.* The book of Judges is the history of Israel's failure as the witness of the Lord. Joshua sets before us the energy of faith, which, grounding itself on the promise of God, and trusting Him, loyally addressed itself to the appointed task. In Judges we see the miserable state of the nation now become unfaithful; and at the same time the gracious interventions of God for their deliverance from the calamities into which their unfaithfulness had brought them. These interventions correspond with *revivals* in the history of the Christian church. The Hebrews found it more convenient to use the heathen people than to expel them; and so these became "thorns in their sides, and snares for their feet." Note some of the bad effects. (1) Idolatry, with its licentious accompaniments, was largely practiced, xvii. We read often of the Baalim, Ashteroth, of the groves, of idols and idol-worship. These plural names (Baalim, Ashteroth) are significant, one general object of worship, but idols without number of that object. Just as in Italy there is but one madonna, but she has a hundred different images and shrines. (2) Frequent and rash use of vows was another feature of this age. It was contracted mainly from the heathen, particularly the Phoenicians. At Carthage, old Hamilcar exacted of his son Hannibal, the vow, so solemn in its origin, so grand in its consequences, of eternal undying war with Rome

By the way, the name Hannibal points to Baal, as also Asdrubal, Maherbal, etc. So hasty and disastrous vows were common in the times of the Judges. Witness that of all Israel against Benjamin, xxi:1; of Jephthah, the most tragic of all, xi:30, 31; of Saul, which almost cost Jonathan his life, 1 Sam. xiv:24. (3) Lawlessness, amounting almost to anarchy, prevailed. "The highways were unoccupied and the travelers walked through byways," v:6. How vivid the picture! The thoroughfares were abandoned, because infested, no doubt, by highwaymen, who robbed as they listed, and there was no strong government to restrain. Travelers had to creep through byways to escape the dangerous roads. (See xvii:6; xviii:1, 7; xix:1, etc.) (4) Crimes seem to have been common. Witness the raid of the Danites, xviii; the awful wickedness of the men of Gibeah, xix; and the fierce slaughter of Benjamin by the other tribes, xx. (5) Stubborn persistence in evil was another feature of the time, ii:17-19; Ps. cvi:34-43. This is a world-picture. Sin abounds, but grace super-abounds. Human obstinacy and unbelief never defeat the gracious purpose of God.

Brief notes on some of the Judges are appended.

Shamgar, iii:31. The account of him is confined to this single verse. Yet it is enough to mark him as a hero. It reminds one of the mention of Jabez, 1 Chron. iv:9, 10, or of the condensed histories in Heb. xi. With an ignoble weapon, a paltry oxgoad, Shamgar wrought a deed of valor which set him among the Hebrew worthies. How much may be done by the most trifling means if one is working with God! Moses had only a rod, Samson a jaw-bone, Jonathan a spear, Esther her beauty and her tongue; but with them all was the power of God.

Deborah and Barak, iv, v. Deborah appears in the line of Israel's deliverers. Although no warrior, she inspired with courage and enthusiasm the warriors of her people, and the victory was in reality her's. There had been no deliverance had not this woman lifted up her voice like a trumpet. "A mother in Israel," she named herself. *Mater patriae*, the mother of her country, her people might have called her. Woman's influence—who can measure it? Sarah, Rahab, Ruth, Deborah, Hannah, Elizabeth, Mary, Dorcas: Blandina the martyr, Monica the mother of Augustine, the mother of the Wesleys, the daughter of John Knox, Jennie Geddes—their names, and of scores more, will never be forgotten.

Gideon, vi, vii. Let us not attribute his hesitancy, his request for more proof that God had called him, to unbelief. It was his native modesty that held him back; the agony of uncertainty—his need of being sure and doubly sure. *Then*, forward! It is thus with great souls. Luther shrank from the mighty task set him; Knox hid himself; Calvin sought to flee till Farel with his tremendous adjuration arrested him. Gideon was fitted at length for decisive service. His three hundred were men of like faith and fearlessness with himself. Soldiers with conscience and convictions are the bravest. Cromwell wanted no other sort. He loved the "godly;" loved to lead those who went to battle from prayer and praise. Gideon's strategy has been called "inspired tactics." Very different from the charge of the Old Guard at Waterloo, and of the Six Hundred at Balaklava, it was even more notable. "Lamps, pitchers and trumpets:" the means were wholly inadequate to the end. But God fought with the three hundred; for He "works with minorities who work with Him." What an invincible thing faith is!

Jephthah, xi. This captain is mentioned with Gideon, Barak and Samson in the monumental chapter of the New Testament, Heb. xi. Notwithstanding his rashness, his wild roving life, the Spirit has given him rank among some of the noblest of the Old Testament worthies. In spite of the strong arguments urged in support of the view that he actually offered his daughter in sacrifice to God, in accordance with his vow, there is enough ground in the somewhat ambiguous narrative to justify a more humane interpretation. It seems more in harmony with the place given Jephthah among the saints, and with her "bewailing her virginity," that the father devoted his daughter to a life of celibacy and seclusion. Every such vow must be dangerous and sinful. To bind oneself by oath to do something unknown and unknowable is criminally rash. Besides, it is foolish to imagine we can buy the help of God by promising Him devotion in return. A hasty vow that involves one in wrong-doing is better broken than kept. Better still it is, not to contract such obligations at all

Samson's riddle, xiv:14. Samson's riddle is God's riddle. It shows us God and the Enemy at their several work—the enemy doing his work as the Strong and the Eater, and God in gracious and victorious power forcing him to yield both meat and sweetness. The riddle is the shortest and most graphic account of God's ways with the world anywhere to be found. Whether Samson intended it or not, he touched the secret of Providence. God permits the Devil to assert his will and weave his toils and do his work up to a certain stage; and then God interferes, and out of the Enemy's doings evolves His own blessed ends. That is the history of the Fall, of Jacob, Joseph, Moses, Israel, Job, and a hundred more. The death of Christ is a most illustrious example of the truth of Samson's riddle. That death transcends all other events. "A bygone eternity knew no other future; and eternity to come shall know no other past." In the midst, the Cross in lonely majesty; God on the one side with averted face; on the other Satan exulting in his triumph. What a seeming victory for the Eater—victory eclipsing all others. But again, and more and more than ever before, he is compelled to yield meat and sweetness. For by that Cross, Christ hath abolished death, destroyed him that had the power of death, and redeemed His people from a perpetual bondage. That Cross will yet be the destruction of the world's evils, the expulsion of its sorrows, the overthrow of the kingdom of darkness, and the hurling of the Devourer into the Lake of Fire!

RUTH.

Let us rejoice for the book of Ruth! Had we the book of Judges alone, as to the long period of Israel's history between Joshua and Samuel, we should be ready to conclude that all the gentler virtues had fled from the land, and lawlessness and crime were universal. But this book lifts up the curtain which veils the privacy of domestic life, and discloses to us most beautiful views of piety, integrity, self-sacrificing affection, gentleness and charity, growing up amidst the rude scenes of war and strife, and the abominations attendant upon the practice of idolatry. There were still beautiful lives in those times, and bright examples of faith. If the enemy were busy in corrupting the people, God likewise secured the triumph of His love in the hearts of many. The key-word is *faith;* the key-verses 1:16, 17. Even a cursory reader must be impressed with the sublime beauty of this remarkable record. For pathos, sweetness, and unaffected naturalness, it is unsurpassed. So graphic is this "prose idyl," that picture after picture presents itself, and yet there is no confusion, no diminution of descriptive power, and the interest of the reader is held, increased from beginning to end. Its crystalline transparency, and inimitable simplicity stamp the narrative as true. The book is not exactly a history; nor is it biography. It is only a little biographical episode in a history. Just as there were real saints in the darkest periods in the Middle Ages, when popes and prelates vied in wickedness with kings and barons, saints who were hidden away in quiet nooks and corners of Christendom—so in the midnight of Hebrew history there were some who worshipped not Baal, who in wondrous simplicity of character and genuine fidelity, lived near to God, and kept the light of true religion burning brightly. Such was the household of Elimelech, of Boaz and no doubt of many others.

I. *The principal figure in the book is Ruth.* She was a Moabitess. Her nationality was particularly odious to the Jew. An Egyptian or an Edomite was not so abhorrent, for one from these people might, according to law, be incorporated into the congregation in the third generation, Deu. xxiii:8. But a Moabite and an Ammonite seem to have been interdicted from entering Israel forever, Deu. xxiii:3. At least, they could not enter till the tenth generation. Moab and Ammon had their origin in one of the darkest crimes recorded in the Old Testament, Gen. xix. But grace triumphed over every barrier, and this book shows us its glorious victory in the presence of the most adverse circumstances.

II. *Efforts to escape from trouble*, i:1-5. Famine, the frequent attendant on war, came to Bethlehem and the inhabitants suffered want. "The house of bread" (Bethlehem so means) was without bread. It may have been that the famine was brought about by the incursion of the Midianites and Amalekites, Judges vi:1-6. Sure we may be that the affliction came in consequence of Israel's disobedience and sin. Elimelech and his family determined to seek support in the land of Moab. The name Elimelech signifies "My God is King." The faith which is imbedded in the name of this good man ought to have shone out more brightly in the time of trial than it appears to have done. It is bad enough when in the midst of difficulties the people of God come down into the world to find help and comfort; it is worse when they abide there. And yet we should not condemn Elimelech and his household, for the inspired record gives no hint that the step taken was blamed. However, migration, flight, does not fly trouble. New and worse afflictions fell upon the refugees. First, the godly husband died, the two sons married Moabite women, and they too died, and Naomi was left a childless widow. Three widows in one house! If the Elimelech family were backsliders, they found as all such unfaithful professors of godliness must find, that distance from God is loss, disappointment and death. Nearness to God is rest, peace, blessedness, Ps. xvi:11. Naomi proved this to the uttermost. When she returned to Bethlehem, and the old neighbors gathered about her to ask, "Is not this Naomi?"—she answered out of a heart that had supped on sorrow, "Call me not Naomi [pleasant], call me Mara [bitter]; for the Almighty hath dealt very bitterly with me. I went out full, and the Lord hath brought me home again empty," i:20, 21. People who fly from one sort of trouble are likely to encounter worse. We may escape from famine but we cannot escape death.

III. *Faith and devotion*, i:8-18. The Hebrew family had not held the relation to God in secret in the land of Moab. They were not ashamed of Israel's Saviour. Some one of them, perhaps all of them, must have taught the truth about Jehovah to the wives ot Mahlon and Chilion. Most likely it was Naomi who did so. And the teaching was not fruitless. No witness for God ever is. How far it extended in this case we have no means of knowing; but we do know that it bore the richest fruit in one instance—that of Ruth. Orpah was not so deeply impressed, i:15. "But Ruth clave unto her," vs. 14. All sincere souls are tested. Adam and Eve, Abraham, Peter were. So, too, was Ruth. "Return thou after thy sister-in-law," Naomi said to her. But she stood the test. She had learned something, perhaps much, of the merciful Lord of Israel; she knew that to be with them was to share the blessings and promises which they enjoyed. The beauty and attractiveness of the people whose God is the Lord she had seen and felt in the Elimelech family; and part from them she could not. Her reply to Naomi's dismissal is surpassingly fine.

> "Insist not on me forsaking thee,
>   To return from following thee;
> For whither thou goest, I will go;
>   And wherever thou lodgest, I will lodge;
> Thy people is my people,
>   And thy God my God;
> Wheresoever thou diest I will die,
>   And there will I be buried.
> Jehovah do so to me,
>   And still more,
> If aught but death part thee and me," i:16, 17.

"Nothing could be said more fine, more brave" (Matthew Henry). "Her vow has stamped itself on the very heart of the world; and that not because of the beauty of its form simply, though even in our English version it sounds like a sweet and noble music, but because it expresses in a worthy form, and once for all, the utter devotion of a genuine and self-conquering love" (S. Cox). Let it be noted, that the devoted attachment of Ruth to Naomi springs out of a true and firm faith. Her choice of Naomi's God to be her own is the proof of it. It was no doubt a glad companionship to Naomi. "Thus God never forsaketh His; but when one comfort faileth, findeth them out another; as when Sarah died, Rebekah came in her room. Yea, God Himself stood by Paul when all men forsook him" (John Trapp).

IV. *Salutations*, ii:4. Boaz, "a mighty man of wealth," ii:1, saluting his reapers with the devout benediction, "The Lord be with you," and the hearty response of the workman, "The Lord bless thee," is a pleasant picture of old-world life, and of the deep religious feeling which prevailed among this frank and guileless people. With them it was no meaningless form, no mere custom out of which the life had flown. It was the expression of those who loved the Lord and hence loved one another, Ps. cxxix:8. Gideon was saluted thus: "The Lord is with thee," and Mary thus: " Hail, highly favored one! the Lord is with thee"—the greetings of angels. Jesus was wont to greet His disciples saying, "Peace be unto you." The apostles closed their letters with blessings—"The Lord be with you all." In the case of pious persons such salutations are prayers for those addressed. How many of our common greetings have their origin in prayer!

"Good-bye"—God be with you; "Farewell," "Good night," are prayers. *Addio*, say the Italians: To God I commend you! Once these expressions meant all that true hearts wished for each other. Now they are like old coins, of which the image and superscription are rubbed out.

V. *The Kinsman Redeemer*, iii, iv:1-16. The duties of a Kinsman-redeemer were both varied and important. Lev. xxv:25-28, 47-50, treats of the redemption of the property and person of a "brother" who might be reduced to penury. But there is another feature connected with the functions of the redeemer which is brought before us in this book, viz., the levirate law, as it is called, i. e., the law of the near of kin (brother-in-law), founded on Deu. xxv:5, 6. There can be scarcely any doubt but that this law acted in the case of the kinsman-redeemer. At least, it is recognized in the transaction between Boaz, the kinsman nearer than Boaz, and Ruth. She is persistently faithful to her duty to her dead husband; Boaz to the law of Moses; the "near kinsman" considerate only of his selfish interests. And Boaz buys both the alienated land, and redeems the person of Ruth. Neither of the two women could sell or restore the property. Ruth could glean, but she could neither buy herself nor the estate of her deceased husband. Boaz, the "mighty man of wealth," is both able and willing to undertake and accomplish. How like our Kinsman Redeemer, the Lord Jesus Christ, who buys us, and redeems our alienated heritage, 1 Cor. vi:19, 20; 1 Pet. i:3-5. Let the reader note the three majestic adjectives in Peter: "incorruptible, undefiled, and that fadeth not away." Of no inheritance in this world can so much be said. Ours is, in its nature incorruptible, in its possession without a stain, and in its enjoyment everlastingly fresh and satisfying.

VI. *Genealogy of David*, iv:17-22; *genealogy of Christ*, Matt. i:5. And so David the king descends through two Gentile women, on the name of each of whom there rests a blot, Rahab and Ruth. The one was a harlot, the other was a Moabitess whose paternal ancestor, Moab, was the child of incest! And Jesus traces His human lineage through this same line. Marvelous grace and condescension! He links Himself, not with a race of righteous people, but with sinners. He claims kindred with the poorest and the worst of men, and He saves them, too, who will but trust Him. No more need Naomi call herself Mara, but the pleased and pleasant ancestress of Obed, Jesse, David, Jesus.

VII. *Worldwide events often hinge upon a little incident, a trifling act*, ii:3. "Her *hap* was to light on a part of the field of Boaz." Her hap! And yet that "hap" turned out to be her marriage, and the births, ultimately, of David and of Jesus. Out of insignificant trifles, as men name them, God weaves His mighty ends. An arrow is shot across a deep chasm through which a turbulent stream rushes. To the arrow a thread is attached, to the thread a cord, then a cable; and in due time a bridge spans the huge trench, and men pass and repass at their pleasure.

The sleepless night of a king turns out to be the salvation of a proscribed nation, Esther vi:1. A young widow happens to enter a harvest-field to gather a little food for herself and a dependent mother-in-law. There follow that simple act, a marriage, the birth of a son, a great king, and finally a mighty Saviour. Our God is One whose providence is so special and minute that nothing escapes it, nothing is too small for it, and all things are bent to fulfill His wise and blessed ends. Let us trust Him; for He sees the end from the beginning

FIRST SAMUEL.

The key-word of First Samuel is, "Kingdom·" the key-verse, 1 Sam. x:25.

These two books take their name from the great man whose history they relate, the prophet Samuel. In some of the oldest translations they are designated as "First and Second Kings," and those which follow as "Third and Fourth Kings." All four relate to the kingdom of Israel. The general history, interrupted by Ruth, is again taken up and carrried forward to the captivity.

First Samuel is divided into two parts: Part I., the theocracy under Eli and Samuel; chapters i-vii. Part II., anointing of Saul as king, and his reign; chapters viii-xxxi.

First Samuel narrates a radical change in the re lations of the chosen people with God. Up to this point Jehovah was their king. Now in answer to their unbelieving clamor (1 Sam. viii:5-9), a king was given them. To the king they were directly responsible; indirectly to Jehovah, as through the king. A new office was introduced in connection with the change of relationship, viz., the office of prophet. Prophets there were before; Moses was such and others, Num. xii:6-8. But now the office becomes a part of the national life, as we may say; and prophecy implies failure. Yet out of it all God wrought infinite good. How much we owe to this office cannot be computed. By it we have the revelation of the grace and counsels of God. First Samuel shows us the failure of the people, the breaking up of the old relationship, the appointment of a king, and the office of the prophet inaugurated.

The fall of Shiloh contributed much to the change. The first place where the sanctuary was located after the passage of the Jordan was Gilgal, Josh. v:10. It was ere long established at Shiloh, Josh. xviii:1, and there it remained until captured by the Philistines, 1 Sam. iv. Afterward it was located at Kirjath-jearim, 1 Sam. vii:1, 2; and was finally brought to Jerusalem by David, where it remained, 2 Sam. vi. Wherever the ark was, there was the "house of God," Ju. xviii:31; 1 Sam. iii:3. There were other places where worship was offered, but the tabernacle was pre-eminent. The other sanctuaries held a relation to the tabernacle such as the synagogues held to the temple. They were altogether subordinate.

There are three great names about which most of the events of these books of Samuel may be grouped, Samuel, Saul and David.

I. *Samuel.* His birth was the answer to his mother's agonizing prayer, 1 Sam. i:10, 11. He was asked of God, given by Him, and his happy mother named him Samuel—"asked of God," i:20. Two things are noteworthy as to Hannah's conduct: First, after her very earnest prayer, "the woman went her way and did eat, and her countenance was no more sad," vs. 18. An example of faith! Her tears and sighs all gone. Second, her song of joy.

ii:1-10. It is a very noble hymn, the outpouring of a glad heart which could not but sing. There is a close resemblance between it and Mary's song, Lu. i: 46-55. Both thrill with the deepest fervor and piety.

1. *Samuel throughout his long life was a Nazarite*, i:11. Given in answer to prayer he was consecrated to God from infancy, and brought up in the sacred tent at Shiloh. Simple, devout, true, he was strong in will, unflinching in the discharge of the most painful duties, iii:17, 18; xv:26.

2. *He was a man of prayer*, 1 Sam. iii; vii:8, 9, etc. Stanley holds that the "cry" for which Samuel was noted, was shrill and piercing, and was uttered in all his intercessions for the people, when they were in danger of trouble. All the very great men of the Bible and of the Church were men of prayer, of persevering, believing, importunate prayer.

3. *His influence was felt throughout the whole nation.* Of all the judges of Israel, Samuel, the last of them, wielded the greatest power. Men trembled at his presence, 1 Sam. xvi:4. Saul himself feared him. His influence lay not in military exploits, nor in diplomatic skill, nor in political shrewdness, but in his unswerving integrity, his splendid loyalty. In his old age, when the time was come for him to lay down the heavy burden he had so long borne, he could challenge all Israel to point out a single instance of his selfishness or unrighteousness, 1 Sam. xii:1-5.

4. *Samuel was a prophet, and the first of the long line of prophets which closes with the Old Testament*, Acts iii:24; xiii:20; Heb. xi:32. With him the office and order began a distinct feature of the Hebrew polity.

Prior to Samuel "the word of the Lord was precious [rare] in those days; there was no open vision," iii: 1. With him the "revelations" through prophecy (which means a message from God) began, iii:21. Of the nature of these revelations, suffice it to say now, that they were not by intuition or genius or imagination of the prophet, but by direct communication from God, 2 Pet. i:20, 21; Heb. i:1, 2, cf. Jer. xxiii:16, 21. We learn something of the nature of prophecy from the word used about Samuel, viz., "Seer," 1 Sam. ix:9. This was the most ancient name for the office; and it seems to intimate that the prophet was gifted with a preternatural sight, the faculty and power of vision as to unseen things which ordinary men do not possess. Balaam defines it, "to have the eyes open, to hear the words of God and to see the vision of the Almighty, falling into a trance, but having the eyes open," Num. xxiv:3, 4, 15, 16.

5. *The schools of the prophets.* These were founded by Samuel, and were designed to make the office permanent and effective. One was located at Ramah, of which Samuel seems to have been at the head, 1 Sam. xix:19, 20; and others at other places, 1 Sam. x:5. Still others, afterward, at Bethel, 2 Kings ii:3; at Jericho, 2 Kings ii:5; at Gilgal, 2 Kings iv:38. The chief study of the young men in these schools, no doubt, was the law and its interpretation; but we gather from 1 Sam. x:5, cf. 1 Chron. xxv:1-3, that the cultivation of music was a part of their labors. The art was not an integral part of the office of prophecy, but its accompaniment; for in the rapt ecstatic condition of soul into which he was thrown when the spirit of prophecy

came upon him, his utterances rushed forth in a tuneful flow, and very naturally he accompanied them with a musical instrument, 2 Kings iii:15.

6. *Samuel, as prophet, was the channel of communication between the Lord and the people.* The priest was so no longer; nor the judge. Whatever message the Lord had for His people was addressed to them through the prophet. It was he who, acting under divine direction, inaugurated the kingdom and anointed the king, viii; x:1; who announced the forfeiture of the throne by the first king, 1 Sam. xv:28; who anointed his successor, xvi:12, 13. This high place the office maintained until the fall of Israel. It was the change of relation with God consequent upon the establishment of the kingdom which made it so. Through the priest the people drew near to God; through the prophet God drew near to the people. In Heb. iii:1 the two offices are united in Christ. As Apostle He pleads God's cause with us; as Priest He pleads our cause with God.

II. *Saul.* He was of the tribe of Benjamin, the son of Kish, of the family of Abiel. Abner, his chief officer, was his near kinsman, probably his uncle. The family was one of wealth and influence, 1 Sam. ix:1.

1. *In Saul we have man acting in the energy of the flesh, with small spiritual force.* He was of gigantic stature; his physical powers enormous. At the close of his first interview with Samuel, he "turned his shoulder [margin] to go"—one can almost see that massive shoulder wheel round, suggestive of strength, and endurance, 1 Sam. x:9. Indecision and irresolution mark his life throughout. He had the military qualities of a leader, and was

something of a statesman, but he was destitute of true spiritual power. The gift promised and conferred upon him, 1 Sam. x:6, 9, had to do with his ruling and leadership. It does not mean the new birth.

2. *Condition of Israel at Saul's inauguration.* It was as bad as it could well be. The nation's helplessness appears in the graphic words of 1 Sam. xiii: 19; no smith in all Israel; no sword or spear, save those of Saul and Jonathan. Could national disarmament and prostration be greater?

3. *His jealous disposition.* This is seen in his treatment of his own son Jonathan, a better man than his father, 1 Sam. xiv:38-44; xx:30; of David the truest friend he had in the whole realm, xxiii; of Ahimelech, the high priest, and of the priests, xxii. Saul's life was one long tragedy. A strange frenzy took possession of him. The Scripture calls it an evil spirit, 1 Sam. xvi:14-16; xviii:10; xix:9, etc. He became suspicious, distrustful, violent. Dark thoughts tormented him. Wild passions shook his huge frame, with fierce spasms of conscience and murderous moods of jealousy—in fact, he seems at times to have been mad. He fell into melancholy, and his courtiers trembled before him as he sat in his house with his javelin in his hand, and the evil spirit brooding over him. His courage forsook him, and he who had been admired for his stature and strength, whose armor no ordinary man could wear, sometimes fought with desperation, and sometimes was craven. So fully had come to pass the words of the prophet about him and the people, 1 Sam. viii:18; xii:12, 13, 25. To such an end "the flesh" at length arrives.

4. *His rejection.* Two acts of disobedience marked his downward course. The first was his rash sacrifice. He had been bidden to tarry until Samuel should arrive. About the hardest thing a weak and impulsive man can do is patiently to wait in the presence of uncertainty or perplexity. Samuel plainly intimated to him that the kingdom should pass away from him, 1 Sam. xiii:14. It was Saul's first distinct warning of the doom that awaited him and his house. The second was his refusal to execute on Agag the punishment his crimes merited, 1 Sam. xv. This was a wilful violation of the Lord's command, Ex. xvii:16; Deu. xxv:19. This time Samuel pronounced the decisive sentence, 1 Sam. xv:22, 23, 27-29. One of the strange leaves in human history here turns. Saul refused to punish Agag the Amalekite; and at his death the fallen king is stripped of his crown and his ornaments by a prowling son of Amalek, 2 Sam. i:10. Slay your enemy, sin, and it will be well with you, spare your enemy, sin, and it will despoil and murder you. The reprisals of sin and of law—how awful they are!

5. *Saul's death*, 1 Sam. xxviii, xxxi. He was in sore distress; his kingdom was in imminent peril; himself forsaken of God; he felt that the fatal net was fast closing in upon him; that escape was now impossible; and in his dire extremity, goaded to desperation, he tried the experiment of consulting the witch of En-dor. "All human history has failed to record a despair deeper or more tragic than his, who, having forsaken God, and being of God forsaken, is now seeking to move hell, since heaven is inexorable to him; and infinitely guilty as he is, assuredly there is something unutterably pathetic

in that yearning of the disanointed king, now in his utter desolation, to change words once more with the friend and counselor of his youth, and if he must hear his doom, to hear it from no other lips but his" (Trench).

As to the question of Samuel's appearance in response to the witch's incantations, let the following be considered:—(1) Saul testified that God no longer answered him at all, xxviii:15. Is it likely that God, who refused to hold intercourse with Saul by any appointed channels of communication, would send Samuel in answer to the conjuring of this hag? Would He so far recognize the "black art"? (2) Vs. 15. That the power of the necromancer could reach to the abode of the saintly dead, and "disquiet" them is incredible. (3) "God brought Samuel up to pronounce his doom. The sorceress had nothing to do with it." But He had pronounced his doom, xvi:1. The spectre foretells nothing that was not already known, save his approaching death; and in the state in which the king and all Israel were at the time, it would not be difficult to predict the issue of the impending battle. On the face of it, this strange account bears evidence of the tricks of a juggler, and the powers of both the clairvoyant and ventriloquist. And it is noteworthy that the name of the witch in the Septuagint version is, *ventriloquist*. The next day Saul died. "I gave thee a king in mine anger, and took him away in my wrath," Hos. xiii:11. There is an apparent discrepancy in the two accounts of Saul's death which we have. In 1 Sam. xxxi:4, 5, we are told he died by his own hand; but in 2 Sam. i:10 the Amalekite tells David that he slew him. John

Trapp is right: "An artificially composed speech, but scarce ever a true word. This Amalekite, which signifieth a licking-people, would, like a cur dog, have sucked David's blood only with licking, but was happily disappointed."

SECOND SAMUEL.

The key-word is "Kingdom"; the key-verse, 1 Sam. xvi:1. The unity of plan and the design of these books of Samuel is quite apparent. The main theme is the establishment of the Kingdom in Israel, and the transfer of the crown from the tribe of Benjamin to that of Judah. The king given in answer to the clamors of the restless people—given in anger and taken away in wrath, is by divine interposition succeeded by one who "is after God's own heart," David. The books of Samuel afford an illustration of Samson's riddle, Judges xiv:14. The eater is made to yield meat, the strong, sweetness. Samson's riddle is God's riddle. David is the prominent figure in these books; for his name becomes in due time associated with the name of his Son and Lord; his throne merges into the throne of the Messiah. Even his splendid son Solomon sinks to a lower place. Broadly, it may be said that First Samuel records David's wondrous training for his mission; Second Samuel, his reign. In the first, he is at school; in the second, on the throne. Discipline! How large a place it fills in God's purposes touching His best servants! Moses, Joshua, Samuel, David, Daniel, John the Baptist, and Paul, are the proof of it. No man in this world ever has achieved much who has not been in God's school.

Second Samuel contains the history of the reign

of David. The book may be conveniently divided into three parts. Part I., chapters i-x: David enthroned as king, first over Judah, and then over all Israel. Part II., chapters xi-xx: David's sin and its dreadful consequences—some of its consequences are, incest and rebellion in his own family, and Joab's insolence and lawlessness—a frightful crop followed his sowing! Part III., chapters xxi-xxiv: David's last acts and last words, and his mighty men.

1. *David's prominence in the Bible.* No Old Testament character surpasses him in this regard. He ranks with Moses and Abraham. Indeed, in frequency of mention and the reverence paid him, hardly another equals him. Jerusalem is called after him, 2 Sam. v:9; Bethlehem, likewise, Lu. ii:4, 11. Again and again we read of the "house of David," Zech. xii:7; Lu. i:27, 69; of the "tabernacle of David," Acts xv:16. The relation which Christ sustains to David is manifold. He is of the seed of David, Rom. i:3; cf. Ps. lxxxix:36; the Son of David Matt. i:1; xxii:42; the Heir to throne of David, Lu i:32; Acts ii:30; and He hath the key of David, Rev iii:7; cf. Is. xxii:22. Scripture associates David with Christ in the closest way; the one ever fore shadows the other; his "house" is the kingdom of David, and this is the fore-gleam of Christ's kingdom; his "key" is the symbol of the authority he had over his house, and this in the hand of Christ is expressive of supreme sovereignty. All this gives David a pre-eminence that belongs to few, if any other, in the Bible.

2. *His birth and youth*, 1 Sam. xvi; xvii:15, 34, etc. Bethlehem, famous for its well, 1 Chron. xi:17,

was the place of his birth, as also the birthplace of his august son and heir, Matt. ii:4-6. He was the youngest of eight sons. His lineage is carefully preserved in Ruth iv and 1 Chron. ii:11-15. (Note: in 1 Chron. ii David is called the seventh son. Probably one of the brothers had died early, and so in this list he would naturally be omitted.) In the genealogy of Matthew he is distinguished by the royal title, "David the king." His early manhood was spent in the duties of a shepherd, an occupation attended with personal hazard. So the sheperd-king tells us that in defence of his flock he slew a lion and a bear, 1 Sam. xvii:34-36. Out of his shepherd-life grew one of his sweetest psalms, the matchless Twenty-third; and no doubt his sojourn in the wide country, and his nights in the field, gazing on the starry heavens so dazzlingly brilliant in the east, suggested some of the images in that finest anthem of creation, the Eighth Psalm.

3. *His anointing*, 1 Sam. xvi:1-13. The sons of Jesse passed before Samuel in a sort of review. The eldest, Eliab, seemed to recommend himself to the prophet as the successor of Saul by his physical qualifications. But all glorying in the flesh and its birthright is now to be set aside. In the sad example of Saul it has been demonstrated to all spiritual minds that the flesh profiteth nothing. The external appearance, the fine proportions and lofty stature must give place to the energy of faith in the inner man. The youngest in Jesse's family, the despised and forgotten one, is the chosen of the Lord, "for the Lord seeth not as man seeth; for man looketh on the outward appearance, but the Lord looketh on the heart." This anointing of David

was private, secret. Publicly he was anointed over Judah, 2 Sam. ii:4, and over all Israel, 2 Sam. v:3. Note, Saul and Jehu were anointed with a vial of oil, 1 Sam. x:1; 2 Kings ix:1 (R. V.); David and Solomon with a horn of oil. But Christ was anointed with the oil of gladness above His fellows, Heb. i:9. It was because Christ fulfilled all righteousness, did perfectly the will of His Father, that He was raised to the throne of God amid the acclamations of the heavenly host.

We have a little glimpse of David's personal appearance here. He is said to have been "ruddy"—with auburn hair, and the bloom of youth on his cheek. Tradition says that his lowly descendant, Mary, had also auburn or golden hair. He was of a "beautiful countenance," had "fair eyes," the margin has it; "beautiful eyes," the ancient Septuagint reads. Richly endowed as he was, a poet of the highest order, a man of faith, zeal, devotedness, energy, no wonder his powers were seen in his brilliant and piercing eyes.

3. *David's training for the great destiny that God had marked for him.* It was a singular one, but perfectly adapted to the end in view. First of all, there was his association with the prophet Samuel, which must have been of incalculable benefit to him. There can be no reasonable doubt but that Samuel taught his apt and gifted pupil much; probably reading, writing, music, 1 Sam. xix:18-24. But Samuel gave him something far better than mere accomplishments, viz., the knowledge of the law of God, and the beauty of a devoted and godly life. No one could spend any time with Samuel, no one of the temperament and piety of David, without vast good to his

own soul. Saul himself could not come into his presence without benefit. The influence of the prophet on the future king of Israel was never lost.

But the main factor in his remarkable education was his afflictions and persecutions at the hands of Saul and other enemies. God sent His servant to that school and set him down to those books which were exactly suited to His purpose respecting him. He could not have been the man and the king he was had he not suffered as he did. He could not have written the psalms that he did, humanly speaking, had he not waded deep in trouble and sorrow. He could not have been the type of the Lord Jesus he is, had he not been hated, persecuted, hunted like a partridge on the mountains. Because he stood in peculiar relations to God; because his life was filled with the strangest vicissitudes, swinging through an arc that embraced much if not all of human experience, an arc that touched the highest point of fame and grandeur, and yet dipped down to the lowest humiliation and sorrow; because of his fullness of experience; he could write psalms that suit all men in all ages and conditions, psalms that go to the heart of all. Edward Irving finely says of him, "Every angel of joy and of sorrow swept, as he passed, over the chords of David's harp, and the hearts of a hundred men strove and struggled together within the narrow continent of his single heart."

Three personal blessings came to David from his trials. The first was, his prudence was unfolded. Again and again it is mentioned to his credit, 1 Sam. xviii:14, 15, 30; 2 Sam. xiv:20; Ps. xxxv:14. Second, his magnanimity. We see it all through his life, with a few painful exceptions, and especially in his forbearance toward Saul. Third, his dependence on God. It grew out of his exposure to so many and varied perils, and out of his hair-breadth escapes. How often he says, in memory of the dangers he has passed, "The Lord that hath redeemed me out of adversity." Thus he constantly refers to the Lord as his "rock," "strength," etc. Indeed much of the imagery of his Psalms is taken from the hiding-places and fastnesses that saved him from the pursuers.

5. *Foundation of Jerusalem, the capital of Israel*, 2 Sam. v, vi. It was still in the possession of the heathen Jebusites, Josh. xv:63. But David, and his chief captain, the able but unscrupulous Joab, 1 Chron. xi:6, captured it. Thus the ancient city of Melchizedek became the seat of the theocratic kingdom; and from hence onward it was called "the city of David," and "the city of God." Thither, also, amid universal rejoicing, the ark was borne, and God in this symbol of His presence, dwelt among His people. Psalms cxxxii was written in commemoration of the glorious event.

6. *The royal covenant*, 2 Sam. vii:12-16; 1 Chron. xvii:11-14. It is on the ground of this great covenant that Christ is David's Heir, Matt. i:1; Acts ii: 29-36. Whether Solomon is in it at all is questioned by some. If he is, it is in altogether a subordinate way, as in vs. 14. Bishop Horsley (quoted by Bishop Nicholson) renders vs. 14 thus: "When guilt is laid upon him, I will chasten him with the rod of men." With what gratitude does David reply to the gracious covenant made with him and his house? In vs. 19, is a very peculiar expression,

"And is this the manner of men, O Lord God?" cf. 1 Chron. xvii:17. Commentators puzzle over it not a little. It certainly refers to the Messiah. The Sept. version renders, "But this is the law of the man, O, Lord God." The meaning seems to be, "this is the law about the man," the man promised, the Son and Lord of David.

7. *David's failures and crimes.* They were neither few nor small. (1) When persecuted by Saul he sought refuge once and again among Israel's enemies. The first time he was extricated only after deep humiliation and disgrace, 1 Sam. xxi. The second time he does so, he suffers loss, 1 Sam. xxx: 1-8. But he is mercifully preserved from fighting against his own people. (2) His plurality of wives. He established a harem after the manner of oriental monarchs. To the two wives he had in the wilderness he added others, 2 Sam. v:13. The results of his sin were seen in the disorderly and turbulent family that grew up around him, and in the kindling of fierce passions in himself which led him into dreadful sin at length. (3) His close alliance with the bloody sons of Zeruiah, with Joab more particularly, who murdered as he listed, and David seemed powerless to punish, was another grievous mistake of his. (4) The crime as to Bathsheba and Uriah. The record of this dark deed sets out with the statement that when the army marched against Rabbah the king tarried at Jerusalem, 2 Sam. xi:1. "David's giving himself to ease and pleasure was the root of all his wretchedness. Standing waters gather filth. As the crab-fish seizeth upon the oyster gaping, so doth Satan upon the idle" (Trapp). Our peril is greatest when we are neglecting duty. What a sad

history! What unworthiness, that he, a king from God, honored of God with such a covenant as was made with him, to be guilty of such crimes! How much happier when hunted as a partridge! But even here grace, amazing grace, does not fail. He is restored, and writes the most pitiful wail of confession ever inspired by the Spirit of God, Ps. li, and the joy of forgiveness, Ps. xxxii. Unpunished he did not go. Amnon's sin, Absalom's rebellion, Joab's insolence, Sheba's rebellion, and Adonijah's attempt to seize the throne, were the legitimate fruits of his guilt. Ps. xcix:8. (5) His numbering the people, 2 Sam. xxiv. With all his faults and sins, David, nevertheless, was one of the truest and most faithful men Israel ever had. At heart, in the inmost core of him, David was right with God. Posture of soul toward God—that is the final test. Here David fails not.

FIRST AND SECOND KINGS.

The design of these books is to trace the history of the Hebrew kingdom through its most prosperous period to its decline and fall. They record Israel's glory while monarch and people serve the Lord; their shame and misery when they turn away from Him. The momentous lesson the books teach is obedience and blessing, apostasy and ruin.

Key-word, 'Royalty;' key-verse, 1 Kings ii:12; xi: 13" (Pierson).

Division—First Kings—Part I., David's death and Solomon's glorious reign, i-xi. Part II., revolt of Jeroboam, and establishment of the two kingdoms, xii-xxii. Second Kings—Part I., history of the two kingdoms to the captivity of Israel (northern kingdom), i-xvii. Part II., decline and captivity of Judah, xviii-xxv.

1. *Solomon's reign,* 1 Kings i-xi. His name was given him by his mother, but the Lord through the prophet Nathan, called him Jedidiah, i. e., "Beloved of Jehovah," perhaps as an assurance to David that his sin was forgiven, 2 Sam. xii:24, 25. The name Solomon, which signifies "the Peaceful," received the divine sanction, 1 Chron. xxii:9.

(1) His wisdom. 1 Kings iii:5-14. In answer to his prayer, God gave him a singularly comprehensive mind, power of observation and reflection, and a strong grasp on the great problems of human life.

He was a botanist, zoologist, architect, poet, and moral philosopher; in short, he was the first man for intellect of his day, and indeed of any time, 1 Kings iv:29-34.

(2) Extent of his empire, 1 Kings iv:21. By "the river" is meant the Euphrates, cf. Gen. xv:18; Josh. i:4.

(3) Promotion of commerce. By alliances with trading peoples contiguous to Israel he furthered commerce to such an extent that the ships of Solomon and Hiram ran on the Red sea, it is thought, as far as the Indian ocean, and on the west by the Mediterranean to Tarshish, perhaps on the coast of Spain, 2 Chron. ix:10, 21, and brought from thence gold, silver, ivory, sandal-wood, and new forms of animal life, "apes and peacocks."

(4) His magnificence. It appears in his gorgeous throne of ivory with its twelve massive lions, 2 Chron. ix:18, 19; in the sumptuous provision for his table, 1 Kings iv:22, 23; in the plentifulness of the precious metals, 2 Chron. ix:27; 1 Kings x:27; in the presence of horses and chariots in Jerusalem, for the first time, 1 Kings x:26-29; 2 Chron. i:16.

(5) The temple, 1 King vi-viii. This was Solomon's greatest work. In form the temple was an exact reproduction of the tabernacle of the wilderness, only double in size. The temple, in reality, was the sacred Tent in marble and gold. The site was Mt. Moriah, memorable as the place where Abraham's faith had been tried, and where David offered and the plague was staid, 1 Chron. xxi:28. The amount of labor, wealth, and skill expended on this magnificent sanctuary almost passes belief, 1 Chron. xxii:14-16; 1 Kings v:13-18, etc. Never,

perhaps, has the world seen a costlier structure, or one more dazzlingly beautiful. The second temple was far from being its equal, Ezra iii:12. It stood with its facade to the east. From the foundation to the roof, the front was clothed over with solid plates of gold. When the morning sun arose, the gold and marble sent back his rays with an added glory so great that a gazer standing on the Mount of Olives opposite, had to shade his eyes when looking to the temple mount. The prayer of dedication, 1 Kings viii, and God's acceptance of the house, 2 Chron. vii: 1-4, afford precious instruction.

(6) Solomon's fall, 1 Kings xi.—Through the fatal institution of polygamy he was corrupted and his court demoralized. Heathen rites were introduced; idolatrous altars arose hard by the Temple of Jehovah, vs. 6-8. The great prince sank lower and lower, seduced by the multitude of his wives and mistresses; and he disappears from the history under the deepest cloud—though the book of Ecclesiastes gives some evidence of his repentance. "Behold a greater than Solomon is here." Failure in David; failure in Solomon; failure everywhere, save in Him who is the Witness faithful and true, Jesus Christ. What a creature man is! How vain, unstable, puerile, fallible, worthless; but "Jesus Christ is the same yesterday, and today, and forever," Heb. xiii:8.

2. *Revolt of the Ten Tribes*, 1 Kings xii. Rehoboam, Solomon's son and successor, appears to have been a vain, supercilious young man, one of "foolish sons" of whom his father so often speaks. Notwithstanding the hundreds of wives Solomon had, this is the only son we read of, and he none of the wisest.

Probably his father had him in mind when he wrote the bitter words of Ecc. ii:18, 19.

Rehoboam's obstinacy and pride alienated his people; and ten tribes seceded from the house of David, and formed a separate kingdom with Jeroboam at its head. It was only because of the Lord's love for David that his throne remained for him in Jerusalem, 1 Kings xi. Four times in that chapter occur the words, "David my servant's sake;" God would prove faithful to His covenant, though David's son would not.

Jeroboam's sin, 1 Kings xii:26-30. Political motives led to its commission. To make the division complete and perpetuate his dynasty, he founded two sanctuaries, one at Dan, the other at Bethel; he placed in them beast-idols, the calves of Egypt, and with the old cry of the wilderness, Ex. xxxii:4, saluted them, "Behold thy gods, O Israel, which brought thee up out of Egypt." This distinctively was Jeroboam's sin. And from that time forward he is described as "Jeroboam, the son of Nebat, who made Israel to sin." To him directly the northern kingdom owed its ruin; to him indirectly Judah likewise her fall.

3. *The Prophets*, 1 Kings xiii, xvii, xx, etc. Prophecy implies failure, "a light that shineth in a dark place." As the transgressions of Israel and Judah increased, God's testimony by the mouth of His prophets became more and more energetic and intense. Great prophets succeed each other rapidly; sometimes they appear singly, sometimes in groups; sometimes many of them are in action together. Their solemn voices in warning are heard all over the two kingdoms, and swell and deepen as apos-

tasy grows apace, and the catastrophe approaches. Elijah, Elisha, Hosea, Amos, Isaiah, Jeremiah— what great names are associated with Israel's and Judah's decline and fall!—the greatest the world has ever known. Prophet after prophet, prophets side by side with prophets, mingling their stern and awful voices, lifting them up, making their appeals and their warnings and their threats, in the name of Jehovah, mightier and still more passionate; and yet even they, sanctioning their messages by judicial signs and wonders, are powerless to arrest the apostasy, and the end comes at last in fire and sword, tears and blood. And poor Israel's sun goes down into a dismal night that still lasts!

4. *Elijah.* Of the large number of God's witnesses during this period, to this prophet alone must a few words be devoted. Elijah's miracles, like those of Moses, are *judicial.* He shuts heaven over the rebellious people, 1 Kings xvii:1; Jas. v:17, proves at Carmel that Jehovah alone is God, and the people execute judgment on the priests of Baal, 1 King xviii, brings down fire upon the captains sent to arrest him, 2 Kings i. The Two Witnesses of Rev. xi will exercise the like power in working similar signs for the same space of time, three years and a half. His miracles were signs to Israel; theirs will be signs to the world. So, too, his last journeys when he was about to be taken away, were signs. Four places he visited in his last tours just before his rapture:

(1) Gilgal, 2 Kings ii:1—the starting point. It was the spot where God "rolled away the reproach of Egypt from Israel," when Joshua had circumcised the people, Josh. v:9. But this spot was memorable

for the sin of Saul which cost him his throne, 1 Sam. xv. Transgression was multiplied at Gilgal, Hos. ix:15; Amos iv:4. The point of departure in a double sense! Elijah cannot stay at Gilgal because of sin.

(2) Bethel, 2 Kings ii:2. A place of extraordinary visions and promises, Gen. xxviii; xxxi:13, etc. But at Bethel, Jeroboam had set up the golden calf, and there Israel had worshipped and sinned, Hos. x: 15; Amos iv:4. The prophet cannot remain at Bethel; sin meets him there.

(3) Jericho, 2 Kings ii:4. Formerly the power of the enemy barred Israel's way at this point. God smote the place, and pronounced a curse against it. Man rebuilt it notwithstanding the curse, 1 Kings xvi: 34. The prophet cannot remain here, for sin again confronts him. Elijah passes the Jordan, and out beyond the territory of Israel and into the world of the Gentiles. How deep the lesson if the people had eyes to see, minds to understand. What was all this but a symbolical representation of the Lord's departure from Israel, the prophetic light going out, the candlestick being removed? But Israel would not see nor heed.

5. *Captivity of Israel*, 2 Kings xvii. "The course of iniquity had been run. The stream grew darker in its downward flow. Every commandment of God was broken. People and king vied in debauchery." Is it any surprise God should name them Lo-ruhamah, no-mercy, and Lo-ammi, not my people? Hos i. The last king of Israel was Hoshea, a better man than most of his predecessors, 2 Kings xvii:1, 2. Nevertheless, the catastrophe came in his day. A more devout ruler could not have averted it. Louis

XVI. was one of the best of French kings, yet under him burst forth the revolution which consumed him and his queen. Seeds which ripen into a harvest of judgment are sown long before the reaping-time.

6. *Captivity of Judah*, 2 Kings xxiv, xxv. Many faithful kings Judah had who ruled in the fear of God, and who earnestly sought the reformation of the land, as Joash, Hezekiah, Josiah; but more were disloyal who walked in the ways of the kings of Israel. A fatal mistake was the introduction of the idolatrous house of Ahab into the line of David, by the marriage of Jehoram with Athalia, 2 Chron. xxi: 6, one of the wickedest of princesses, a true daughter of the hateful Jezebel. The last kings of Judah, Manasseh, Jehoiakim, Jehoiakin, and Zedekiah, were about as bad as they well could be. It was then that Babylon appeared in the field and Judah went into a captivity of seventy years; Babylon, the inventress of idolatry, became the instrument of executing judgment on idolatrous Judah.

Three times the army of Nebuchadnezzar invaded Judah. First, when Jehoiakim was reigning, the king who ruthlessly cut with his penknife the scroll of Jeremiah and cast the pieces into the brazier of coals whereat he warmed himself, Jer. xxxvi:23. Jehoiakim surrendered to the Chaldeans, and some of the principal men went into captivity, among whom were Daniel and his friends, Dan. i:1, 6. The second invasion was under Jehoiakin, when a much larger deportation of Jews to Babylon took place. The third, at the rebellion of Zedekiah, when the city was destroyed, and untold suffering endured. It was during these stirring times that the powerful ministry of Jeremiah was exercised.

7. *Gentile supremacy.* With the fall of Israel and Judah, the world's power passed into the hands of the Gentiles. Babylon was summoned to the place of imperial power, of world empire, Jer. xxvii:5-7; Dan. ii:37, 38. "Thou art this head of gold." "The times of the Gentiles" then began, and they run on still. Israel has never been reset in the place of independence and of distinct nationality from that day to this.

What then? Is this all? Is there nothing more for this poor, dismembered, dispersed people of Israel? Surely. God who cannot lie has declared they shall yet be Ammi, my people. And their restoration and conversion will be blessing for the whole world, as their casting away has been blessing to the Gentiles, Rom. xi.

FIRST AND SECOND CHRONICLES.

The Books of the Kings give us the general and public history of the government of Israel; its glory in the reigns of David and Solomon; its fall, and the causes which led to it.

The Books of Chronicles, while traversing substantially the same ground, have another purpose, a well-defined aim, viz., that of tracing the history of Judah, and the house of David. Israel (the kingdom of Samaria) does not enter into these books save as its kings come into contact with those of Judah. In Chronicles there seems to be a kind of studied avoidance of any mention of the northern kingdom, and the attention of the reader is held steadily to Judah, Jerusalem, the temple and its priests and services, as if God was now concerned exclusively with these.

The key-word is "Election;" the key-verses, 1 Chron. xvii:7, 8, 27; xxviii:5.

Chronicles serves well as a title, if we understand it to mean the equivalent of "Acts," or "History." "Things Omitted" (the title of the Sept.) is inaccurate. The books are not a supplement to other books of Scripture; they are an independent work, having their own plan and end.

1. *The time of composition can be approximately fixed.* The books were written at the close of the Babylonian exile. The genealogy of the house of

David is carried down to Zerubbabel, if not a little lower, iii:17-19. In 1 Chron. vi:15 the captivity is spoken of in such a way as to make it evident that the author was writing in a time subsequent to that event. It is generally believed that Ezra was the author. Certainly no man of that time could be found better fitted for the work.

2. *Contents.* These may be conveniently distributed into four groups.

I. *Genealogical tables, from Adam to the return from the exile*, 1 Chron. i-ix. It is important to observe that throughout these long lists of names there is traceable the sovereign choice of God. The lines follow mainly the track of a blessed generation, a separated race. Thus, beginning with Adam, we have the family of Seth down to Noah. Then after a brief list of the families of Japheth and of Ham, the family of Shem, whose God is the Lord, is taken up and traced to Abraham who becomes, as it were, a fresh stock. His posterity after the flesh is first given; then Isaac, the child of promise, a fresh stock, because a child of election, follows, with Jacob and his twelve sons, of whom Judah is the central object of the inspired writer, for he is the royal tribe, from whom the Messiah is to spring; and the family of David is given the pre-eminence in the line of Judah. Two of the sons of Israel are omitted, Dan and Zebulun; no genealogy of them is given. All through it is the sovereign action of grace in the selection of those who are brought nigh to God that is prominent.

II. *David's reign*, 1 Chron. x-xxix:22. After a brief account of Saul, 1 Chron. ix:35; x, David's throne is the theme, the kingdom, looked at as ordained of God for blessing. And accordingly David's sufferings and faults are passed over in silence, except that of numbering the people, 1 Chron. xxi.

III. *Account of the kingdom under Solomon*, 1 Chron. xxix:28-30; 2 Chron. i-ix. "Then Solomon sat on the throne of the Lord as king, instead of David, his father, and prospered"—a remarkable expression not found elsewhere (cf. 1 Chron. xxviii:5). The throne was God's; and people and king should have sought the realization of the august idea. They did not, yet the idea is not lost sight of or abandoned, for the Messiah is to fulfill it perfectly. So David and Solomon become types in these books of the future glory of the true Son and Heir.

IV. *Account of the kingdom of Judah from the disruption to the captivity*, 2 Chron. x-xxxvi.

3. *Design of First and Second Chronicles.* Their object is manifold. Some of these purposes may be pointed out. First, God's dispensational ways. Obviously, with the opening of Chronicles a new era begins. Through all the preceding books we have the record of God's ways with His chosen people, the seed of Abraham. The record is carried forward through the second Book of Kings, when it is broken off, no less in sorrow than in anger. With Chronicles the sacred writer goes back to the beginning and starts again with Adam, Seth, etc., and dwells with great minuteness on the tribe of Judah, and the house of David. With Chronicles, therefore, begins the second great division of the Bible. Up to this point failure has marked the whole history. A fresh start is now made; and David's Divine Son, in whom all will be made good, comes more and more into prominence. The Books

of Chronicles are related to the new order of things, not to the old. They are not linked with Samuel and Kings, but with Ezra and Nehemiah, with Zechariah and Malachi. They do not look back, but forward. The antediluvian economy failed through man's sin; the patriarchal likewise; the Jewish next, in its national capacity. But here begins a new epoch. A remnant according to the election of grace returns from captivity to the land of promise; and the Spirit of God turns their faces toward Him who is promised, who will not fail.

A second purpose is, to secure the genealogy of Christ, as the Son of David. Hence the lineage of David's house, and indeed of the whole tribe of Judah, is very fully given. Evidently, Matthew and Luke availed themselves of Chronicles in tracing the human descent of our Lord.

Another practical object was to confirm the returned captives in their allegiance and fidelity to the Lord. It is pointed out in an impressive manner that ordinarily temporal blessing ensued when King and people renounced idolatry, destroyed the idols, and served the Lord; while punishment followed disobedience and apostasy. Such teaching was calculated to settle the Jews in the conviction that the fate of the nation was in their hands.

4. *David's arrangements for the worship of God*, 1 Chron. xxiii-xxvi. These provisions relate to the services of the temple, and are quite full and explicit. The priests, sons of Aaron, were divided into twenty-four orders or courses: the Levites into twenty-four courses of singers and musicians, porters, keepers of the treasures of the house of God, officers and judges. It is singular that nothing

touching these arrangements is recorded in the books of Samuel or of Kings. The reason for the omission of them in those books probably is this: in the disorder and confusion consequent upon the captivity, much of the knowledge of the order and manner of God's worship would be lost, and such a guide as here is given would be both necessary and useful, indeed, indispensable. Hence they are recorded here alone.

5. *Dedication of the Temple*, 2 Chron. v. The splendid structure reared on Mt. Moriah was at length completed. The Cherubim, let it be observed, stood at the lower end of the house, and really looked outward, 2 Chron. iii:13 [margin] as if intimating that a wider field of blessing ere long would be enjoyed. The priests began the dedicatory services, but it was only when the singers and players on musical instruments sang and played "as one, to make one sound to be heard in praising and thanking the Lord; and when they lifted up their voices with the trumpets and cymbals and instruments of music, and praised the Lord, for He is good; for His mercy endureth forever; that then the house was filled with a cloud, even the house of the Lord," vss. 13, 14. So, too, when the disciples "were all with one accord in one place," Acts ii:1, the blessing came—the Holy Spirit was poured out upon them in richest profusion. Unity of will, of heart, of voice and mind brings the blessing. Our discords and jarring purposes and wishes, hinder our prayers and worship

6. *Deliverances wrought for the house of David.* There are four of them, and they mark a kind of progress, and were significant signs to Judah.

(1) Abijah, son of Rehoboam, gained a great victory over Jeroboam, 2 Chron. xiii (not recorded in Kings). Abijah was completely surrounded by the forces of Israel, and escape seemed impossible. Judah cried to the Lord, the priests sounded with the trumpets, and the men gave a shout, "and God smote Jeroboam and all Israel before Abijah and Judah." "Thus the children of Israel were brought under at that time and the children of Judah prevailed, because they relied upon the Lord God of their fathers."

(2) Asa, son of Abijah and a better man, found himself confronted by a prodigious host of Ethiopians, 2 Chron. xiv (not recorded in Kings). The battle was not yet joined when Asa appealed to God in the noble words of faith: "Lord, it is nothing with thee to help, whether with many, or with them that have no power; help us, O Lord our God, for we rest on Thee, and in Thy name we go against this multitude. O Lord, Thou art our God; let not man prevail against Thee." The Lord in answer to the appeal gave him at once the mastery over the enemy.

(3) Jehoshaphat had a still more remarkable deliverance, 2 Chron. xx (not recorded in Kings). He was threatened by a formidable combination of Moabites, Ammonites, and Edomites. In this crisis of impending danger he proclaimed a fast throughout his kingdom, and summoned a national prayer-meeting at Jerusalem. The pious monarch led the devotions of the people; and in his prayer he spoke of Abraham as the "friend of God," cf. Isa. xli:8; Jas. ii:23. He marched out against the enemy, in this extraordinary order: in the fore-front of his

battle-line he put singers who should praise the Lord, and who sang the refrain of the Temple-hymn, "Praise the Lord, for his mercy endureth forever." The army of Judah drew no sword, shot no arrow. The Lord turned the arms of the hostile allies against each other; and Judah was delivered without striking a blow.

(4) Hezekiah's deliverance was even yet more wonderful, 2 Chron. xxxii; 2 Kings xviii, xix. The occasion of it was the visit and insulting letter of Sennacherib, king of Assyria. The godly monarch met the crisis as a man who trusted in God. The enemy relied on "chariots and horses," but Hezekiah remembered the name of Jehovah. Sennacherib would have laughed, and thought him in an agony of fear had he seen the king on his knees with the open letter spread out before the Lord. The proud boast of the Assyrian was but brief. In this case, there was no blare of trumpet, no call to arms, no marching of an army. In the silence of the night, and unattended by any human agency, the angel of the Lord smote the camp of the Assyrians, and with shame, defeated and broken, the proud king turned back to his own land.

7. *A main cause of Judah's fall*, 2 Chron. xxxvi: 21; cf. Lev. xxvi:34. A striking fulfillment of prophecy, and the shining proof of its truth. Nearly nine hundred years before the event God said that the people should be carried away from the land, and it should have its rest. And here is the accomplishment. To violate any command of His is to bring upon one's self certain punishment.

There are some apparent discrepancies in these books of Chronicles with others of the Old Testament. But all of them can be easily explained, or are due altogether to errors of transcribers. We ought to be thankful that copyists of the Bible, in the days before printing, adhered so faithfully to the text, and refused to tamper with it in the slightest degree. For example, how easily might a transcriber have changed 2 Sam. viii:4 so as to harmonize with 1 Chron. xviii:4; or 2 Chron. xxxvi:9 with 2 Kings xxiv:8. But none of the copyists did so. Their reverence for the Word of God was too deep and true to allow them for a moment to do anything of the sort. How different are some who live in our day whose pens are far more reckless and daring than Jehoiakim's pen-knife!

EZRA.

With Ezra and Nehemiah a new era of Jewish history begins. The exile has terminated; a remnant of the chosen people has returned to their land; the temple is rebuilt; and a new order of things inaugurated. The two books relate to the restoration and reorganization, and to the reformation of abuses which had crept in. They extend over a period of about one hundred years. Key-word, "Restoration." Key-verse, Ezra i:5; Neh. ii:5.

1. *New names meet us in these books.* Babylon, the haughty power that made Judah captive, slew Zedekiah's sons before his eyes and rudely blinded him forever, has been overthrown, as it had been predicted, Jer. l:1-3. God had used that proud nation to chastise His guilty people; but it exceeded its commission, and was in turn punished, Isa. xlvii:6. Persia now sways the scepter of universal dominion. For the first time we encounter the name of *Jews*. Hitherto Israel is the title by which the chosen people were called; now it alternates with the name that came in with the exile of Judah and at length almost entirely supplanted it. In Ezra and Nehemiah both are found, while in Esther, Jews alone are mentioned.

2. *The decree of Cyrus*, Ezra. i:1-4. It was issued in the first year of his reign at Babylon, B. C. 536, and had for its scope the return of the Jews to Pal-

estine and the rebuilding of the temple at Jerusalem. Many things are remarkable touching this decree: (1) It was promulgated by a heathen king, spontaneously as it would seem, although resulting from the exertion of divine influence on his mind, vs. 1. (2) It recognizes one supreme God, "the Lord God of heaven," vs. 2. (3) It declares that the supreme God had "charged" the king to rebuild the temple. (4) It urges the return of the captives to their own land, and blesses them in the name of the Lord God of Israel, vs. 3. (5) It directs that gifts be made for the building of the temple, vs. 4. The secret of God's government of the world is here, in part, open to us, and we see how great political events, anteriorly improbable, are brought about by His action on men's hearts, Prov. xxi:1. We infer also from the decree that either monotheism still prevailed in Persia or that Cyrus through contact with the Jews had come to know the God of heaven. About fifty thousand Jews availed themselves of the privileges of Cyrus' decree, and returned to their homes in Judea, Ez. ii.

3. *Building and dedication of the temple*, Ez. iii-vi. Never has any work for God been undertaken which did not meet with opposition. It was so in the building of the second temple. The leaders in the good work were Zerubbabel, a prince of the house of David, and Jeshua (or Joshua) the high priest. For a brief time they were permitted to prosecute their task unmolested; but ere long the enemy began to throw hindrances in the way. Satan will never allow any inroad on his kingdom without resenting it. A proposition to join in the work was made the builders by the half-heathen Samaritans,

the mongrel population that had been settled in the territory of the Ten Tribes by the Assyrian conqueror. The overture was declined; and the Samaritans became the open and avowed enemies of the Jews. During three reigns, the remainder of that of Cyrus, of Cambyses, and the Pseudo-Smerdis, they stopped the work on the temple. Beginning again, Ez. v:2, the satrap Tatnai and others interfered, but failed to arrest it. Then a letter was sent Darius the king, asking that search be made as to the existence of the Cyrus decree of which doubt seems to have been entertained. No copy of it was to be found at the capital, so effectually had the usurper, Smerdis, destroyed everything of the previous reigns. But at Ecbatana, vi:2, it was discovered; and Darius confirmed it by a decree of his own, and even directed that aid should be given the Jews from the royal taxes that the house of God might be completed. Moreover, the voice of prophecy, silent since the "third of Cyrus," when Daniel uttered his last warning (Dan. x:1), is once more heard. Haggai and Zechariah exhort, entreat, warn and encourage the people in the good work in which they are engaged; and at length they see the happy accomplishment of the great undertaking. After twenty-one years the sanctuary, the "second temple," is completed and dedicated with appropriate ceremonies, Ez. vi:14-18.

The golden and silver vessels that Nebuchadnezzar had seized and carried to Babylon were restored. It was a time of great emotion, loud weeping and louder joy. Aged Jews who had seen the first gorgeous Temple could not refrain from tears.

The passover was observed for the first time for

seventy years at least. Six memorable passovers are recorded in the Old Testament: the first in Egypt, Ex. xii; the second in the wilderness, Num. ix; the third at Gilgal, Josh. v; the fourth in the reign of Hezekiah, 2 Chron. xxx; the fifth in the eighteenth year of Josiah, 2 Kings xxiii; the sixth this of the restored exiles, Ez. vi:19. If we add that in connection with which our Lord was crucified, we have seven notable observances of this feast in the history of Israel.

4. *Second return of Jews under Ezra, and reforms*, Ez. vii-x. Fifty-seven years after the dedication of the temple, a further return of Israelites from captivity took place under the leadership of Ezra. His authority to execute the objects he had in view was derived from a decree issued to Ezra by Artaxerxes in the seventh year of his reign, vii:8, 12-26. The royal commission contemplated (1) the return of all so minded with Ezra to Jerusalem, vs. 13. According to chapter viii, 1,773 adult male colonists accompanied Ezra. "Counting five to a family this would give a total of nearly 9,000 souls;" (2) the decree invested Ezra with the chief authority over the whole district "beyond the river," vss. 25, 26; (3) an exemption from taxation of every kind was granted to all grades of Levites, vs. 24; (4) conveying of certain offerings of the king and his officers to Jerusalem, vss. 15, 19. There can be hardly any doubt but that numbers of the ten tribes returned with Ezra to Judea. The term Israel which occurs frequently in both Ezra and Nehemiah, indicates this, Ez. ii:70; vii:28, etc. Besides, sacrifices were offered for the twelve tribes, Ez. vi:16, 17· viii:35· Priests and Levites were found in considerable num-

bers among the restored captives, even the descendants of the high priest as was Ezra himself, for he was of the lineage of Hilkiah and Aaron, Ez. vii:1, 5. Many Jews remained in the provinces of Babylon, as we know from the book of Esther, and they established there schools which gave birth at length to the Babylonian Talmud, the most influential of all the Jewish uninspired writings. Mr. Wilkinson, of the Mildmay Mission to the Jews, in his book, "Israel My Glory," demonstrates that on the return from the captivity of Babylon all the tribes of Israel were represented in the resettlement of Palestine; and this fact helps to solve not a few problems, as e. g. that of the lost ten tribes, the address of James to the twelve tribes, Jas. i:1, etc. Of course, it is not denied that there are remnants of those lost tribes scattered over the world who will be restored when God sets His hand a second time to bring back His people, Is. xi:11, but it may be well for us to reflect that among the Israelites known to us in Asia, Europe and America, there are descendants of the twelve tribes; not those of Judah and Benjamin alone.

5. *Ezra as a reformer.* All through his book there are evidences that his chief aim was to reorganize the worship of God, to instruct the people in the law, and to restore the ancient rights and customs. That he was competent for such work is clear from the fact of his being "a ready scribe in the law of Moses," Ez. vii:6. By this is meant that he was not only a careful and accurate transcriber, but also a sound interpreter of the law. His influence over the Jews of his time and of succeeding ages was very great. He ranked with David and Moses.

(1) He brought about the repudiation of heathen wives, Ez. x:10. Out of the whole population there were 112 cases of mixed marriages to which the law of Moses was applied and obeyed.

(2) He was an expounder of the law to the people, Neh. viii. His public teaching was of the most effective kind, for it was followed by the very best results, viz., reformation, penitence, and genuine sorrow for sin.

(3) A persistent Jewish tradition ascribes to him the founding of that beneficent institution of later Judaism, the synagogue.

(4) He had much to do, it is very generally believed, with the arrangement of the canon of the Old Testament. The order in which the book of Psalms comes to us, it has been long held, is due to Ezra. That he was in a position to do such important work is evident from the fact of his being learned in the Word of God and the inspiration of the Spirit of God which he enjoyed.

NEHEMIAH.

Nehemiah was an official of rank at the court of the Persian monarch, Artaxerxes Longimanus. He is not to be confounded with the Nehemiah who returned from the exile to Jerusalem under Zerubbabel and Joshua, Ezra ii:2. The "cup-bearer" to the king flourished and wrought his good work under God in behalf of the restored captives nearly one hundred years after Zerubbabel reached Judea. This book extends over a period of about twelve years, viz., from B. C. 445 to 433. It contains the account of Nehemiah himself and of certain proceedings in which he was engaged between the twentieth and thirty-second or thirty-third years of Artaxerxes' reign. It is the last of the Old Testament historical books. Its design is to supplement and complete the account of the return of the Jews from captivity recorded in Ezra, to record the circumstances attending the rebuilding of the walls of Jerusalem and the reforms which were introduced. While Nehemiah is almost universally admitted to be the author, there are evidences that he availed himself of documents existing in his day for certain portions of his work. Its date is B. C. 430-432.

The contents may be distributed thus: Introductory, chapters i, ii; in which the writer narrates the circumstances under which he engaged in the work of reconstructing the walls of the city, and the authority given him by the king so to do. The main narrative, chapters iii-vii:5; where it is interrupted by a list of the families that returned in the first expedition; then, from the close of chapter vii, the narrative is resumed and continued, with other lists inserted, to the end of the book. It will be observed that Neh. vii and Ezra ii are identical, or nearly so. Which list is the original, and which the copy? Or did these two writers copy from some genealogical register extant in their times? Nehemiah tells us vii:5, that he found a register of the genealogy of those who went up at the first—language which plainly signifies that the list he gives was one which he found already existing, and the fair supposition is that it was either that of Ezra ii, or some document that preserved the family records of the Jews. Probably the former supposition is nearer the truth.

Nehemiah gives a vivid picture of the condition of the Jews at the time of the restoration. Their feebleness and paucity of numbers are very noticeable. The sneer of Sanballat that a fox might break down their walls suggests much. The list in chapter vii gives of "the whole congregation together" 42,360, and of servants, 7,337, and 245 singers. The weakness of the congregation is seen when this number is compared with the times when Judah alone numbered 470,000 warriors, 1 Chron. xxi:5.

Ezra was a great reformer, and he was ably supported in the work of reorganization by this earnest and uncompromising champion of pure Judaism—Nehemiah. News of the afflictions of his people at Jerusalem and of the ruined condition of the walls of the holy city reached him at the Persian court, and caused him profound grief. He sought and obtained leave of his sovereign to go up to Jerusalem and rebuild the broken walls of the city. This was about twelve or thirteen years after the first visit of Ezra. Keeping his mission secret, Nehemiah planned the work he had set himself to do; partitioned out the task among a large number of working-parties, all acting simultaneously; and in a little more than seven weeks the entire wall was repaired and restored to its full height, Neh. vi:15. Strong doors were set in the gateway, guards established, and the gates were kept closed from nightfall "until the sun was hot," vii:3. Nehemiah's administration at Jerusalem was not less than thirteen years, and he governed with the same vigor, promptness, and energy which marked the opening months of his work.

(1) His hospitality, dispensed both towards natives and foreigners, was generous, v:14-18.

(2) He augmented the population of Jerusalem by bringing men in from the country districts, xi:1.

(3) He redeemed large numbers of Jews who had been sold into slavery among the heathen, and restored them to their native land; and put an end to a system of borrowing money of the most oppressive sort, v:1-13; x:31.

(4) He enforced the strict observance of the Sabbath, x:31; xiii:15-22; and the annual payment for the temple-service, x:32-37.

(5) Like Ezra, he compelled all those who had married foreign wives to divorce them, xiii:1-3, 23-28. Strict, prompt, uncompromising, he would allow no relaxation of the old law, no departure from the old ways, no consorting with foreigners. He found that Tobiah the Ammonite, was living in one

of the chambers of the house of God by the sanction of Eliashib, the guardian of the temple, and forthwith Nehemiah of his own authority turned all the furniture into the street, xiii:7, 8. Ezra was the ecclesiastical reformer of his times, Nehemiah the civil. The one reorganized the priesthood, the other society. Both labored untiringly to bring back the returned captives to the law of Moses, and the practice of strict Judaism. What is most striking in these books is the intense monotheism, the Jewish nationalism which would have nothing to do even with the Samaritans.

Results of the captivity. (1) It cured the Jews of all hankering after strange gods. They returned to their land with deep abhorrence of idol worship, and resumed their places as witnesses to the supreme and sole Deity of Jehovah. To this day they have never forgotten the lesson. Into whatever earthliness and blindness of heart they may have fallen, they have never returned to the idolatry of Ahaz and Manasseh. The mother of idols, Babylon, crushed the spirit of idolatry in Israel.

(2) The restoration did not set Israel in the place they had lost. There was no Shechinah in the Most Holy Place, no Urim or Thummim with the priest, no national independence as formerly. They were subject to the Persians, the Greeks, the Romans, who finally demolished the temple, trod the city into the dust, and led forth the people into an exile which still endures. From the return from Babylon to the appearing of the Messiah we read of no miracle or miraculous intervention of God. In the expressive language of the Epistle to the Hebrews the dispensation "was waxing old, and ready

to perish," viii:13. God might visit in grace and mercy, as we know He did, but there was no more the visible power of former times. When an economy has been spoiled and ruined by man's unfaithfulness and sin, God does not restore it to its original purity and power; He removes it to introduce something better.

ESTHER.

The book of Esther chronologically falls into the interval between the first and the second expeditions to Jerusalem from Babylon, a period embracing about eighty years. Ahashuerus' reign began in B. C. 486, and ended in B. C. 465—twenty-one years. In the third year of his reign the events narrated in this book commenced. The book is anonymous, but it must have been written not long after the death of Ahashuerus—Rawlinson thinks within twenty years from the death of that monarch. It is a deeply interesting book, one of the inspired commentaries on God's marvelous providence.

The key-word is "Providence"; the key-verse, iv: 14.

1. Principal characters of the book—*dramatis personæ:*

(1) Ahashuerus. No doubt this is the Hebrew name for the famous Persian king, Xerxes. *Khshayarsha* is said to be his Persian name; and the similarity between it and the Hebrew is so great as to be almost identical. The Greeks turned it into Xerxes. This is the man who played so important a part in Grecian history; who marched his army against Greece; who insanely attempted to chain the Hellespont, and madly beat the sea with whips because forsooth it broke up his boats.

(2) Mordecai, a Jew dwelling at Shushan and in-

timate at court; an upright, intelligent, and farsighted man, to whose noble heart the people of Israel were very dear. He was of the family of Kish and of the tribe of Benjamin. He was the first cousin of Esther, whom he had brought up as his own daughter. Her Hebrew name was Hadassah, Esther being probably Persian. She was an orphan, and a woman not only of great beauty, but also of sagacity and devotion. Her "woman's wit" was more than a match for the astute and malignant Haman.

(3) Haman was a high officer at the court of Xerxes, was possessed of princely wealth, v:11, stood nearest the throne, was entrusted with the king's signet-ring, and had the power of life and death over the subjects of the empire, iii:1, 10-12. But withal he was a man of utmost vanity, blindest prejudices, and capable of the deadliest enmity; a timeserving, selfish, implacable, swaggering bully, a man whose mind was covered over at the top so as to shut out all lofty aspirations, and closed in at the sides so as to shut out all kindness, and open only at the bottom for the incoming of base passions, pride, haughtiness and hate. Singular, when all the world was bowing down to him, Haman would go home to boast of his riches, his children, his high standing with the king and queen, and yet wind up the list of his successes with the doleful note, "Yet all this availeth me nothing so long as I see Mordecai, the Jew, sitting at the king's gate;" supremely unhappy because one poor man refused to stand up with turban in his hand as he passed in and out of the palace-gate. Haman was an Agagite, probably a descendant of Amalek; and being such Mordecai could not pay him homage, Ex. xvii:16.

2. The design of the book is to show God's providential care of His people. It also illustrates the nature and ways of Divine Providence. Multitudes of Jews remained in the region of Babylon after the publication of Cyrus' decree for the return to Judea. They had been born and reared there and would not exchange it even for Jerusalem. The same God who watched over the builders of the temple and the walls of the holy city also guarded these stranger Jews in the one hundred and twenty provinces of Ahashuerus' empire, and this book is the record of His care for them. "No weapon that is formed against thee" is the lesson it teaches. It is an inspired commentary on the great promise, "I will not fail nor forsake thee," Deu. xxxi:6; Heb. xiii:5. Note some of the characteristic features.

3. Providence is secret, mysterious, and even unintelligible until its ends are revealed. One peculiarity of the book is that the name of God is not found in it. In this it differs from all other portions of the word of God. Even the shortest Psalm has it. "The author avoids, as if by design, the name of God," writes Ewald. And yet there are few parts of Scripture where He is more obviously present than in this. There must be a reason for this omission of the name. (1) The Jews' relation to God. They were out of the land of promise and of the covenant, and were in that of the stranger; they held no longer any position owned of God. So God acts toward them in accordance with the facts. He stands at a distance from them, as we may say; does not show Himself openly; watches over them from afar, and in a nameless way; and therefore, characteristically, His name does not appear in this book just as

He Himself is not seen in open interposition in their behalf. Infinite goodness delivers them, but in a way in exact accordance with the relation they sustain to Him. But this is likewise the distinctive feature of Providence in the broadest sense. It is mysterious, nameless, often paradoxical and inexplicable; yet to faith the finger of God is visible in every event, His hand is discovered in the strange weaving that goes on. Men and women appear to be the chief actors in this drama: Ahashuerus, Vashti, Esther, Mordecai, Haman and the rest, these are the prominent figures; these seem to be doing all that is done. But back of the screen there stands One who is infinitely wise and loving and patient, who guides all things for the accomplishment of His glorious purposes, and for the good of His people. His name is not mentioned, as He Himself is not seen save as faith discovers Him; yet in all that occurs He is present. We live in a world governed by a system of laws invariable and constant, so we are told. Doubtless. But back of all law, natural or otherwise, One is who upholds and controls all, and uses them for His glory, Heb. i:3. Here is a great manufactory. Thousands of spindles are twirling, numberless wheels and shafts and belts are revolving; men and women run here and there, receiving the finished material, supplying the machinery with fresh. Who turns all that vast and complicated mechanism? Itself? The men and women attending it? No. Outside, in the little brick building pulses and throbs the strong engine that moves all within. Who shape and guide the events of the world? Statesmen, politicians, armies? Only in a very subordinate way. Every wheel and screw, every shaft, pivot and belt in the complicated machinery of human affairs is under the hand of Him, who is unseen and nameless, and yet who controls and conducts all things according to His sovereign will. Nevertheless, He seems to stand apart from them, and at a distance. It is appropriate, therefore, that in a book devoted to the elucidation of God's mysterious providence His name should be omitted.

(2) Another characteristic is, attention to minutia and detail. Providence in this book takes up the little things, the trifles as men name them, and out of these works its far-reaching aims. Out of the whim of Ahashuerus during his great feast the queen Vashti was set aside, and Esther, the orphan Jewess, chosen in her stead, i, ii. A sleepless night on the part of the king led to the consultation of the court journals and the discovery of Modecai's fidelity whereby the king's life had been saved, which brought him into royal favor and set him in a position effectively to counteract and checkmate the cruel plots of the enemy, Haman, against the Jews, vi. In its marvelous unfoldings, Providence never neglects what men may be disposed to regard as things of no moment. It takes up the details, the minutia, the shreds and ravelings of life, and it combines and twists them together into a mighty cable by which irresistibly the purposes of God are drawn forward and accomplished. All revolutions, changes, achievements whatsoever, greatest and smallest, which the world has ever beheld, have often, in the course of their genesis, depended on the merest trifles, on the turning of straws, we might say.

It is the delight of the historian to trace the starting-point of the French revolution to the cast of a camp kettle over the head of a Marquis Riqueti as he lay wounded on a bridge at the battle of Cosano. That marquis, thus saved from death, became the grandfather of the fiery Mirabeau who was the prime leader in the movement which culminated in the horrors of the Revolution. It was the flight of birds from north toward the south which turned the prows of Columbus' little ships to the southern half of the western hemisphere, and which led ultimately to the settlement of that section of the world by the peoples of the Latin race. God's Providence meant that this northern continent should be reserved for a very different people, a Protestant people, with an open Bible, and with church and state completely separated. History is filled with similar instances of the very greatest and most far-reaching consequences following small divergences at the starting-point. As with nations so with the individual.

Many a one's whole life-current has been changed by a trivial circumstance; by going around the square of a city in one direction rather than in another, by meeting casually with another whose words exert a lasting influence.

(3) The intelligence and wisdom of Providence is another feature which the book reveals. Fate is blind. Providence has eyes. Fatalism says, Whatever is, must be. Providence says, Whatever God ordains must be; but God never ordains anything without a benevolent purpose. Esther strikingly illustrates all this. We see how exactly God adjusts everything to accomplish His will. Queen Esther comes to the throne for just such a time of distress

and exigency as that through which the Jews were to pass, iv:14, 16. Sleep is taken from Ahashuerus at precisely the right time, vi:1-3. A day sooner or a day later might have been fatal. Mordecai is brought into prominence at the right juncture, vi:10-13. On the thirteenth day of the first month the lot was cast by the superstitious Haman for the slaughter of the innocent people of Mordecai; and it fixed the day of execution on the thirteenth of the twelfth month, one year hence. God ordered it so that sufficient time should intervene, that there might be ample opportunity for counteraction and ultimate deliverance, iii:7; viii:9-17; ix:1, 2.

4. *Alleged difficulties.* Some have objected to the contents of Esther as improbable. It has been said that it is unlikely that the Persian monarch would issue an order for the destruction of the Jews, and afterward a counter-order authorizing them to slay their enemies, his own subjects. But if it be true as related by an ancient historian (Diodorus Siculus), that Xerxes put the Medians forward at Thermopylae that they might be all killed because he believed they were not reconciled to the loss of their national supremacy, it is surely not incredible that he should grant permission to his chief officer to destroy strangers who were represented as dangerous to the well-being of the state. Besides, we are to remember that the events of the book transpired after the disastrous expedition to Greece. Xerxes, we may well believe, was exasperated with the result, and in no humor to show clemency. Haman insinuated that vast revenues would flow into the king's treasury from the plundered Jews, and in the exhausted condition of the finances the plot must

have commended itself to the king of the Persians.

Furthermore, we must remember that the stupid custom of the Medes and Persians as to the irreversible nature of a royal decree still prevailed, and Xerxes himself, autocrat as he was, could not annul it. The only thing to be done was to authorize the Jews to defend themselves, and this the king did. The feast of Purim, instituted at the time, became a national observance, and has remained to this day as the most cherished of Jewish usages, and is proof of the integrity and validity of the book.

JOB.

The book of Job is one of the noblest poems in existence. The splendor of imagery which glows on every page; the personages introduced into it; the mysterious problems which it discusses; the action which sweeps through every emotion of the soul and strikes every chord of the human heart, invest the book with peculiar interest.

"The key-word is "Chastisement;" the key-verse, xxxiv:31, 32.

It is anonymous. It has been ascribed to Job himself, to Elihu, to Solomon, Ezra, Moses and others. The question of its authorship can never be finally settled. There is something very attractive in the view that while Moses was sojourning in Midian he came in contact with those who told of Job's great trial and of his happy deliverance, and that he wrote this majestic poem; but we cannot verify it. The anonymous character of the book, however, does not invalidate it. The authorship of Esther and of the Epistle to the Hebrews is unknown, yet their canonicity is not questioned.

1. *Is Job a real or fictitious character?* The actual existence of the patriarch has been denied by many. Rabbi Maimonides, of the twelfth century, appears to have been the first to advance this notion. In current literature one meets with it almost con-

stantly. We hold that the contents of this book are veritable history. The extreme circumstantiality of the details; the description of Job, of his family and friends, with their names and special designations, his country, property, and many other points of the like nature, mark the history rather than fiction. Besides, the Bible itself settles this matter for all who receive it as God's Word. The prophet Ezekiel associates him with Noah and Daniel, in a way to make his identity as real as those other servants of God, Ezek. xiv:14, 20. If Daniel and Noah were persons, then was Job also, Jas. **v**: 11; "Ye have heard of the patience of Job, and have seen the end of the Lord; that the Lord is very pitiful, and of tender mercy." That reference would be wholly without point, and an impeachment of the apostle's inspiration if Job were mythical.

2. *The age in which Job lived.* Usher's chronology fixes it at B. C. 1520, twenty-nine years before the Exodus. But if the book were contemporary with the deliverance from Egypt, we might expect some reference to the events connected therewith, and more particularly in a debate in which human suffering, and God's providence are the theme. Silence here is inexplicable. That Job lived in patriarchal times is very probable. He survived his sore trial one hundred and forty years, xlii:16. He must have been of considerable age when the trial began, for he was the father of ten children, seven sons and three daughters, i:2. He could be hardly less than fifty when the reverses came upon him; and his entire life must have been about two hundred years. Men had ceased long before the time of Moses to live to this age. Terah lived two hundred and five

years; Abraham, one hundred and seventy-five; Isaac, one hundred and eighty; Jacob, one hundred and forty-seven; Joseph, one hundred and ten; Moses, one hundred and twenty. Job must have lived nearer to Abraham than to Moses; and this book was composed probably long before the first book of Moses; and so is no doubt the oldest record in the world. The sacrifice which Job offered for his children is patriarchal, combining with it the essential idea of the sin-offering, and he acts as the priest, being the head of his family, as was the common practice of the patriarchs. From the four constellations mentioned in xxxviii:31, 32, three mathematicians have computed that Job's trial took place about B. C. 2100. There may be error, of course, in these calculations, as it is confessedly difficult to identify the constellations mentioned in the chapter; still, it is remarkable that three independent and scholarly investigators should arrive at about the same results, there being only forty-two years difference between them.

2. *Structure of the book.* It consists of three parts. Part I., Introductory narrative in prose, chapters i, ii. Part II., The poem, iii-xlii:6. Part III., Concluding narrative in prose, xlii:7-17.

It will be observed that the poem is very regular and simple in form. Its order is natural throughout. And yet it is replete with art the most subtle and attractive. With admirable skill and wonderful force the problem is introduced, the frightful disproportion of happiness and misery in this world. The sad plight of Job, the dreadful losses he sustains, the horrible disease which consumes his flesh and racks his frame, the agonizing wail he at length pours forth, the dark questions that haunt his mind, the black doubts that assail his faith, the gulf of infidelity that yawns to receive him—these in awful grandeur are set before the three philosophers with masterly hand. And the philosophers are utterly powerless to grapple with the problem. After three speeches each, save Zophar, who speaks but twice, they succumb and are silent. Then follow the splendid monologues of Elihu, who, although he goes far toward answering the questions and solving the problem, leaves it still in doubt and darkness. But his addresses prepare the way for the appearing of the Lord on the scene, who speaks, sets Job right, and full blessing ensues.

4. *Design of the book.* It is threefold. 1. To refute the slander of Satan. 2. To discuss the question of human suffering, and particularly the suffering of the righteous. 3. To reveal Job to himself, and remove the self-righteousness which prevented the full measure of blessing which God had in store for him.

5. *Job's happy estate*, i:1-5; xxix. It is clear enough from these sections of the book that he was wealthy, influential, devout, benevolent, and highly esteemed —in short, a mighty Sheik in the land of Uz.

Touching his nationality little is known. There is no account of his ancestry, no mention of his parentage. We only know that he belonged to the great Shemitic family to which almost all God's revelations have been made. He comes before us in mature manhood, whence no one knows (even the location of Uz is conjectural): he disappears in the grave when his fitful life with its strange vicissitudes is over. This is characteristic. It is the problem God keeps before us—the mystery of Providence, the malice of Satan, the good enclosed in suffering. These he would have us see, not the man so much.

Job's prosperity for a time was uninterrupted. In his own striking imagery, "I washed my steps with butter, and the rock poured me out rivers of oil." His personal character is thus described: "And that man was perfect and upright and one that feared God and eschewed evil," i:1, 8. He was honest and straightforward and sincere in his guilelessness. No duplicity either toward God or man was found in him. In his solicitude for his children and in his kindness and helpfulness to all about him, the genuineness of his piety was exhibited. He was happy in his relationship with God, happy in his family, possessed of princely wealth, loved and trusted by his fellows—in short, the most powerful Sheik in the East. But in a day his joy fled, his prosperity blighted, his children cold in death, himself smitten with pain and anguish beyond the lot of men. What is the meaning of the dreadful reverses which befell him? This leads us to the contemplation of one of the main designs of the book.

6. *Satan's slander against Job*, i:9-11; ii:4, 5. The singular spectacle is presented of the Prince of Darkness appearing in the train of the Most High. But Satan is there for a definite purpose, viz., to accuse and malign, Rev. xii:10. One question he starts, as full of subtlety as of malice: "Doth Job serve for naught?" 'Is not the allegiance which receives such direct and tangible rewards only a refined form of selfishness? His fealty is mercenary, his attachment is for hire;' "he serveth not God,

but himself upon God." And Satan boldly asserts that if these external blessings were withdrawn, Job's allegiance would be cast off—"he will curse thee to thy face." One main feature of the problem which the book discusses is thus distinctly propounded: Can goodness exist irrespective of reward? Can the fear of God live when every inducement is withdrawn? Is allegiance to God based on the love and knowledge of Him, or does it exist only for the advantages it secures, the immunities it enjoys? The problem is one of infinite moment; for if the love and grace of God only serve to produce a refined selfishness, then His whole work is abortive, and God is unable to retrieve the ruin of sin.

There was no method by which these slanderous accusations could be more effectively silenced than by the removal of those things on which the adversary asserted Job's fidelity depended. And so the servant of God was tested to the uttermost. The trial was twofold. First, his wealth and his children were suddenly snatched away from him. The book clearly teaches that it was through Satanic agency, in the mysterious government of God, that these dreadful losses were sustained. But out of this furnace Job issues without the smell of fire on his garments, i:21. 22; "In all this, Job sinned not, nor charged God foolishly." In this assault Satan was forbidden to touch Job's person, i:12. He next affirms that Job will give up all for his life, ii:4. That this is also a lie, the devil knows perfectly well. Myriads of God's dear people have gone to the worst forms of death for the name and the love of Christ. Permission, however, is given, up to the point only this side of death, and he is smitten with a loathsome disease—elephantiasis it is thought to have been, a disease believed by many in the East to be the judgment of God. The patriarch sat down on the ash-heap in unspeakable desolation, anguish and woe, bereft of property, children, health; his wife advising him to renounce the God whom he had served so long. Will he finally break with God? Is there anything left to keep him faithful? Blessed be God for sustaining and conquering grace! Out of the final trial Job comes forth triumphantly: "In all this did not Job sin with his lips," ii:10.

It is proved, therefore, once for all, and never more to be disputed, that Job's loyalty is not grounded in selfishness, that true piety lives when all external advantages are withdrawn, and that God's grace is more than a match for Satan's malice and the deep-rooted egotism of sin. Thus, one prime object of the book stands disclosed. But God had other and greater ends in the sufferings of his servant, which will appear in the sequel. It was not needful to send Job to such a terrible school of affliction merely to prove the Devil a liar. He was that from the beginning, Jno. viii:44. There must be ulterior designs.

7. Let the reader note how prominent Satan is in the earlier chapters of the book. We know that he was the real instigator of Job's woes. Probably the patriarch himself did not; and so all the more inexplicable and mysterious his sufferings must have appeared to him and his friends, the comforters. Now, some things respecting this great Evil Spirit we gather from this inspired record. (1) His

personality. Satan is no myth. Every attribute, quality, action, mark, and sign which can indicate personality, are ascribed to him with a precision of language which refuses to be explained away. If we attempt to interpret this and the like Scripture as only meaning the principle of evil and not a person, then there is an end to all rules of fixed thought, and the Bible may mean anything and everything we please. (2) His power. It is simply tremendous. He brought fire from heaven to consume the sheep [electricity]; the storm from the desert, which crushed the house where the young people were feasting: i. e., he can, when permitted, wield the forces of nature for the accomplishment of his wicked designs. (3) His enmity is even greater than his power. He pursues his evil ends with tireless energy and sleepless vigilance. (4) Still, he is subordinate. He can afflict only so far and when God for inscrutable purposes permits him. There was a "hedge" about Job through which Satan could not break. No doubt, like the lion he is, 1 Pet. v:8, he travelled round and round that hedge, but always on the outside. "He can go only the length of his chain."

It is noteworthy that nearly all the revelation we have of this great evil spirit is found in the New Testament. Rarely is he mentioned in the Old—in Eden, in Job, David, Joshua the High Priest. God delayed the full disclosure of him to later times, and then gave him twenty-eight names which fully describe him.

The other great features of the poem are now to be pointed out. These are two: The meaning of human suffering, particularly the suffering of the righteous; and the revelation of Job to himself. The first is the theme of the great Debate, chapters iv, xxxi. The second is traceable through the entire poem from chapter iii to chapter xlii, and is this: that the patriarch, with all his pre-eminent excellencies, secretly cherished and probably unwittingly cherished, somewhat of self-righteousness, a kind of religious pride which marred his lovely character and hindered the blessing God would bestow upon him; and this, cost what it might, must be cut up by the roots.

Many a citadel is proof against assault which yet may be obliged to succumb to the slow and steady progress of a siege. The first onset of pain is not so formidable as its protracted endurance. Job is now in this stage, the worst of all. Day after day he is compelled to drag his weary burden, how long we know not. Some time elapsed between the first wild outburst of trouble and the arrival of his friends.

The comforters were men of experience and wisdom, and profoundly religious. Piety and the fear of the Lord breathe throughout all their discourses. They cherished the kindliest feelings toward their stricken friend, and had come expressly to minister to his wounded spirit, ii:11-13. Their visit, their sitting with him in silence for seven days with torn garments and dust on their heads, prove the sincerity of their sympathy. Nevertheless, their presence only served to exasperate him, and aggravate his misery.

1. *Job's first monologue*, iii. It is unexampled for its expression of anguish and for its pathos. What language is there, and what imagery? He curses

his birthday, and hurls anathemas upon his life; asks that God may expunge that day from His calendar of time, that it may be frightened with horrible sounds, and chased forever by devouring death, that in eternity it may be a sunless day and a starless night. A similar instance of the effect of accumulated sorrows is found in the life of Jeremiah, xx: 14-18. It does not appear that the friends had uttered a word. Job opened the dialogue. They sat in total silence, covered with dust, gazing on a grief too profound for them to reach. As we read these utterances, choked with passion and with tears, we feel that Job had very imperfectly learned to say, "Thy will be done." He broke down in the very thing for which he was noted—patience. But let us remember Job did not know himself. He was complacently resting in his "integrity," which is another name for self-righteousness. There was a root of bitterness in him of which he seems to have been ignorant, but which must be eradicated. He had to learn the lesson to which all the saints are set down, viz., that the egotism of nature is offensive to God; that there is no confidence to be put in the flesh. And so, one aim of the book is to reveal Job to himself, and thus deliver him from the evil his afflictions were meant to remove. But let it be remembered that he curses his day, not his God, as Satan would have him do. He curses the day of his natural birth, not the day of his new birth. Amid all his doubts and darkness never for a moment does his faith in God waver— "Though he slay me, yet will I trust in Him," is his magnificent resolution.

2 *The debate.* It consists of three rounds. Each of the three philosophers speaks three times, save

Zophar, who speaks but twice, and Job replies to each in succession, chapters iv, xxxi.

The first round, chapters iv, xiv. The question is propounded by Eliphaz very skillfully and strongly, iv, v. God blesses the just, punishes the unjust. The proposition of Eliphaz is this: He that sins must suffer; as Job is a dreadful sufferer, he must be guilty of some grievous sin. Job replies, vi, vii, complaining that there is no adequate cause for his afflictions, that God treats him as if an irrational being, a sea or a sea-monster. His plaint resembles that of chapter iii, only more subdued and humble. Bildad follows in the same strain of Eliphaz, viii. "If thou wert pure and upright, surely now he would awake for thee;" and since He does not, something must be frightfully wrong. Job stoutly resists the imputation, and appeals to God, who knows that he is not wicked, as charged, ix, x. Zophar urges that he is certainly guilty, and exhorts him to repentance, xi. Job's reply, xii-xiv, is remarkable. He shows how the wicked often prosper, how God does as He pleases with great and small, and appeals from them to God.

In the second round, chapters xv-xxi, the comforters increase in the severity of their tone, and urge with considerable vehemence that it is the wicked who are scourged, not the righteous, and assail the integrity of Job, intimating broadly that he is guilty of some secret sin, some colossal crime. Zophar, the most impetuous and severe of all, insinuates that there is hypocrisy in the case, that God has at length torn the mask from the false face and he now stands revealed in his true character. The patriarch refutes the reasoning, proves that the wicked often grow old and prosper, that apparently God treats the good and the bad alike in this life, and the dark doubts which the Psalmist felt (Ps. lxxiii), haunt and harass his mind. With righteous indignation he flings from him the unworthy innuendos of the comforters and accuses them of intensifying his misery. After giving his wonderful confession of faith, xix:25-28, he points his argument with these telling words: "But ye should say, Why persecute we him? seeing the root of the matter is in me. Be afraid of the sword."

In the third round, chapters xxii-xxvi, the comforters are turned into headlong accusers. Invective now takes the place of calm reasoning; and Job instead of getting better grows worse, and even yearns to appear before the throne of God, declaring that if he could do so he would order his cause before him, and fill his mouth with arguments, xxiii:3, 4. "Job's disputing with God is as terrible as it is pitiable. It is terrible, because he uplifts himself, Titan-like, against God; and pitiable, because the God against whom he fights, is not the God he has known, but a phantom which his temptation has presented to his dim vision."

3. *The cause of the failure of the disputants.* The mistake of the comforters was this: they insisted that God was dealing with Job *retributively*. They labored to convict him of high-handed wickedness. They hint again and again that if all were told nothing would be too bad to impute to him. "Who ever perished being innocent, and when were the righteous cut off?" is the foundation of their reasoning. They totally failed to discover the true cause for his suffering. They applied many princi-

ples of the moral government of God to the wrong case; and hence their argument only served to exasperate him. No wonder he reproached them for their cruelty, and in the bitterness of an insulted character and wounded spirit, covered them with scorn and contempt. Nor was Job less wrong. He insisted that God acted *arbitrarily;* that having the power to do as He pleased with him, He did so. Because he was not guilty of any crime, of notorious sin, as the philosophers sought to make out, he infers that his affliction is without adequate grounds, that it is altogether disproportionate to his case, and therefore unjust and arbitrary.

4. *Job's second monologue,* chapters xxvii-xxxi. It was now Zophar's turn to speak, but he is silent, and the others also hold their peace, virtually admitting defeat. The great debate has ended without concluding anything. The mystery of the affliction of the godly remains unexplained. This second monologue is in many ways very remarkable. Its diction and imagery, its deep insight into man's powers and discoveries, its earnest piety coupled with its recognition of God's unfathomableness, its inimitable pathos, and its passionate appeals are unsurpassed in the whole field of literature. The touching description of his misery as contrasted with his former happiness, the gloom that has settled down upon him, the exposure to shame and ignominy, the inward terrors, and unanswered prayers—how graphically it is all portrayed. And yet never once does he abate his claim to innocency. He clings as tenaciously as ever to his integrity. That he has been wrong he will not allow. He is a spotless person, according to his

own account of himself, chapter xxix. In chapter xxxi:35, 36, he expresses the desire that the Almighty would answer him, draw up charges against him (such is the meaning of "adversary writing a book"); he would make answer. What language for a sinful mortal to use toward the infinite God! This is the secret of the book and the key to Job's trial. Let us not read it as if the aim were merely to prove the devil a liar, or to discuss the mysterious government of the world, or to vindicate God's wisdom and goodness, or to demonstrate Job's sincerity. All this is in it; but all this is not the main design. As God's dealing with him was personal, some personal reason or cause there must have been in the patriarch for it. A survey of his monologues and replies to his friends reveals the very important fact that he had not in any measure learned that in him, that is, in his flesh, there dwelt no good thing; that before God he had absolutely nothing to recommend him to the divine favor. And this truth is forcibly brought out by the addresses of Elihu.

5. *Elihu's ministry*, chapters xxxii-xxxvii. Who he was or where his home was is not definitely known. His name means "God is he," or "He is my God;" his father's name, Barachel, "God blesses." Obviously the knowledge and fear of the Lord found a place in his family. He was present during the debate, but being a young man he modestly remained silent while his elders struggled with the deep question of God's providence and human suffering. In two terse sentences the whole preceding discussion is condensed: "Against Job was his wrath kindled, because he justified himself rather

than God. Also against his three friends was his wrath kindled, because they had found no answer, and yet had condemned Job," xxxii:2, 3. There it is in a nut-shell. If the friends cannot answer him, why should they condemn him? Moreover, Job's justification of himself is virtually God's condemnation. God's chastising hand was upon him in sore affliction, in order that the evil in him might be disclosed, judged, and put away, and his self-vindication really meant the defeat of His gracious purpose, so far as he could defeat it. For to justify himself was to take his stand on the ground of law, or his own righteousness, and there condemnation must be his portion.

Elihu pours a flood of light on the subject of afflictions. He shows why these are sent on the godly, and what they accomplish, xxxiii:17, 30; xxxiv:31, 32. In visiting suffering on His people God is not occupied with the penal side of their sins. Their afflictions are not judgments, but chastisements. The object of them is to keep back the soul of the saint from the pit, and to hide pride from him. Hence sufferings, instead of being an expression of His wrath, flow from divine tenderness and love. The doctrine of Elihu is as distant as the poles from that of Eliphaz and his companions. Job recognizes the truth of it, for it is self-evidencing, and is silent. Besides, he shows Job what false notions he entertained about himself. "I am clean without transgression, I am innocent; neither is there iniquity in me," xxxiii:9; cf. ix:21; xii:4; xvi:17. What language for a sinner to use with whom God was having some sort of controversy, and upon whom such awful sorrows had come! And yet Job adds: "Behold, he findeth occasions against me, He counteth me for his enemy," xxxiii:10. Now here is a palpable discrepancy. Could a holy and just God find fault with a pure and innocent man? Impossible. Either Job is self-deceived, or God is unrighteous. Elihu brings this out; then pronounces sentence: "Behold, in this thou art not just; I will answer thee, that God is greater than man." What a simple truth; and yet how appropriate to the case in hand. If God be greater than man, clearly he and not man must be the judge of what is right.

6. *The Lord's presence*, chapters xxxviii-xlii. All Job's misconceptions of the divine character and government, all his rash criticisms on the Lord's ways, and all his fancied goodness vanish instantly before that majestic Presence. "Who is he that hideth counsel without knowledge? therefore have I uttered that I understood not; things too wonderful for me which I knew not. I have heard of thee by the hearing of the ear; but now mine eye seeth thee. Wherefore I abhor myself, and repent in dust and ashes," xlii:3, 5, 6. What a thorough breakdown. Once Job wanted to be in His presence that he might debate the question of his suffering with Him. Now he is there, and this is the issue: profoundest humiliation and repentance. All egotism is gone, and pride is in the dust. The final end and aim of his sorrows are at length attained, and full blessing ensues.

7. And now as a fitting close to the poem, Job becomes an intercessor for the three philosophers who had not spoken the right thing as the patriarch had done, xlii:8, 9. The friends also who appear to

have stood aloof from him in the day of his calamity now gather about him with their gifts; and the Lord Himself doubles for His servant all that he had lost, save His children. And yet these are doubled likewise. Ten waited him on the other side, and ten were given here. Thus, the oldest book in the world teaches the doctrine of immortality.

The ancient Version of the Seventy adds to the Hebrew closing of Job, these suggestive words (with others): "It is written that he will rise again with those whom the Lord raiseth."

PSALMS.

In Luke xxiv:44 our Lord refers to what is written "in the law of Moses, and in the prophets, and in the Psalms" concerning Himself. This is an authoritative division of the Old Testament. By the law of Moses is meant the Pentateuch, or Fivefold Book. The prophets include not only the prophetic writings, but also Joshua, Judges, the Samuels and Kings. The remaining books are the Holy Writings (Hagiographa), and receive the name of Psalms because this book stands, in the Hebrew Bible, at the head of the division.

The Hebrew title to this precious Scripture is Praises, or the Book of Praises, a title which designates the main object of the book, viz., The worship of God. Our word Psalms is the anglicized form of the Greek name for the book, a word which seems to involve the idea of instrumental accompaniment in the rendition of these inspired lyrics in the worship of God. The early Christian fathers called it, The Psalter.

The book of Psalms has evidently a peculiar character. It is not the history of God's people, or of God's ways with them, nor is it the inculcation of positive doctrines or duties, nor the formal prophetic announcement of coming events. These are in the Psalms, it is true, but only in a subordinate way. History, prophecy, providence, doctrine and law are all here, but these form nothing more than the frame around which the Spirit of God has built the praise, prayer, and adoration of the Lord's people.

"The first three Psalms are keys to the whole collection; the themes are the Scriptures, the Messiah, and the believer's experience." Worship, in its broadest application, is the central idea of the Psalter. Many of the Psalms, in whole or in part, are prayers—intercessions for the psalmist himself and for those of a like precious faith with himself, for the Lord's cause in the earth, and for the reign of righteousness and peace. Many of them express deep and poignant sorrow for sin, and plead for pardon. Many of them are descriptive of the godly man, of his character, ways, afflictions, and deliverances. Others are didactic and predictive. And others pour forth the fervid praises of a glad and happy heart. But all of them are worship. They carry the worshiper directly into the divine presence, and deal with all that is in him and belongs to him as before God. Of the book as a whole the following points may be noted:

1. The Psalms are pre-eminently devotional. They exhale the very spirit of worship, they breathe the atmosphere of devotion. They magnify and praise the Lord, they ascribe to Him the majesty and glory which are due to Him alone. They exalt His attributes, His name, His word, His providence, and His presence in all the affairs of the world. All that comes into the life of the saint they refer to Him. The difficulties, perils, temptations, enemies, sorrows, joys, in short, all the vast experiences of God's people are brought into His presence, are ascribed to Him. The Psalms, unlike the

sentiments of most in our day, never stop short with second causes—with the laws and forces of nature, as if everything here were tied up in the environment, as men call it—they go beyond these, to God Himself, and to that infinite Source who is present in all the works of His hands, they attribute whatever happens to the believer. The heart of the worshiper ever turns to Him. Very significant is the frequent exhortation to "lift up" the heart or the soul to God, an expression which still lingers in the Roman Catholic Missal—*sursum corda*, "Up Heart"—surviving amid the corruption and superstition that there abound like the peak of a submerged world. Worship, the devotion of the heart, is a prominent feature of the Psalms.

2. The Psalms are remarkably fruitful of experience. It would almost seem as if the Spirit of God had gathered into these one hundred and fifty lyrics all the varied exercises of soul of which the redeemed have knowledge in the world. There is no state or exigency, no circumstance or set of circumstances of what nature soever, prosperous and adverse, bad and good, near and remote, but it may find a faithful expression in this inimitable book. Here is mirrored all that the saint desires and seeks, loves and hates. His hopes, fears, confidence, weaknesses, strength, triumph and failure are here. Here, too, are his temptations and trials, his conflicts with foes both within and without, his defeats and his victories. In short, the life of the believer, with its intricate mazes, its vast alterations, is here laid bare.

No doubt the human experiences recorded in the Psalms have a basis in the history of those who were their authors; but not all of them. There are not a few in which no human experience finds any counterpart. We must look to the Lord Jesus Christ to find any adequate expression for them. Nevertheless, most of those written by David sprang from his own personal experience, and this fact explains why his life should have had such a wonderful range. He was called to write, by the inspiration of the Spirit, songs that would go to the heart of universal man, and so his life ran up and down through the entire gamut of human emotions. It is the same, in degree, with the other Psalms not belonging to David. They are all the products of the inner life, "openings to the light of day from the strong hidden currents which have been flowing underneath."

3. But there is much more. The Psalms are full of Christ. They speak of His humiliation and exaltation, of His rejection by the world and of His final triumph over all opposition. But they go deeper, as we may say; deeper even than the gospels; they let us into His thoughts and feelings when the billows of wrath were rolling over Him, when the heavy cloud of judgment which was all our own burst upon His devoted head. Such particularly are the Twenty-second and the Sixty-ninth.

4. Authors of the Psalms. At the head of the list, of course, stands David, the poet-king, and prophet, Acts ii:30. He was naturally most gifted, possessed in a very high degree that rarest of endowments, a poetic genius. Far beyond all this, he enjoyed the inspiration of the Spirit, 2 Sam. xxiii:2. Besides, David stood in a peculiar relation to God, was a

man after His own heart, 1 Sam. xiii:14. In the historical books of the Old Testament it is not easy to see how David's character comports with this remarkable testimony; but in the Psalms we put our finger on the beating of his heart-pulse, and feel the very throbbings and movements of his soul. Preeminently he was the friend of God. Seventy-three are by David, fifty are anonymous. and it is thought by many that some of them were composed by him likewise. Moses is declared to be the author of the Ninetieth. All the internal evidences corroborate the heading. It is emphatically a wilderness and pilgrim song, a true "Psalm of Life." To Solomon two are ascribed, the Seventy-second and the One hundred and twenty-seventh. The latter is a temple song; the former closes with "The prayers of David, the son of Jesse, are ended," words that seem to suggest a Davidic authorship. The meaning is, that, when the predictions of the Psalms are fulfilled, the grand objects for which David prayed will then be realized. Asaph, Jeduthun (or Ethan), and the sons of Korah were probably the authors of those which bear their names.

5. The collection and arrangement of the Psalter. It is very generally believed that David arranged those existing at his time. We infer this from his careful ordering the service of song in the worship of the sanctuary, 1 Chron. xxv. Probably Ezra collected and arranged the book as we now have it. The principle by which he was guided was not that of chronology, or the respective ages of the various Psalms, but the "succession of thought," and the two great names of God, as we shall presently see.

6. The inscriptions are worthy of note, though

so ancient that their meaning was only partially known when the Septuagint version was made [nearly three centuries before Christ]; at least some of them are not translated. *Michtam* is a golden, *maschil* a didactic Psalm. *Selah* is thought by many to be a musical sign of some sort. If so, then Hab. iii was intended to be musically rendered, for it is found there. It is always connected with some striking passage, is a kind of index finger, as if saying, "Pause and consider." Jerome says that the words with which Selah stands are of eternal moment. The significance of the other headings is only conjectural. Two translations of the Sept., however, are suggestive:—Ps. xxii: "To the chief musician upon Aijeleth—Shahar," i. e., "The hind of the morning;" an allusion to the plaint of the Messiah compassed about by baying dogs, like the hunted hind. Ps. lvi: "The silent dove in far-off lands," in allusion perhaps to David's exile life.

7. The book is divided into five parts, each division being marked by a doxology, The revision is a signal improvement on the authorized version of the Old Testament, for it faithfully represents these divisions. Some have seen in the Psalter the image of the Pentateuch. Delitzsch calls it "the congregation's five-fold word to the Lord, even as the Thorah [the Law] is the Lord's five-fold word to the congregation." The One hundred and fiftieth is the doxology of the fifth book, and of the entire collection. It begins with the noble word Hallelujah, and ends with it, and in every verse lying between, it is found. The Psalm has the same number of verses as the first, but how different the two, and how much lies between them. Through struggle

and conflict, defeat and victory, the people and cause of God have pressed on, and now at length His vast purposes find their fulfillment, and everything that hath breath is summoned to praise Him. It is the climax, the *finale* of all toward which He has been working and moving through the past ages and dispensations, and the goal is now reached; and so the magnificent shout of a redeemed creation is Hallelujah.

8. Variation of the divine names in the Psalms. Reference is made more particularly to the two great titles by which the Supreme Being is commonly designated in the Old Testament, viz., Lord (Jehovah) and God (Elohim). The use of these two divine names in the Psalter is very noticeable and interesting. In book first, Ps. i-xli, Lord (or Jehovah) occurs about 277 times, and God (Elohim) only about forty-seven times. In book second, Ps. xlii-lxxii, the order is reversed, God being found some 194 times, and Lord only some twenty-seven times. Book Third, lxxiii-lxxxix, employs them with approximate uniformity, or to speak a little more accurately, the book is made up of about fifty-seven Elohim (God) and forty-six Jehovah Psalms. The title of God is found much more frequently in the first half than in the last; and conversely, Lord less in the first than in the last half, i. e.. Ps. lxxiii-lxxxii have God about forty times, and Lord only about ten times; while in lxxxiii-lxxxix God occurs seventeen, and Lord thirty-three times. In the fourth and fifth books the name God recedes more and more, being found about forty times, while Lord comes into remarkable prominence, occuring nearly 380 times. (Note: Ps. cviii

is made up of two Psalms from the second book.)

The Spirit uses these divine names, not at random as men so often do, but always with an intelligent purpose, whether we be able to discover His design or not. It is believed God is the wider title, the more general name, and designates Him as the Creator, Governor and Judge of all; Lord as the self-existent One who stands in covenant relationship with His people. In Gen. i it is God who creates; while it is Jehovah who makes the covenant with Abraham and with Israel. *God* refers to His natural attributes (His power, wisdom, etc.), whereas *Jehovah* (while not excluding the other) refers more especially to His moral attributes (holiness, mercy, etc.) (Forbes).

Let it be carefully observed that the Psalms are arranged according to these great names of God, and not according to the dates of their composition at all. Some of the oldest are toward the end of the collection, as that ascribed to Moses which is numbered as the 90th, and the 145th is David's, while some that are supposed to have been written about the time of the Babylonian exile are nearly in the middle of the book. Chronology, therefore, had no place in the arrangement of the Psalms. The divine names are the key to their order. This appears from the 32d and 51st, both of which relate to the sin of David. The 32d is in the first book and has the title, Lord, throughout, for it is the joy of forgiveness and restoration of divine favor which are there celebrated; whereas in the 51st, where the awful crime is so touchingly confessed, the name is God exclusively, save in verse 15, which has Lord (Adonai), Master. And yet in the order of time the 51st takes the precedence, for pardon follows confession; but the 51st is in the second book. Why are they placed thus? The explanation seems to be this: In the 51st David recognizes that his sin has in reality interrupted the covenant relation he sustains to God, that it is a virtual breach of it, and hence he does not appeal to Jehovah, but to God, the Judge and Governor, who stands at a distance from the sinner, ready, as we may say, to hear his confession, judge his sin, and restore him to favor; but in the 32d he joyfully reclaims the covenant relation, re-enters into communion with his Redeemer, and hence Jehovah is the great title of his address.

The Psalter gives evidence of what we may call structural inspiration. It is firmly believed that none other but the Spirit of God arranged these Psalms as we now have them; and that there is a profound meaning in their order. The whole book is a sort of mirror of God's ways with His people, and with the world. In the first book Israel is in the covenant relation with God, and therefore the covenant name, *Jehovah*, is prominent; in the second, the people have fallen from their first love, have gone into apostacy and unbelief, and *God* takes the pre-eminence, God, the Judge and the Governor; in the third, they are viewed as returning to their allegiance, under the loving and faithful dealing of God, as He is revealed to them in the double name of God and Lord; while in the remaining books, Israel, according to all the prophets and Paul in the 11th of the Romans, is brought again and finally into full favor and fellowship, and all the earth rejoices in the fullness of redemption, and the great Hallelujah Chorus is sung. Like some majestic oratorio, some sublime symphony, is this book of Psalms, with the theme sometimes receding, then again advancing, now in the minor, then in the major, and anon in the chromatic scales, struggling through difficulties, triumphing over obstacles, steadily moving forward to the climax when all the voices and all the instruments, the parts and the chorus unite and combine in the final and overwhelming Hallelujah. One can hardly doubt but that the close of the Psalter celebrates the glorious time when the voices of angels, redeemed men, and every creature in heaven and on earth and under the earth, and such as are in the sea, will join in the thrilling anthem, "Blessing, and honor, and glory, and power, be unto Him that sitteth upon the throne, and unto the Lamb for ever and ever, Amen"—Hallelujah, Rev. v, 11-14. The book of Psalms, it is firmly believed, is prophetic. The Spirit of God has ordered these His songs in the way He has, that the believer might here, as in so much else of Holy Scripture, have the assurance of the blessed outcome of God's ways with the world.

But there is progress in the book likewise. The first and second books give us David's experience, and God's dealings with him. But we do not stop with doctrine and discipline as an ultimate attainment. And so the other books go on, rising higher and higher until they culminate in the exultant burst of jubilant praise of the Hallelujah Psalms at the close.

The Songs of Degrees, or Ascents, Ps. cxx-cxxxiv, were probably sung by the caravan pilgrims as they went up from various sections of the country to keep the annual feasts at Jerusalem. How appropriate they are for such devout companies is apparent to every attentive reader. No doubt it was with thanksgiving and joy that the travelers sang, "I was glad when they said unto me, Let us go into the house of the Lord," cxxii. As the hills of Judea arose before them with equal gladness they sang, "I will lift up mine eyes unto the hills from whence cometh my help," cxxi. The safety and stability of those who trust in the Lord found expression in the noble words of Ps. cxxv. It adds a charming feature to these fifteen Psalms when we think of them as the songs of God's wandering people. It is no spiritualizing process which declares that these also are our pilgrim Psalms, our mighty and inspired road songs.

There are several acrostic Psalms, or better, "A B C Psalms," as the Latin fathers named them (*Psalmi abecedari*). The most notable is the one hundred and nineteenth, each verse of which in the entire twenty-two parts begins with its own acrostic letter.

9. *The imprecatory Psalms.* Besides isolated and minor passages which occur throughout the book, there are at least three, viz., xxxv, lxix, cix, which invoke the most awful judgments upon the heads of enemies. They seem to breathe the very spirit of hatred and revenge. The believing heart of many is staggered by the fierce wrath and indignation which these Psalms display. Let us calmly study them, and learn what we may of their import.

(1) We are to offer no apology for these and the like Scriptures. If we believe in the plenary inspiration of the Bible, we are to hold firmly to the

truth that these Psalms, terrible as they may be to us who see so little of the real nature of sin and its heinousness and of God's unalterable purpose to punish it forever, are the expression of the mind of the Spirit concerning evil and persistent, incorrigible evil doers. Nor should it be forgotten that the Lord Jesus Himself, that meek and lowly One, employed as appalling language about the wicked as is found in the Psalter, Matt. xxiii, 13-36; Mar. ix, 42-49, etc. Men who charge the writers of the Psalms in question with bloody-mindedness bring the same accusation against the Son of God.

(2) The imprecatory Psalms with few exceptions are ascribed to David. That king was as devoid of vindictiveness as any public character that can well be named. His noble conduct toward Saul, the meekness with which he bore the bitter reproaches of Shimei, his gentleness and humility, remove him far enough from the charge of bloodthirstiness, and the lust of vengeance. Compare him with the rulers of so-called Christian nations, since the reformation —the kings of Germany, the Charleses of England to say nothing of those of Austria, Spain, France, Russia—all Christian at least in name, and it will be seen that not one of them stands higher than David in the qualities of mercy and justice; nay, most of them fall far below him. When David's whole career is intelligently and fairly reviewed, it leaves on the mind the impression of a man who possessed as meek and placable a temper as any monarch of history. The imprecatory Psalms he wrote are extraordinary, and out of his common way of acting and feeling.

(3) These are not the utterances of resentment

for private injuries, or of a desire to see personal enemies laid low. The inspired writer speaks in a public character, as the anointed king of Israel, the chosen servant of the Lord. It is for the vindication of the cause he represents, the cause of God and of righteousness, he asks.

(4) These Psalms are associated with the Lord Jesus Christ. Peter quotes the one hundred and ninth and applies it directly to Judas Iscariot and his betrayal of Jesus, Acts i, 20. Five times the sixty-ninth is quoted in the New Testament, besides being often alluded to, Jno. ii, 17; xv, 25; xix, 28, 30; Rom. xi, 9; xv, 3. The circumstances in which they are quoted are as remarkable as the quotations themselves. In the guest chamber Jesus cited lxix, 4: "They hated me without a cause," and He represents it as a prediction of the people's hatred of the Father and Himself, Jno. xv, 25. When He drove the hucksters from the temple the disciples remembered it is written, "The zeal of thy house hath eaten me up," Ps. lxix, 9; and the words reveal His mind at the time.

(5) They express Christ's righteous indignation against the malice and enmity of incorrigible and impenitent sinners; and His determination to visit condign punishment upon them. In these and similar Scriptures the Lord asks that justice, rigorous and inflexible, be done on His foes; and God's justice, when executed as He only can, is approved by all right minded beings.

(6) It is believed that what Jesus encountered at the hands of His implacable foes during His early life, and especially at its close, will be repeated in some measure in the world's crisis. Judas will have

his counterpart and far more in the man of sin; the mocking rabble of Jerusalem will have theirs in the mad outburst of godlessness when the world, led on by Satan and deceived by a lie, shall wheel into line and march to battle against the Lord God and His Christ; and then these "cursing Psalms," and the awful predictions of Isaiah, Daniel, Jesus, Paul, and John shall have their final and complete fulfillment.

10. *Christ in the Psalms.* That Christ is in the book is universally admitted. All students recognize it. There may be difference of opinion as to the Messianic character of some, and as to the sense of particular passages, but the broad fact is incontrovertible. But how is He here presented? Almost as fully as in the New Testament.

He is revealed as the Prophet. In Ps. xxii, 22 He says, "I will declare thy name unto my brethren; in the midst of the congregation will I praise thee." These words are quoted in Heb. ii, 12, as proof that Christ is not ashamed to call His people His brethren. It may be also that He had these words in mind when, in the intercessory prayer, he said, "I have declared thy name unto them, and will declare it," Jno. xvii, 26—a compendium of all that He taught His disciples, and of all He continues to teach them; for His one supreme work was and is, to reveal the Father to His people, and to bring them into His glorious presence, Heb. ii, 13. Ps. xl. 9, 10, exhibits Him as preaching, and the theme of the great Preacher is, righteousness, faithfulness, salvation, lovingkindness, and truth; and these all as of God, for before each of the words on which He discourses stands "thy." In the New Testament He reveals "The righteousness of God by faith." So likewise He is the Prophet in Ps. xlv; lxxxix; cxix; cii, etc.

His priestly office is made very prominent. In Ps. xl, 6, 8 we have the object of His mission announced, and the perfection of His work as contrasted with the inefficiency of the Levitical sacrifices. In Ps. xxii and lxix the intensity and awfulness of His sufferings as Priest and Victim are depicted with graphic power. A remarkable feature in these two Psalms is that the language is that of history, the past tense, such as He uses in His prayer in John xvii, as if all were an accomplished fact, a consummated thing. The human experience of the writer has little or nothing to do with the indescribable anguish of these Psalms, for suffering in them passes into a region where no mere mortal ever enters. In Gethsemane and at the cross alone is the fulfillment to be seen. The twenty-second ends with the striking words, " They shall come and declare His righteousness unto a people that shall be born, that He hath done this." *He hath done it*, is translated by Him into "It is finished," as Hengstenberg has shown. It is noteworthy that the word priest in the singular occurs but once in the Psalter. In Ps. cx is found this unexpected verse (i. e., so abruptly is it introduced), "The Lord hath sworn, and will not repent, Thou art a priest forever after the order of Melchizedek." The King is also the Priest whose office is everlasting, all succession being cut off. The divinely instituted Aaronic priesthood is passed by, and a still more ancient order that has lain dormant for a thousand years, is revived and perpetuated in this new Priest-king. The doctrine of the oath of God as to Christ the King and Priest is fully drawn out in

Heb. vii. The sixteenth declares the Messiah's death and resurrection, which Peter on the day of Pentecost uses with wonderful power. The sixty-eighth tells of His ascension and its results, cf Eph. iv, 8-12; Acts ii, 30-34.

His kingly office is celebrated in very many, e. g., ii, xxi, xlv, lxxii, etc. The King and His kingdom in these and the like Psalms is infinitely more glorious and mighty than that of David or Solomon, than of any and all the kings of earth. In exact accordance with the teaching of the New Testament the Psalms ground Christ's kingdom upon His perfect sacrifice, as the second, one hundred and tenth, and others clearly show. In fact, all through the Psalter there is a constant blending of Messiah's offices in the same Psalm, e. g., in the twenty-second He is Prophet and Priest, in the one hundred and tenth King and Priest, etc. His offices are interdependent and inhere in the one person of the Mediator; and this great fact proves incontrovertibly that the Messianic Psalms cannot apply to any human king like David, or Hezekiah, or Josiah; to any priest like Aaron, or Hilkiah; to any prophet like Moses, or Elijah; for no one of them, good and great men as they were, ever combined all these offices in his own person. They find their perfection only in Him who was the Prophet greater than Jonah, who was the King greater than Solomon, who was the Priest greater than Aaron and Melchizedek.

His sufferings are delineated minutely. We are taught in the Psalms that He suffered from three sources. First, He suffered from God. This solemn truth is brought out vividly in the twenty-second. The very words He uttered on the cross are here found, made ready to His hand. He ascribes His exceeding sorrow to God, and to His treatment of Him as the surety and substitute of His people. Atonement is unquestionably taught in this book. Second, He suffered from the hand of man, i. e., for righteousness' sake. His patience, humility, benevolence, love, and piety call out the fiercest enmity of wicked men and of Satan against Him. This side of our Lord's sufferings is most fully dwelt on. With amazing force and accuracy the rage and fury of His foes are depicted. They rush upon Him open-mouthed, like ferocious beasts. They roar about Him, like savage bulls of Bashan. He stands in the midst of them as though surrounded by baying dogs—He innocent and guileless, like the hunted hind. They stand staring and gaping upon Him:

> "But I a worm, as no man prized,
> Reproached of men, by all despised;
> All shake the head, they mock and gaze,
> Each scornful lip contempt betrays."

His sorrowful plaint in the sixty-ninth is that every delicacy of feeling is violated by His pitiless enemies. Shame covers His face, reproach breaks His heart. He is the song of the drunkards as they reel through the streets. He is an alien to His mother's children (a proof that Mary had other children after the birth of her Son, lxix, 8). Wretched men dared to spit in His face. And He is all alone in His suffering, with none to pity or to help. Third, He suffered in sympathy with His people. He so entirely identified Himself with them that He became a partaker with them in their afflictions and distresses. The "godly man," "the upright man," the "afflicted man" of the Psalter is ultimately none other than the Son of man who in wondrous sympathy makes the sorrows of believers His own, who shares with them all their human experiences except personal sin. If they are in trouble He enters into it with them; if floods are rolling over them, He likewise is in deep waters. Indeed, we cannot understand much of this profound book unless we see that Christ is intimately associated with His people in all that befalls them. (See the proof, if proof be needed, Heb. ii, 12, 13, where He sings praise like the brethren, and trusts like the brethren —*His* brethren.)

His second coming is foretold, l, xcvii, xcviii, etc. The Psalms, like all other Scriptures, are full of Christ. They speak of His person, offices, sufferings; of His death, resurrection, ascension, and coming again; they set forth the glory of His kingdom when He shall take to Himself His great power and reign in millennial bliss over all the earth.

11. *The Doctrine of Sin in the Psalter.* The law was the revelation of God's mind as to sin. The Psalms are the response of God's people to His declarations on the subject. And the fulness of their teaching on the terrific topic appears: (1) In the copiousness of the vocabulary employed to describe it; as *evil, iniquity, wickedness, sin*—in the abstract, or as a principle; then as manifesting itself in outward acts, as *trespass, transgression, disobedience, wrongs, faults*, etc. (2) In the recognition of natural depravity. Original sin is certainly acknowledged. The taint of sin is born with us. It is not a thing contracted by example or contact with men; its presence in us and with us antedates our birth. (3) In the confession of sin, so full, so intense, so hot burning and choked

with sobs. (4) In its pardon, God exhausts even His vocabulary in revealing His pardoning mercy in the book. He forgives sin, sins, iniquities, transgressions, trespasses; He blots them out, puts them away, covers them over, hides them. That is, the pardon extends to the utmost limit of the being, nature, activities, and pollution of sin. Luther named Ps. xxxii, li, cxxx, cxliii, *Psalmi Paulini*—Pauline Psalms; for they contain the doctrine of Paul as to justification, repentance, and pardon.

12. *Recognition of the Word of God in the Psalms.* This is another prominent feature of the book. According to Ps. i, 2, the "blessed man" is one who among other things makes the law of the Lord his delight and his study night and day. It is no insignificant mark of genuine piety. He who has no desire nor relish for food is sick. In Ps. xix, 7-9, we have "six descriptive titles of the word, six characteristic qualities mentioned, and six divine effects declared;" while in verses ten, eleven, the Holy Spirit gives His estimate of the value of the Word, and the believer's use of it. Ps. cxix—twenty-two alliterative poems, with eight verses in each, the first word in every line beginning with the same letter, celebrates in a very wonderful manner the Word of God. In every verse but one (122) the Scriptures are mentioned by some of their many titles; hence there is ground for this inscription of a certain version, "The Christian's golden ABC of the praise, love, power, and use of the Word of God." In cxxxviii, 2, we have God's exaltation of His Word above all His name.

13. *The doctrine of the future life is prominent in the book.* It is enough to refer the reader to the

following: i; xvi, 8-11; xvii, 15; xxiii; xxxi, 5; xxxiv, 22; l, 1-6, etc.

14. *The Psalms' place in sufferings of the saints.* What a story they could tell if we could but hear it from sick beds, from dungeons, scaffolds, stakes, lonely mountains and bleak moors, from exiles and martyrs, from the fields of battles and the valley of the shadow of death! "What a record that would be, if one could write it down—all the spiritual experiences, the disclosures of the heart, the comforts and the conflicts which men in the course of ages have connected with the words of the Psalms. What a history, if we could discover the place the book has occupied in the inner life of the heroes of the kingdom of God!" (Tholuck.)

It may prove helpful to some if a few incidents of Christian history be given in which the book was the stay and comfort of God's afflicted people. From various sources these now recorded have been gathered, but mainly from Dr. Ker's little volume, "The Psalms in History and Biography."

Ps. ii, 10, 11, was the remonstrance addressed to Henry VIII. of England by John Lambert, who was burned at Smithfield in 1538. His martyrdom was one of the most cruel of that time, and yet his faith was most triumphant, as he lifted his fingers flaming with fire, saying, "None but Christ, none but Christ."

Ps. iv, 6, "Lord, lift up the light of thy countenance upon me," was quoted by James Melville when he was dying, for his comfort, as likewise, xxiii, 4; xxvii, 1. "The candle being behind back, he desired that it should be brought before him, that he might see to die. By occasion thereof, he remembered that Scripture, Ps. xviii, 28, 'The Lord will lighten my candle; He will enlighten my darkness.'" A woman of our own times, wife of Thomas Carlyle, thus wrote in her journal: "Sleep has come to look to me the highest virtue and the greatest happiness; that is, good sleep, untroubled, beautiful, like a child's. Ah, me! have mercy upon me, O Lord; for I am weak. O Lord, heal me; for my bones are vexed. My soul is also sore vexed; but thou, O Lord, how long?"—vi, 2, 3. Not a few know the sweetness of iv, 8; cxxvii, 2, " So He giveth His beloved sleep," when insomnia torments and terrifies them.

Psalm twenty-three fills a very large place in the history of God's children. " It has sung courage to the army of the disappointed. It has poured balm and consolation into the hearts of the sick, of captives in dungeons, of widows in their pinching griefs, of orphans in their loneliness. Dying soldiers have died easier as it was read to them; ghastly hospitals have been illuminated; it has visited the prisoner, and broken his chains, and, like Peter's angel, led him forth in imagination, and sung him back to his home again. It has made the dying Christian slave freer than his master." John Welsh, son-in-law of John Knox, sung it at two in the morning when banished from Scotland, and with other ministers of the reformed faith and a large concourse of people singing and praying with them, set sail for France. Welsh's wife besought the king for her husband, and was offered his liberty on condition of his preaching and teaching no more. The brave daughter of Knox lifted her apron with her hands and said, " I would rather receive his head here, than his liberty at such a price." Two young women, Marion Harvey and

Isabel Alison, on their way to the scaffold for the honor and name of Jesus, were annoyed by the priests who wished to thrust their prayers on them, and the one said to the other, "Come, Isabel, let us sing the Twenty-third Psalm," which they did; and she then said, "I am come here today for avowing Christ to be Head of His church, and King in Zion. O seek Him, sirs, seek Him, and ye shall find Him." Her companion said on the scaffold, "Farewell, all created comforts; farewell, sweet Bible in which I delighted most, and which has been sweet to me since I came to prison; farewell, Christian acquaintances; now into thy hands I commit my spirit, Father, Son, and Holy Ghost." Whereupon the hangman threw her over.

When Edward Irving lay dying he murmured again and again in Hebrew, "The Lord my Shepherd." So, too, when James Inglis was on his deathbed this Twenty-third Psalm was read to him, and the dying saint said, "You will understand me as not speaking boastfully of myself when I say that every word you have read is personal to me, personal to my faith, personal to my soul. And now I will rest, and afterward we will talk of His mercies."

Within the last few days a devoted young woman, recently graduated from college and a teacher in the public schools, was fast nearing the end. Her relatives and a few friends stood round her bed, when she said, "Sing the Twenty-third Psalm." With choking voices they began, and the dying girl joined with them, but had strength to sing but a few words when her voice failed. She said soon after, "I can not see you well; but [looking upward] I see Jesus, and many, O so many who have gone before." And with the word glory, she went away.

Psalm xxxi, 5, holds an extraordinary place among dying believers—"Into thy hands I commit my spirit"—the words rise from saint after saint. They were the last spoken by the Lord Jesus on the cross, Lu. xxiii, 46; the last of Stephen, Acts vii, 59; of Polycarp, Basil, St. Louis, Columbus, and of the poor Italian prisoner of our own times, Silvio Pellico. On the 6th of July, 1415, John Huss of Bohemia was burned to death in a field near the ancient city of Constance, his safe conduct being violated by the Emperor Sigismund for which the pope gave absolution. A brass tablet marks the spot where Huss stood. While seven bishops removed his priestly dress piece by piece, and placed on his head a paper crown painted with demons, they addressed him, "We deliver thy soul unto Satan." "But I," he said, "commend it into thy hands, Lord Jesus Christ, who hast redeemed me." One hundred and thirty-one years after, Luther died (1546). Among his last words were these: "I pray thee, O Lord Jesus Christ, to take my soul into thy keeping." Then he said thrice, "Father, into thy hands I commend my spirit, thou hast redeemed me, Lord God of truth." Twenty-six years after (1572), John Knox died, saying, "Now, for the last time, I commend my spirit, soul and body," touching three of his fingers, "into thy hand, O Lord." Nearly a century after this, Hugh M'Kail, the gifted martyr of Scotland, took hold of the ladder to go up to his death, having sung these same words, saying as he went up, "I care no more to go up this ladder, and over it, than if I were going to my father's house."

He called to his friends and fellow sufferers below, "Be not afraid. Every step of this ladder is a degree nearer heaven."

In the reign of Queen Mary (1554), William Hunter, nineteen years of age, was brought to the stake for the gospel, and recited the Eighty-fourth Psalm while being bound. When the fire was kindled, he cast his Psalter into his brother's hand who said, "William, think of the holy passion of Christ, and be not afraid." And William answered, "I am not afraid." Then, lifting up his hands to heaven, he cried, "Lord, Lord, Lord, receive my spirit."

Jerome Savonarola and his brother monks chanted the sixty-eighth as they marched into the Piazza of Florence to meet the trial of fire (1498). He spent the brief respite allowed him before his execution in meditating on the fifty-first, the sorrowful *Miserere*. "O Lord, a thousand times thou hast cancelled my iniquities, and a thousand times I have fallen, but thou wilt yet have me secure. I will hope, therefore, in the Lord, and speedily be delivered from every trouble. By whose merits? Mine? Never, but by thine, O Lord." Luther afterward translated Savonarola's meditation with these memorable words affixed: "Although somewhat of scholastic mud did still cleave to the feet of this good man, he nevertheless upheld justification by faith without the works of the law, and was in consequence burned by the pope. But, lo, he lives in blessedness, and Christ by my means now canonizes and crowns him, even though the pope and the papists should burst with rage."

In the autumn of 1689 a band of eight hundred Waldenses who had been banished from North Italy into Switzerland returned to their valleys, crossing the Alps not far from the tracks pursued by Hannibal and Napoleon. They were led by their hero-minister, Henri Arnaud; and, after incredible perils and sufferings, they re-entered their old homes, singing the seventy-fourth and one hundred and twenty-ninth Psalms.

David Livingstone read the one hundred and twenty-first and one hundred and thirty-fifth, and prayed with his old father and sister, as he set out from his Scottish home for Africa; and his mother-in-law, Mrs. Moffat, wrote him at Linyanti, on the threshold of his perilous journey, that the ninety-first and one hundred and thirty-first Psalms were constantly with her as she thought of and prayed for him.

"No book which is without the assurance of immortality could have cheated so many dying saints and deceived so many generations of mourners. There is not a pall of darkness over the Psalms; no odor of the charnel-house exhales from them. The hopes of eternity trickle like drops of light from the pens of their writers. They come to us like the breath of violets in a letter which reaches us from a land of sunshine. The Easter bells are always ringing in the Psalter."

PROVERBS.

The authorship of this book is announced in the preface, "The proverbs of Solomon, the son of David, king of Israel," i, 1. It is the first book of the Bible to name the author at the beginning. Solomon lived long before the sages of Greece, five hundred years before the "seven wise men," and seven hundred before Socrates and Aristotle. There is little foundation for the Rabbinical tradition that some of the Grecian writers borrowed largely from Solomon, and certainly there is less for the notion that the book borrowed from them. He was peculiarly qualified, apart from the inspiration of the Holy Spirit, to write such books as are ascribed to him in the Bible, viz.: Proverbs, Ecclesiastes, and the Song; for he possessed in an extraordinary degree a remarkable comprehensiveness of mind. "Wisdom and understanding exceeding much, and largeness of heart, even as the sand that is on the sea shore," is the description in 1 Kings iv, 29. He was a philosopher, a poet, a botanist, zoologist, architect, as well as king, 1 Kings iv, 32-34. His mental grasp is perhaps more clearly seen in his character as moralist than in any other aspect. Yet he had very unusual powers of analysis and classification. To Solomon belonged the rare distinction of possessing that subtle, piercing intuitiveness of mind which sees at a glance what others less gifted reach only by laborious processes of reasoning. To have this seeing faculty in its fullness is to have the loftiest human endowment; and it was bestowed upon him in the highest degree. His analytical power is exhibited in his thorough acquaintance with and description of human character. In all its phases and manifestations; in its fullness and poverty, its strength and weakness, he is familiar with it. He sees the springs of all action; he understands the motives and passions and propensities which sway men and which make them what they are. Nor is his acquaintance with human character confined to any one class, as for example, the ruling class with which he was personally identified. He knows by an inspired intuition universal man; the peasant equally well with the monarch, the philosopher as well as the simpleton. With swift and unerring hand he labels each man according to the character he has discovered in him, and instantly sets him in his proper place. Like the other inspired writers, Solomon knows but two classes among men: the righteous and the wicked, or, as he generally designates them, the wise and the fools. He no sooner fastens his gaze on a fellow mortal than he determines, by the prevailing temper he has detected in him, to which company he belongs, and he fixes his standing accordingly.

"Wisdom" is the key-word, and i, 7, the key-verse of the book.

1. The proverb:—"A master sentence," "maxim or brief sententious saying," "enigmatical utterance," etc. Such are some of the more common definitions of a proverb. That given by an English statesman is full of significance—"The wisdom of many and the wit of one." Proverbs are very abun

dant among all peoples. Many of them, although they sound new to us and wonderfully apposite, have descended from the remotest antiquity. Some are worthless, many are wicked, but generally proverbs are the product of the wisdom and experience of the ages. Those of this book are not only true, but given us by the unerring Spirit of God, and of course must be filled with the best instruction. The proverb of the Bible follows the general rule of Hebrew poetry. It presents a great truth by a very apt comparison, or by a sharp and striking contrast. A parable is truth set forth in a lengthened similitude or narrative; a proverb is truth in the form of a sententious aphorism, a concentrated, pithy and pregnant saying.

2. The design of this book is quite clearly indicated in i, 2-4: "To know wisdom and instruction; to perceive the words of understanding; to receive the instruction of wisdom, justice, judgment and equity; to give subtilty to the simple, to the young man knowledge and discretion." A noble aim, worthy of the Spirit of God. Its main object is to instruct the believer in the things of God; to furnish him with those mighty and enduring principles according to which he is to order his life so as to escape the perils of the wicked, and establish his way in righteousness and peace. Dr. Arnot's title for the book is a good description of its chief design: "Laws from Heaven for Life on Earth." It is the application of that wisdom which created the heavens and the earth to the details of life in this world of confusion and evil. We have in it the ways of God, the divine path for human conduct, and the discernment of what the world is. It has to do with

God's government of the world, and with our own happiness here, if we maintain our earthly relationships according to God. It keeps turning a powerful light on the dark and dangerous places; it unfolds that deep law which applies so universally, "Whatsoever a man soweth, that shall he also reap;" it points out with marvelous clearness that a false step may lead to bitter consequences; and it contrasts false ways with right, the path of life with the path of death.

3. Analysis of the book. It naturally falls into two great sections: (1) Chaps. i-ix, which give the general principles in broad outlines; (2) chaps. x-xxxi, Proverbs proper.

A more particular and exhaustive division would arrange the contents of the book into five parts, as follows:

(1) Chaps. i-ix, in which are contained wise and fatherly exhortations addressed mainly to the young, together with a masterly description of wisdom. The thought in this section is more consecutive than in Proverbs proper.

(2) Chaps. x-xxii, 16. Moral aphorisms, or master sentences, bearing on practical life.

(3) Chaps. xxii, 17; xxiv, in which the method of more or less connected thought is resumed, as in the first section.

(4) Chaps. xxv-xxix. The proverbs of this part are said to be those of Solomon "which the men of Hezekiah, king of Judah, copied out." It is difficult to determine precisely what this statement means. It hardly warrants us in affirming a different authorship for this section. The sayings are attributed to Solomon; it is only said that these men "copied

out," arranged and compiled them. The memory of these learned men of Hezekiah's court is perpetuated in Jewish tradition. In the Talmud they are called a "society," or "academy," and it is declared that "Hezekiah and his academy wrote Isaiah, Proverbs, the Song, and Ecclesiastes," which can only mean that they compiled and arranged them. Perhaps the true explanation is, that the proverbs of this section had been transmitted orally from Solomon to the time of Hezekiah, and that the work of Hezekiah's men was that of collecting and editing them in this permanent form. This view seems to be confirmed by the fact that many of the proverbs of these chapters are repetitions, with slight variations, of some which occur in the preceding section.

(5) Chaps. xxx, xxxi, which may be considered as a sort of an appendix to the whole book, and of which the authorship is a problem that cannot be solved. The thirtieth is ascribed to Agur the son of Jakeh. Who he was it seems next to impossible to determine. The word "prophecy" with which the chapter begins, or oracle, as the revision translates it, points to a higher character, if we may so say, than other portions of the book. Verses 4, 19, 24-28, 30, 31, remind one of Job, while the oft recurring "three" and "four" recall Amos. The chapter is addressed to Ithiel and Ucal. Who they were, or whether these are proper names or symbolical titles, is not known. So also the "King Lemuel" of the thirty-first is supposed by the older students of the book to be another name for Solomon, and by later ones as symbolical. From beginning to end, there is but one subject, the delineation of a perfect wife. Trapp is of the opinion that Lemuel is Solomon, and his

mother, Bath-sheba, was the author of this surpassingly fine description of the perfect wife.

4. Principal topics of Proverbs.

(1) Wisdom, viii. Clearly something more than an attribute is meant by the Wisdom of this chapter. We might conceive God's wisdom personified using the language of vs. 22, but when we proceed to vss. 23-31, nay, even to the end of the chapter, we are irresistibly led to think, not of a poetic personification, but of the personal God Himself, in His awful majesty and holiness. There is a remarkable similarity between wisdom as described here, and Christ as He is set before us in the New Testament. It is quite surprising how the parallel between them can be exactly traced. Wisdom is represented as dwelling with God from eternity; so also is Christ, Jno. i, 1, 2. Wisdom is before all things, so also is Christ, Col. i, 17. Wisdom is the eldest child of God; Christ is the first-born of the whole creation, Col. i, 15, the only Begotten of the Father, Jno. i, 14. Indeed, the parallel may be followed out to the greatest length and with the utmost minutia. It can not be reasonably doubted, therefore, that the Wisdom of Solomon is identical with the Lord Jesus of later Scripture; and by this title and portraiture Solomon adumbrated the God-man Messiah.

(2) Filial piety. In the law given at Sinai, the obligation to honor parents was placed first after duties to God. It underlay all morality in Israel. It underlies all morality still. As might be expected, this subject occupies a prominent place in Proverbs; e. g., i, 8, 9; vi, 20, 21; xiii, 1; xv, 20; xix, 26; xxx, 17, etc.

(3) Bad company. The warnings in respect to

this are very urgent and solemn, for they are of immeasurable importance: i, 10-19; iv, 14-19; xiii, 20; xxiv, 1, 2; xxix, 24.

(4) **Licentiousness.** Solomon calls the harlot "the strange woman," a title which reminds one of "the strange gods" which the prophets so often and so fiercely denounce. She is regarded as a foreigner, an alien; for from the days of Balaam, when at his foul instigation Midianite women beguiled Israel to sin, female influence had again and again brought immoral practices and lewdness into the land. It was by foreign wives and concubines that the great king himself was led astray, 1 Kings xi, 4. She is well named—a stranger to all good, purity, happiness, the foe of herself and of all her kind. The prevalence and danger of this sin are so great as to make the revelation about it very full and explicit: ii, 16-19; v, 3-20; vi, 23-35; vii, 4-27; xxii, 14.

(5) **Intemperance.** This and the sin of uncleanness are twin serpents infinitely more deadly than the fabled snakes of Laocoon. Nothing can exceed the vividness with which Solomon portrays the evils of intemperance. No other Scripture more abounds with the details of its horrors. Here are found some of the most powerful texts from which to preach against this dreadful sin: xx, 1; xxiii, 1-3, 29-35; xxxi, 4-6.

(6) **Contention.** Strifes, disputings, family brawls, quarrels, etc.; their causes and consequences are very fully treated: iii, 30; x, 12; xiii, 10; xv, 1, 2, 4, 18; xvi, 27, 28; xviii, 6-8, etc.

(7) **Lying.** Truthfulness and honesty need to be strongly pressed, for the natural tendency of men is to deceive in order to gain an advantage or elude a

loss; consequently the book emphatically condemns such conduct: vi, 16, 17; xii, 13, 14, 21, 22; xix, 5-9.

(8) The tongue. Bridling the tongue: iv, 24; x, 19; xv, 4; xxi, 23.

(9) Sloth. Paul as earnestly denounces idleness as Solomon. His terse and sufficient rule is, "If any man will not work let him not eat," 2 Thess. iii, 10, revised version. It is well to ponder, in these days. the forcible teaching of Solomon: vi, 6-11; x, 4, 5; xiii, 4; xxiv, 30-34.

(10) Pride and its consequences, viii, 13; xi, 2; xvi, 18; xxix, 23.

(11) Riches. How true is the description: xi, 4, 28; xxiii, 5; xxvii, 24; xxx, 8.

(12) Liberality: iii, 9, 10; xi, 24, 25; xiii, 7; xix, 17: "He that hath pity on the poor lendeth unto the Lord; and that which he hath given will He pay him again." This was the text chosen by the eccentric Rowland Hill for a "charity sermon" he had been asked to preach. Reading it slowly and carefully to the congregation, the preacher began with this sentence, "If ye are satisfied with the security, down with the dust."

ECCLESIASTES.

The word ecclesiastes means *preacher*. The book bearing the name is a sort of sermon, and the speaker is the son of David, king of Jerusalem, i, 1, 12. If this statement of the book is accepted as true, the question of its authorship is settled. There was but one son of David, humanly speaking, who is capable of writing such a treatise as this, Solomon.

The key-phrase is "Under the sun;" the key-verse, i, 2.

1. Style of Ecclesiastes. The tone of a portion of it is sorrowful and apparently skeptical. Unbelievers and scoffers often appeal to it as a sanction for their doubts and a ground of attack against the general faith of the Bible. Voltaire and Frederick the Great are said to have been fond of certain parts, especially of those in which Solomon records his apparent infidelity. The book reads like the experiences of one who had tried the world to the utmost, who had sounded its lowest depths, and found it false and hollow to the core, its pleasures delusions, its riches transient, its honors empty, its enjoyments and happiness Sodom apples that turn to ashes on the lips. Hence its sad and disappointed tone. In all the Bible there is not a sadder. The nearest approach to it in this regard is the Eighty-eighth Psalm. A profound melancholy runs through it—melancholy which arises from a wide survey of human life and

the doings of men, lit up here and there with a faint gleam of a brighter hope. The prevailing cry is that of weariness and despair: "Vanity of vanities; vanity of vanities; all is vanity." This feeling of the preacher deepens into one of perplexity and apparent unbelief, iii, 19; ix, 2, 11; etc. It is just such a cry as we often hear from the inquiring and skeptical spirits of our own age. It is not the voice of abstract right, or truth, or religion, but the bitter and agonizing utterance of one who has known much, felt much, tried much, been admired much, and yet who has seen through all the enormous pretensions and shams of the world.

Is the book skeptical? What is its purpose? How shall we interpret it? In some respects it is difficult to understand; it is very easy to misunderstand it.

2. Its character is earthly. It looks at things as connected with the earth; it looks no higher. The key to it is found in the expression, "under the sun"—an expression found twenty-eight times in the book, and nowhere else in the whole Bible. "Under the heaven" is thrice mentioned, and "upon the earth," some seven times. Nearly forty times does the Spirit of God in this book name the earth and things belonging to earth, as if His gaze were fastened on this world alone and were raised no higher. Obviously, the book has to do with this world exclusively. It never gets above the sun until the very last verses are reached.

If life be viewed as altogether apart from God, if it be contemplated exclusively in its relation to the earth, it becomes inexplicable, and divine Providence an insoluble problem. Leave God out of the affairs of the world, and the conclusions of Solomon must needs follow that there is no profit under the sun in one's labor; there is nothing new; wicked men are in the place of judgment; there is the oppression of the right, the wrong triumphant; folly and wisdom go the same road and to the same end; chance seems to regulate all things. In short, the beginning, middle and end of life becomes vanity and vexation of spirit. Exclude God from the world, and skepticism and materialism must be the inevitable result.

Such is the chief design of the book—to try and test things in order to prove how inadequate they are to satisfy the deepest and truest longings of the human heart. In the book Solomon is experimenting upon the problem—Can the world, apart from God, meet man's need? The verdict is here recorded—"all is vanity." We will apply this principle to the book.

3. The preacher proves vanity "under the sun" from his own experiences, chaps. i, ii. He sets out with the thought of the world's monotony. Generations come and go. The sun rises and sets. The winds fly their rounds. The rivers run into the sea, yet the sea is not full. Some of his observations of natural phenomena are far in advance of anything known in his day by the students of nature. What he says about air currents in i, 6, is a matter of discovery only within the present age; and still more is this remark true of the statement of vs. 7. The Mediterranean, for instance, drains in part three continents. Into that sea the Nile, the Orontes, the Po, the Rhone, constantly flow; the Atlantic rushes into it through one mouth, the Black Sea pours into it through another. What becomes of the surplus water that is continuously poured into the Mediter-

ranean? This was the question which puzzled geographers for centuries. At length, a London chemist discovered the secret—that the clouds receive the surplus: evaporation accounts for all. How close is Solomon to this solution: "All the rivers run into the sea, yet the sea is not full; unto the place from whence the rivers come, thither they return." The preacher pertinently asks, "Is there anything whereof it may be said, see, this is new?" And he answers that it has been before. All is a weary go-round, nothing but a shifting of the old materials, a tiresome repetition, till life itself stiffens into dreadful monotony. "Nothing new under the sun"—"vanity."

The preacher made proof, next, of pleasure as promising satisfaction for the soul, ii, 1-3. Mirth, amusements, wine, were tried. He gave banquets, balls, had shows and displays of every kind, and no doubt gained for himself the title of the "Merry Monarch." But it was sheer failure—vanity he wrote upon this effort.

He then tried riches, and the peculiar treasure of kings, as likewise the gratification of his æsthetic tastes, ii, 4-11. He builded and planted, adorned and beautified. At his command palaces arose, fountains played, servants attended and musicians regaled his leisure hours. He affected art, increased his wealth and rejoiced in the success of his splendid projects. But once more complete disappointment was the issue—"all was vanity and a striving after wind."

His weariness and disgust ensued, ii, 12-26. Confused, perplexed at the strange inexplicable fact that the wise man and the fool apparently fare alike under the sun, that they travel the same road, he "hated" life, took no pleasure in it, saw no advantage in it. With the pessimistic spirits of our restless age, Solomon is perilously near answering the question, Is life worth living?—in the negative. And no wonder. A soul made for God, striving to feed itself on husks, and seeking to gratify its infinite longings on things under the sun, can do no otherwise than become at length weary and disgusted with it all, and wish itself well out of the world.

4. The preacher proves vanity under the sun from his wide observation, iii-viii, 15.

He observes, first of all, the regularity and unchangeableness of natural law, iii. Immutable continuity, inexorable law; men and beasts are alike in the presence of these mighty forces; one event befalls both; "as the one dieth, so dieth the other."

He next notes the wrongs and injustices practiced in the world, iv. Oppression, tyranny, envy, strife, division, they are to be seen everywhere, and the roots of them, too, insatiable greed.

Observations on religion, on riches, and the uselessness of money as a means to satisfy the soul, follow, v, vi.

He next looks upon the inequality of rewards and punishments of the righteous and wicked under the sun, vii, viii, 15, the problem which has puzzled God's people through all time. (Note vii, 15; viii, 14, which open this part of the book.)

5. The preacher's perplexity and apparent skepticism, viii, 16-xi. Let the reader ponder over chaps. viii, 14, 15; ix, 2-6; x, 5-11; xi, 8-10; and he will discover that the wisest of men, Solomon, was totally unable to unravel the mysteries by which he

was surrounded under the sun. He even goes the length of seeming to affirm that death ends all, that there is little, if any, difference in the treatment of the righteous and the wicked here. With all their boasted progress the men of our times who live only under the sun have gotten no further. Life and its vicissitudes, viewed only as to this world and sphere (under the sun) become for the strongest intellect a tangled web whose meshes no mortal hand can disengage. Is it really surprising that the philosophers who speculate as to things under the sun, should at length in a sort of desperation declare the problem insoluble and name themselves very fittingly, *agnostics*—know-nothings? The experiment of Solomon, alas, is being made by multitudes even in our day, and with the like result—"vanity and vexation of spirit."

6. The solution, xii, 13, 14. Here Solomon gets above the sun and things begin at once to disentangle and straighten. The "fear of God" is the Old Testament description of the New Testament "love of God." Love God, obey Him, trust Him and all will be well with you, for the judgment approaches in which all wrongs will be righted and all mysteries cleared up, and you will be made glad with a joy unspeakable. This is the key of the book. Live under the sun, rise no higher and doubt and unbelief will ensue. Live above the sun, spend the days with God, and light and peace you shall have.

Dr. McCook imagines a conversation between a bird and a mole which has pushed its head out of the ground: "What are you making such a noise about?" he asked the bird as it was swinging and singing on a branch of the tree. "O, the sunshine, the trees, the grasses, the shining stream yonder, and the white clouds on the mountain side. The world is full of beauty." "Nonsense!" said Mr. Mole. "I have lived longer in the world than you have, and I have gone deeper into it; I have traversed it and tunneled it, and I know what I am talking about, and I tell you there is nothing in it but fishing worms." Let a man live "under the sun," let him burrow in the earth and strive to get satisfaction for his soul out of it and he will have the experience of the mole. There will come the time, the bitter hour, when he will say with plash of tears and sobs of secret longing, "My soul hath no pleasure in it," "I hate my life." But let him rise above the sun and bask in the splendor of God's light and presence and he will sing.

Ecclesiastes may be regarded as a sermon: Text, i, 2, 3.

Part First.—Text proved:
1. By the preacher's experience, chaps. i, ii.
2. By his observation, chaps, iii, iv.

Part Second.—Text unfolded:
1. The miseries of life.
2. The hypocrisies of life.
3. The wrongs and injustices of life
4. The riches and poverty of life.
5. The uncertainties of life.
6. The best way to get on through this dangerous life.
7. Live above the sun and all will be well.

THE SONG.

Angus assigns this book of Scripture to B.C. 1001. The universal voice of antiquity ascribes it to Solomon, and internal evidence confirms this testimony. His songs were a thousand and five, 1 Kings iv, 32; and this is called the "song of songs," because the best of them all.

Key-word, "Beloved"; key-verse, vi, 3.

Origen and Jerome tell us that the Jews forbade it to be read by any until he was thirty years old. It certainly needs a degree of spiritual maturity to enter aright into the holy mystery of love which it celebrates. It is possible to read the song amiss; but to such as have attained spiritual maturity, of what age soever, it is one of the most edifying of the sacred writings.

Love to Jesus Christ becomes, through the sanctifying influence of the Holy Spirit, the strongest passion which can sway the human heart. Avarice, ambition, love of power may have more of the unnatural vigor attending fever; this carries with it the quiet, enduring energy of health that brings into captivity every thought to the obedience of Christ. Those alone who have experienced the power of this love in its intensity are competent judges whether any language used in expressing it may be exaggerated. If the love of God to us is as incomprehensible as is His eternity and omnipresence, it is not surprising that the love of a grateful heart should struggle and strive to declare itself by appealing to the tenderest ties, by using the boldest imagery; for the love of a believer is but a dim reflection of the measureless love of God.

1. The form of the song is somewhat difficult to determine. A drama it certainly is not, although it has been thus described. It presents little or nothing of the features belonging to the drama. While dialogue is found in it, still it is not of a very sustained kind, nor is it very marked. The feature chiefly lacking is a climax, the culminating *finis* with which the drama is expected to close. Its form seems to be that of a pastoral poem, with characters presenting quasi-dramatic action. The personages introduced into it are the bridegroom and king; the bride, or spouse; the daughters of Jerusalem, or the court ladies of Solomon's palace. There is scarcely traceable any plot, nor dramatic unity, although the poem is one. Most of the addresses, instead of being dialogues, are soliloquies, apostrophes, or monologues. It has changing scenes. Sometimes the scene is laid in a garden; at others in the palace; then in the country amid pastoral quiet and beauty; and in Jerusalem amidst the noise of a great city.

This much may be confidently asserted, that it is a song of love in Oriental language and imagery, with rests and pauses and varying scenery and conversation.

2. The design of the song. There are three interpretations of the poem advanced by as many schools of expositors. Each of these may be briefly mentioned.

The first is that of the merely literal and erotic.

That is, it is held that the poem celebrates the love of Solomon for a young shepherdess who was a member of an agricultural family consisting of a widowed mother and several sons, who lived at Shulem. (The name of the place is derived from the spouse, viz., Shulemite.) The young woman, in the course of her pastoral duties, met with a shepherd to whom, in due time, she became espoused. Her brothers violently opposed the union. She was invited by her lover to accompany him to the fields; but her brothers, to prevent the meeting, sent her to take care of the vineyards. Here, she one day encountered King Solomon, who, assisted by his court ladies, endeavored to win her love. But she remained steadfast to her affianced. The king carried her to the city, made her large promises and sought to overcome her scruples by princely presents; but without avail; and her fidelity was finally rewarded by her marriage with the shepherd and gifts from her reconciled brothers.

According to this theory the scope of the book is to give us an "example of virtue in a young woman who encountered and conquered great temptations, and was eventually rewarded." If this is all, belief in its inspiration must be dismissed; and it has no better right to a place in the Bible than a tale from the Arabian Nights, or the sonnets from Shakespeare. Against this theory there are strong objections: (1) It has been doubted whether there was such a place as Shulem whence the spouse derived her name of the Shulemite. (2) It seems obvious that if we accept this view of the book as true, then we must renounce the belief in Solomon's being the author; for it is altogether unlikely that he could have written so manifest an account of his own defeat. (3) The vast majority of Bible students see no ground or foundation for the story detailed above. They find no shepherd in it; no betrothal of the Shulemite with a shepherd; no effort on the part of the king to supplant another in her affections and steal her from him. In short, the story on which this view rests is pure fiction. (4) If it be no more than a love-poem celebrating one of Solomon's amours it is incredible that it should have been incorporated with the other books of the Bible, and for so many centuries held its place with the other inspired books as one of them. It was in the Old Testament canon when the Septuagint version was made, two hundred and fifty years before the advent of the Savior; it has kept its place there ever since. If it is only a " dissolute love song " God would have found a way to cast it out of His Book ages ago, like the Apocraphal books. (5) The strange and strong hold it has had upon some of the most spiritually minded men the world has ever seen—men like Rutherford, McCheyne, Gill, Moody, Stuart, John and Thomas Goodwin—is inexplicable if the song be nothing more than this hypothesis offers. We must reject this theory.

The second view we mention which has been put forward as an explanation of the design of the book is called the moral. The song is regarded as a description of wedded love in the exercise of its highest and purest affections. In this interpretation no spiritual sense is attached to the poem. The great moral sentiments relating to the holy estate of marriage alone are intended to be inculcated. The foundation for this opinion rests on the union of

Solomon with the daughter of Pharaoh. It is held that the poem sings the praises of that princess, and celebrates the happiness the king enjoyed in union with her.

There are very grave objections which may be urged against this theory. We may safely assert that the Egyptian princess is not meant at all nor can be meant by the Shulemite. Some of the difficulties that lie against it may be stated. The delicate daughter of the haughty Pharaoh could not in any supposable manner have ever been the sunburnt keeper of the vineyards, as the spouse is described to have been, ch. i, 6. She could not have been unveiled and beaten by the watchman of Jerusalem, v, 7. She could not have come from the snowy heights of Lebanon when she had no occasion to be within one hundred and twenty miles of its base, iv, 8. And it is very unlikely that she conducted Solomon into her mother's house, which was in Egypt, iii, 4.

Moreover, on this theory it is impossible to account for the remarkable situation of the spouse. She is found wandering through the streets of the great city by night; is smitten by watchmen; her veil is torn rudely from her face, the gravest insult that could be offered an Eastern woman. In fact, her whole conduct is utterly irreconcilable with the Oriental ideas of womanly seclusion and modesty. If this spouse is a veritable woman, having the experience here ascribed to her, then her character is altogether incompatible with Eastern habits of decorum, and is questionable.

The third view is, that the song is an allegory, that under the guise of human love, the love which passes between two loyal and faithful hearts, is set forth the intimate, tender relationship existing between Christ and His people. The frame, we may reverently say, is human conjugal affection. But through this thin, skillfully carved lattice-work there glance out upon us the joy and bliss, the rapture and ecstacy, the strange, tender wondrous play of the deep abiding love of Jesus for His own, and reciprocally, theirs for Him. The Chaldee Targum, the oldest Jewish commentary on the book, entitles it, "The Songs and Hymns which Solomon the Prophet, King of Israel, Delivered by the Spirit of Prophecy, before Jehovah, the Lord of the Whole Earth." The great body of Christians have always regarded it as a symbolical exhibition of the relations subsisting between the Lord and His people. From first to last, orthodox believers hold it bears the stamp of the allegory. In support of this view the following arguments may be urged: (1) It best accounts for the position of the book in the canon of Scripture. (2) It accords with the instincts of the spiritually-minded. (3) The names of its principal characters indicate that it is an allegory—*Shalomoh*, Solomon, the peaceful one, the prince of peace, and *Shulamith*, also the peaceful one, but feminine—the daughter of peace. These names are believed to be as suggestive, as significant, as Bunyan's "Christian" and "Christiana," or "Faithful" and "Hopeful." Read in this light, we perceive how appropriately the book represents Jesus as the peaceful one, the peace-bringer, and His people as the sharers of His peace, those to whom He gives peace. (4) The fancifulness of some of the scenes and situations render a literal interpretation absurd and impossible. See, for example, ii, 14-17; iii, 1-4; vi, 4-7; iv, 8. The Shulemite is in the clefts of the rock, in the concealments of the precipices; the bridegroom is in the garden, beyond the mountains, in the distant fields. The bride sleeps, the lover knocks at her door in the stillness of the night— withdraws when he receives no answer to his call. She in her remorse arises and wanders about the streets of the city. The rapid transitions, the remarkable situations indicate that the poem is an allegory. (5) This interpretation harmonizes best with the Old Testament representations of the relation between God and His people. This relation is often set forth as one of wedlock. The prophets, Jeremiah, Ezekiel, Hosea, in particular, make the marriage covenant existing between the Lord and Israel the ground of their passionate appeals. Nor is the New Testament silent as to this relation. The union and reciprocal love of Christ and the church are described in language closely akin to that of the song, "He is the Bridegroom who hath the Bride." They rejoice in each other. Their delights are mutual, identical, Matt. ix, 15; John iii, 29; 2 Cor. xi, 2; Eph. v, 25-32; Rev. xix, 7-9; xxi, 7-27.

The sudden pronominal changes indicate that the song is an allegory. "Draw *me, we* will run after thee." "The King hath brought *me* into His chambers; *we* will be glad and rejoice in thee," i, 4. The bride's name is not that of a single individual, but is collective. She is the " daughter of Zion."

3. The teaching of the Song we hold is the following:

(1) The bridegroom is the Messiah, the Redeemer.

(2) The b ride, His people.

(3) The daughters of Jerusalem, are the friends of both, Jno. iii, 29.

(4) The Song describes the love which exists between them. The fountain of all love for Christ is His love to us. To know His love is to love Him in return, 1 Jno. iv, 19.

(5) The time when the Song has its fulfillment is always. But it is believed that it will have a peculiar accomplishment in that day when the Jews are again restored to God's favor and fellowship—and for the second time the marriage bond is ratified and sealed, never again to be violated, Hos. i, ii; Rom. xi, 26-29.

(6) Traits of Christ's love. It is *unconditional*, chap. i, 2-6; comp. Rom. v, 8. *Irresistible*, ii, 8; comp. 1 John iv, 10. *Intense*, ii, 9, 10; comp. John xiv, 1-3. *Sheltering and protective*, ii, 14, 15; comp. Ps. xci, 1-6. *Exacting*, v, 2; comp. Eph. v, 1, 2. *Jealous*, v, 6; comp. Rev. iii, 20.

(7) Traits of a believer's love. It is *self-depreciating*, i, 5. *Eager for communion*, ii, 1-7. *Sometimes interrupted*, iii, 1. *Sorrowful*, v, 6, 7. *Intermittent*, v, 1, 2. *Self-sacrificing*, iii, 2, 3.

4. Structure and summary of contents: (Moody Stewart.)

Canto One.—Subject, the bride seeking and finding the king.

1. The king sought, chap. i, 2-8.
2. The king found, i, 9; ii, 7.

Canto Two. Subject, the sleeping bride awakened.

1. Call to meet the bridegroom, ii, 8-15.
2. Response of the bride, 16; iii, ii, 5.

Canto Three. Subject, the bridegroom with the bride.
1. The king in his bridal chariot, iii, 6-11
2. The beauty of the bride, iv, 1-7.
3. Garden of spices, iv, 8; v, 2.

Canto Four. Subject, bridegroom's withdrawal and reappearance.
1. Sleep and sorrow, v, 3; vi, 3.
2. Bridegroom's return, vi, 4-10.
3. Glory of the bride, vi, 11; vii, 10.
4. Garden in the fields, vii, 11; viii, 4.

Canto Five. Subject, the little sister, viii, 5-14.

PROPHECY.

The subject of prophecy is a vast and important one. It occupies a most prominent place in the Bible. It is found in almost every portion of the Word of God. Sixteen books (i. e., if we reckon Lamentations as a part of Jeremiah) of the Old Testament are devoted to it, and one of the New, Revelation. The moral instruction it contains, the momentous events it announces, the revelation of the divine character and of the nature, establishment, and purpose of the kingdom of God, which it affords, all combine to invest it with the profoundest interest. Before entering upon a study of the prophetic books, some observations on the general subject seem to be required.

Happily the Bible itself furnishes us an authoritative definition of the office and function of the prophet. In Ex. vii, 1, we are told "the Lord said unto Moses, See, I have made thee a god to Pharaoh; and Aaron, thy brother, shall be thy prophet." No statement could be clearer than this. By divine appointment Moses was to be in the place of God to Pharaoh, and Aaron was to act as the prophet of Moses, receiving from him the message and delivering it to the king. This is further illustrated in Ex. iv, 15, 16, where Moses was directed to "speak" to Aaron, "and put words into his mouth," the Lord promising at the same time to be with the mouths of both His servants and to teach them what they should do. Furthermore, Aaron was to be Moses' spokesman unto the people, i. e., he was to act the part of the prophet for Moses, and Moses was to be to him instead of God.

Here, then, we have the Scriptural definition of the prophet. He was one who received a message from God and delivered it to those for whom it was intended. He was God's "spokesman" and "mouth," the bearer and proclaimer of the Lord's will. He was "the man of God;" his message the word of God. Through him God spake, Heb. i, 1.

Prophecy sprang from man's exigencies. It had its origin in man's sore need; its birth was in the day of his sin and apostasy. The first great predictive promise, that which stands at the head of all the rest and leads the long procession, was given after the fall, and because of the fall, Gen. iii, 15. Mercy and grace prompted it, but the ruin wrought by sin was its occasion. It was mainly in consequence of Israel's rejection of God as their glorious King, and their determination to have a king from among themselves and like themselves that Samuel and the prophets that follow after came into such prominence. It was because of the apostasy of the chosen people and the tremendous afflictions which befell them on account of it that the ministries of Jeremiah, Ezekiel, and Daniel assumed such vast importance, and became so significant in all succeeding history. Prophecy, therefore, implies *failure*. Had there been no sin, prophecy would probably have never been given, because not needed. The apostle Peter exhorts believers to take heed to the word of prophecy more confirmed " as unto a light that shineth in a dark place, until the day dawn and the day-star arise in your hearts," 2 Pet. i, 19. "A lamp shining in a dark place" is the inspired description of the nature and object of prophecy. It was when Israel was apostatizing from God that the prophets appeared, uttered their solemn warnings and made their passionate appeals. It was when Jesus knew that the nation had determined on His rejection and murder that He announced the overthrow of the temple, the dismemberment and dispersion of the chosen people. It was when the Spirit of God had detected the germs of declension and apostasy in the professing Christian church that He revealed the guilt, tribulation, and doom of the unfaithful body.

One great aim of prophecy was to testify against the defections and corruptions of the prophet's own times, and to arrest and correct them. Thus, Elijah, Elisha, Hosea, Amos and others bore a faithful witness against the increasing wickedness of the kings and people of Israel (the northern kingdom), and their tone deepened in intensity and earnestness in proportion as the evils grew and the end drew on. So, too, the prophets of Judah cried aloud and spared not in their efforts to check and turn back the tide of evil, but in vain; and Jeremiah sings at length the mournful dirge that tells of Judah's fall. Accordingly, the prophet's message often originated from the circumstances and the exigencies of his own times, and often likewise was addressed to the men of his own generation. But this is not an invariable rule. There is no traceable connection between the temporal conditions of Micah and the prediction of the birth-place of Messiah, Micah v, 2.

Nor is it possible to find any relation between the circumstances in the life of the writer of Psalm twenty-two and the unique experiences therein detailed. The same remark holds in the instances of the covenant and promises made to Abraham, Gen. xv, xxii. The seven great prophetic parables of Matt. xiii, properly speaking, have no " historical setting," as the pet phrase runs. It is a very serious mistake to tie up the messages of the prophets to their own times, and attempt to exhaust their contents in their application to the prophet's contemporaries.

The prophets were predictors of future events. They were the deliverers of the divine communications not only as to the moral state of the men of the prophet's own generation, but more especially as to God's purposes in the future. Often, in fact almost invariably, the messages of the prophets to the people of their own day are intermingled with announcements of events to be realized in the distant future. Such, for example, are many of the predictions of Isaiah, of almost all of Daniel, of our Lord's Olivet prophecy, Matt. xxiv, xxv, and the Apocalypse of John.

Each prophet had both a distinct call to the office, and a message to deliver. Both were from God. No man could assume it, self-appointed; much less could he originate his message. For Moses, see Ex. iii, 2; Samuel, 1 Sam. iii, 10; Isa. vi, 8; Jer. i, 5; Ezek. ii, 4; Dan. ii, 19-23, etc.

The outline of the general subject may be summarized as follows:

1. Prophecy is a miracle of knowledge. That is, it is an accurate foreseeing and foretelling of future

events so that men may perceive that human sagacity, political forecasting, induction by the reason, and intuition, could by no possibility of exertion or premeditation ever predict. Biblical prophecy is not an inference from existing data—nor a deduction. Much less is it a generalization from known facts or shrewd guessing. As it is from God who knows the end from the beginning it can only be a divine revelation. A true prophecy is authenticated by its fulfillment, and remains always a monument of its own origin and truth. Deut. xiii, 1-3; xviii, 20-22; Jer. xxviii, 1-9.

2. It must have been uttered as a prophecy from the beginning. A conjecture, or a happy coincidence, is excluded. An inspired prediction is intentionally given as such, because God, its Author, knows precisely what the event predicted shall be, and He has the power and wisdom to secure its accomplishment.

3. It must have a definite meaning, and inculcate a moral truth. All prophecy is a revelation of the perfections and purposes of God.

4. It must be worthy of God. The puerilities and silliness so often associated with sooth-saying can have no place in predictions which come from God.

5. While it is perspicuous, it is not so detailed and minute as to suggest to human agents ways and methods of working out its accomplishment.

In the study of prophecy it should be borne in mind that it is marked by a certain progress. This is true indeed of the whole Bible. It is a book of growth. The "sundry times and divers manners" of Heb. i, 1, indicates this fact. Gradually, by piecemeal as we might say, God gave forth His communications to the people through His servants, the prophets.

The progress referred to is particularly noticeable in the predictions relating to the Messiah, the promised Deliverer. At first His coming is made public and promiscuous. He might be born anywhere, He might spring from any family of earth. The only thing certain was that He was to be a descendant of Eve, the mother of us all. But ere long a restricting process began which limited the promise and made it more definite and precise. It is announced that He shall be of the seed of Abraham, Gen. xvii, 7; xxii, 18; that He shall be of the tribe of Judah, Gen. xlix, 10; of the house of David, 2 Sam. vii, 14-16; the Son of a Virgin, Isa. vii, 14; born at Bethlehem, Micah v, 2; and in the sixty-ninth week of Daniel's mystic seventy, Dan. ix, 24-26. As the majestic portrait of the coming Messiah grows, new features are added to it by the prophetic hand. He is to be a holy sin-bearer, a silent sufferer, a slaughtered Lamb. The sword is to awake against Him, and He is to know the bitterness of death and the grave. And yet He is to be the conqueror of death, the vanquisher of the grave. From first to last, from the prophetic Psalms to Isaiah and Daniel and Malachi, there is progress, movement, growth.

We should carefully discriminate between prophecy and what in some sort resembles it and with what it has sometimes been confounded, viz., *divination*. According to the Scripture, prophecy does not spring from any natural parts whatsoever, or from any powers of the human spirit. Its origin is always traced to the supernatural working of the Spirit of God on the spirit of the prophet. The prophets disclaim any part in the origination of their messages. Even the words in which the message is conveyed they ascribe to God. Their uniform and authoritative formula is, " The word of the Lord came unto me"—" Thus saith the Lord." The language of the apostle Peter is final on the subject: " For no prophecy ever came by the will of man; but men spake from God, being moved by the Holy Ghost," 2 Pet. i, 21, cf; 1 Pet. i, 10, 11; Lu. i, 70, etc. Soothsaying can claim no such exalted origin. Mark the difference between the two. Prophecy from its nature and design cannot give predictions on all kinds of subjects and things. Divination attempts precisely to do this. Prophecy announces nothing else than events and relations which stand in organic and internal connection with the plan of redemption. Divination undertakes to reveal the future of persons and things without any reference to the divine government or God's purposes of grace. Prophecy has to do with the course and development of God's kingdom in the world. Divination is essentially a puerile kind of fortune-telling. Prophecy is the product of the inspiration of the Holy Spirit. Divination rests upon an imaginary intercourse with an extra-mundane spirit. The prophet spoke the words of the Lord, the words which the Lord had put into his mouth, Jer. i, 9; Ezek. ii, 7. The soothsayer and false prophet spoke out of their own hearts, Jer. xiv, 14; xxiii, 16. The former brought objective truth, the latter a subjective presentiment. The one received his message from without, from beyond the boundaries of his own intelligence. The other evoked his oracle from the depths of his own heart. The prophets had for the object and center of all their communications the Lord Jesus Christ. Divination knows nothing of Christ, cares nothing for Him.

Besides, there is a remarkable harmony and correspondence between the claim of the prophets to be the spokesmen of God and their messages. There is no disparity between them. Their claim and their message square with each other. In all the range of literature there is nothing next to or like this to be found. In this respect the prophecy of Scripture stands without a parallel in the history of the world.

We are not left to conjecture how the divine communications were made to the prophets. In Num. xii, 6-8, the Lord said to Moses, Aaron, and Miriam that He would make Himself known to a prophet in a vision or a dream; but to Moses His servant He would "speak mouth to mouth." In these three ways God made known His will to men. That He spoke to men by an audible voice, giving them a verbal message cannot be doubted, Num. xii, 4, 8; Deut. xxxiv, 10; 1 Sam. iii; Ezek. ii, etc. Through dreams likewise the will of God was revealed. Joseph in Egypt, Joseph the husband of Mary, Nebuchadnezzar and others had communications from God in this way. Most of the contents of the prophetic Scriptures were given through visions vouchsafed the prophets. In the dream and vision the mental state of the prophet is conjectured by Myrick to have been as follows: (1) The bodily senses were closed to external objects as in deep sleep. (2) The reflective and discursive faculty was still and inactive. (3) The spiritual faculty (*the pneuma*) was awakened to the highest state of energy. The spirit of the prophet became, as it were, an ear and an eye, aroused and quickened as he was by the Spirit of God, so that he could hear the voice of the Lord and see the future as it was unfolded to him by the revealing Mind. Anciently the name *Seer* was given the prophet (1 Sam. ix, 9), because pre-eminently he was one who saw, who was endowed with the seeing faculty in the highest degree. He possessed a preternatural sight, and insight; he had power given him to look into the invisible world. That the prophets did not always understand the messages which were communicated to them is evident from 1 Pet. i, 10-12. After receiving the messages they themselves diligently studied them. In both Daniel and the Apocalypse of John there is unmistakable evidence of this fact, Dan. vii, 28; viii, 15-27; x, 7-15; Rev. i, 17; vii, 13, 14; xvii, 6. It follows of necessary consequence that the very words must have been given the prophets by the Lord, for they were incompetent to put into intelligible and accurate language that which they themselves did not understand.

1. The vividness of the visions. The prophets beheld the future as if it were present. In fact, the future was brought before them and became an actual reality by the series of object-visions or pictures in which it was embodied visibly before them. "They saw the future in space rather than in time; the whole, therefore, appears foreshortened and perspective rather than actual distance is regarded." Hence they often speak of the future as if it were past. There is a "prophetic perfect" tense in the language of prophecy. Psalms xxii, lxix, Is. liii, and much of Daniel and Revelation are examples of this use of language. Very graphic are the visions of the

prophets. The picture of the event foretold stands out sharply defined, clear, unmistakable in its outlines, massiveness and action.

2. Symbolism. Prophecy is full of symbols. They correspond to the types of the Mosaic ritual; in both the predominant idea is the pictorial representation of things to come. In Daniel and John the future is portrayed by a series of gorgeous pictures. Symbols, it should be remembered, have a language of their own as definite as any form of speech. They are addressed to the *eye*, while the prophetic discourse is for the *ear*.

Some of the uses of prophecy may be briefly summarized:

1. It substantiates the claims and the mission of the prophet.

2. It is a perduring witness to the person, character and work of the Lord Jesus Christ.

3. It is a chief pillar of Christianity as a divine system.

4. It is an unimpeachable evidence of the plenary inspiration of the Bible.

5. It is the lamp by the light of which the believer is to walk through the darkness of this world.

Some hints touching the study and interpretation of prophecy may not be out of place. Of course, in a paper such as this only the briefest suggestions are given.

1. Ascertain the relation of the prophecy to the prophet himself and to the times in which he lived Often the historical occasion of the divine communication serves to throw much light on its meaning and aim. But this is only partially true. There are

many predictions of which the "historical setting," even if it were discoverable, affords no help.

2. Collect together all that God the Holy Spirit has been pleased to reveal on any subject, and study and compare.

3. Distinguish the form from the truth embodied in it. That is, distinguish figures from what is represented by them. Whatever images the prophet may use the subject of prophecy is never a figure. Back of the picture and behind the image in which the future is revealed lies the reality, the mighty fact which the Spirit of God has been pleased to reveal.

4. Mark the principles of interpretation sanctioned by the New Testament. We there find the true method of prophetic interpretation, viz., that the Bible is an organic unity, that Christ is the center and object of all the divine counsels and purposes, that Israel is not exactly the church of God of our dispensation, and that there is a great and blessed future both for Israel and for the earth itself. If one reverently and earnestly gives himself to the study of prophetic interpretation as furnished by the inspired writers of the New Testament he will discover the divinely sanctioned rule for all the Bible.

5. A common maxim is that history is the expounder of prophecy; that we must await its fulfillment to understand it. The view is only partially correct, is indeed very inadequate. It confounds the interpretation with the confirmation. A prediction is sometimes as difficult to understand after its accomplishment as before. If prophecy can be understood only when it has been fulfilled, then it is practically useless until it has become history. How, then, can it be a lamp shining in a dark place for our

guidance? Prophecy is intended for all God's people. But all cannot know the world's history: hence history is not its final interpreter.

6. The Spirit of God is the infallible interpreter of prophecy, as He is of all Scripture.

ISAIAH.

Of the prophet who bears this name little is known. He was the son of Amoz, a person of course not to be identified with the prophet, Amos. A current Jewish tradition, according to Horne, connected Isaiah with the blood-royal, his father being the son of Joash and brother of Amaziah, king of Judah. Jerome, on the authority of some rabbinical writers, says that the prophet gave his daughter in marriage to King Manasseh, the son of Hezekiah. How much of this traditional information is to be received as worthy of credence it might be difficult to determine, perhaps very little of it. There is more ground for believing that the prophet suffered death in the early reign of Manasseh, being martyred for his infidelity to the truth of which he had borne the noblest and most constant testimony. It is said that he was sawn asunder by order of that bloody tyrant, the Diocletian of Jewish history. Heb. xi, 37, is thought by many to allude to Isaiah's death. His extraordinary call to the office of prophet is recorded in the sixth chapter of his book. It is not meant that Isaiah did not exercise his ministry to some extent before the great vision recorded in chapter six took place. But by it he was inaugurated into the great work to which, in an especial manner, he was now called. It was in the year Uzziah died that the vision was vouchsafed him which changed the whole current of his life and which, as in the case of Saul of Tarsus, made him the man he was. Isaiah saw the Lord seated on a throne high and lifted up. Cherubs, with veiled faces and veiled feet, surrounded the enthroned One as guards round the King. From side to side went up a hymn of praise, the heavenly hosts chanting with tireless energy the holiness of the Lord. All the young man's sins, all the sins of the nation rushed upon him with overwhelming force. "Woe is me, for I am undone," he cried. In the presence of the dazzling brightness and infinite glory of the throne he felt himself to be a man of unclean lips, "the foul-mouthed son of a foul-mouthed race." On those defiled lips the swift seraph laid the flaming coal from the flaming altar. This signified the removing of pollution and the creation of that marvelous style of speech which has entranced the world. From that time forward Isaiah possessed in the highest degree the prophetic gift, a message from God and the power to utter it in the most forcible language. Both the message and the speech were communicated to him from God Himself. The awful voice asked: "Whom shall I send, and who will go for us?" With unhesitating devotion the young man replied, "Here am I; send me." It was his supreme call and commission.

The circle of hearers on whom his ministry was designed immediately to operate was Judah and Jerusalem. Isaiah was the prophet of Judah. While he spoke of Syria, Moab, Egypt, Tyre, Assyria, Babylon, etc., nevertheless these nations were introduced because of their connection with the kingdom of Judah. It was not for their benefit he prophesied, but for the people of Judah alone now become the sole home of Jewish blessings and of hope. His ministry was to be a strangely barren one, vi, 9-13; at least so far as the world judges. The louder he should cry the less would the people hear and understand. Under his testimony, powerful as it should be, worse and more obdurate would they become until judicial blindness, God's heaviest punishment in this world, should settle down upon them. Both the Lord Jesus and Paul allude to the awful effect of refusing the words of God, the hardening process which is sure to follow unbelief, Matt. xiii, 14, 15; Acts xxviii, 25-27. History evermore repeats itself. The Jews of Isaiah's time had their counterpart in those of Jesus' and Paul's day. Nor is it otherwise now. Refuse the divine message, and keep on refusing it; and the time will come when all you can do is to refuse, when the ears cannot hear and the eyes are fast closed in sleep. Besides, Isaiah's ministry was to be one largely made up of the reiterations of "commonplaces." The sad, plaintive cry, "Precept upon precept, precept upon precept; line upon line, line upon line; here a little, there a little," xxviii, 10, 11, was to be a prominent feature in his work and testimony. "Commonplaces!" It is the work of God's messengers still, often sorrowful enough!

Isaiah's ministry extended over a long period, at least over the reigns in whole or in part, of four kings, Uzziah, Jotham, Ahaz, and Hezekiah, i, 1. Probably but little of his prophetic career belonged to the reign of Uzziah. From the book itself it can not be determined whether any prophecy was delivered during the time of Jotham. But it should be remembered that Uzziah was a leper in the closing years of his life, and Jotham, his son, was probably regent during the time, 2 Kings xv, 5; 2 Chron.xxvi, 21 (Uzziah and Azariah are identical). His prophetic activity lasted it is thought by many, for sixty years, perhaps for sixty-five. Rawlinson's conjectural estimate of his lifetime is ninety years—B. B. 780 and B. C. 690—which would make him contemporary with Manasseh for the space of nine years.

Isaiah's character is one of great boldness and earnestness. Toward sin of every kind, he is everywhere uncompromising. Fraud, oppression, dishonesty, hypocrisy, idolatry, apostasy, he denounces with a vehemence that is unparalleled. " He conceals nothing, keeps nothing back, out of a desire for court favor." " Is it a small thing for you to weary men?" he says to one king; " but must ye weary my God also?" vii, 13. " Set thine house in order," he says to another, " for thou shalt die and not live," xxxviii, 1. But he is not all sternness. Some of his passages are unsurpassed for tenderness and compassion and love. Where can anything be found which for pathos equals this, " Comfort ye, comfort ye, my people," xl, 1, 2; " As one whom his mother comforteth, so will I comfort you," lxvi, 13, as if the great God, like a gentle mother, took up into His mighty arms His poor, weeping people, and hushed their sobbings, and rocked them to rest on His own infinite heart. His horizon is broader than that of most of the prophets. While Judah and Jerusalem are the great themes of his prophetic utterances and are nearer his heart than any others, yet the Gentiles are his brother men also, and for them sublime predictions are made, and their future is painted in as glowing colors of beauty and glory as that of Israel itself. Nay, the weary earth and tired nature, the very beasts of the field, together with toiling and suffering man, universal man are yet to share in the glorious salvation of our God.

Then, too, his spirituality and deep reverence should not be overlooked. With David he sees clearly that outward forms and ceremonies are not the true religion, nor sacrifices, nor assemblies of worshiping people, nor days, nor fasts, nor temples, constitute true religion, are of no value in the sight of God if purity of heart and genuine obedience and whole-hearted consecration to the service and worship of God are absent. Isaiah is the evangelical prophet. He speaks of Christ and of His redemption with almost the same clearness and fullness as an evangelist or an apostle.

His name, Isaiah, signifies the salvation of Jehovah, and it, together with the names of his two sons, are thought by Dr. Forbes to be introduced into the prophecies with great beauty and force on the principle of rhetoric known as paranomasia, i. e., play on the name, viz., Maher-shalal-hash-baz ("speed, spoil, hastens the prey"), viii:1, 3; Shear-jashub ("a remnant shall return"), x, 4-34; Isaiah ("Salvation of Jehovah"), xi, xii.

That these three names are wrought into the chapters above cited, can hardly be doubted. The same remark holds likewise as to the name, Immanuel, viii, 5-ix, 7.

1. The title and authentication of the book, chap. i, 1: "The vision of Isaiah, the son of Amoz, which he saw concerning Judah and Jerusalem in the days

of Uzziah, Jotham, Ahaz, and Hezekiah, kings of Judah." This verse is not the preface to the first chapter or to any small portion of the book, as is evident from the enumeration of the four kings; it is a sort of caption to the entire volume. But more, the verse is designed to be a witness and a seal of the source and integrity of the contents of the book. It is very noteworthy that all the prophetic books have just such an endorsement as this of Isaiah, and almost invariably the authentication is found at the opening of the writing. Daniel appears to be an exception; but ch. i, 17, is the voucher for that prophet. The same literary peculiarity, as we may venture to call it, distinguishes the epistolary writings of the New Testament. Paul begins his letters with such an authentication as is found in the prophets. So, likewise, do James, Peter, and Jude. John writes the opening sentence of the Apocalypse with just such an appeal to the divine origin of the predictions contained in his book as the Old Testament seers employ. The Holy Spirit, who is the real Author of the Bible, has thus stamped His majestic *imprimatur* on the great prophetic and epistolary writings. He would be rash and reckless indeed who would essay to remove it!

2. Isaiah may be conveniently divided into three great parts. Part I., chs. i-xxxv. Part II., chs. xxxvi-xxxix. Part III., chs. xl-lxvi. In Parts I. and III. there are three main groups of prophecies, while in Part II. there is but one subject mainly, viz., historical events in connection with the reign of Hezekiah.

Part I. of the book may be distributed into the three following groups of prophecies: (1) Reproofs, warnings, and promises addressed chiefly to Judah and Jerusalem, together with hopes held forth to the Gentiles, chaps. i-xii. This section ends with a glowing announcement of the blessed day coming, the millennial day, when all the promises of God will have their ample fulfillment, chaps. xi-xii. Israel's conversion and the joy of the whole earth in consequence are rapturously described. The antagonisms in nature, the wrongs and oppressions and cruelties practiced by men against one another, in short, the miseries and wretchedness and bitterness of life as it now is in the world, will all be done away, and righteousness and peace and universal rest and blessing cover the whole world as a mantle of joy.

(2) Predictions respecting the nations which were specially hostile to Judah, chaps. xiii-xxiii. Some eight nations are named, among them the great powers of Babylon, Syria, Egypt and Tyre. Their sin and doom are graphically depicted.

(3) Predictions of judgment on the world, on Samaria and Judah and sins and wickedness which provoke the judgment, the Assyrian invasion and destruction of Samaria, the alarm, distress, and final deliverance of Jerusalem, chaps. xxiv-xxxv. The section terminates with another magnificent description of the coming glory, xxxv.

Part II. contains the historical chapters, xxxvi-xxxix. Two of them, xxxvi, xxxvii, relate the story of the Assyrian invasion and its results; the others, xxxviii, xxxix, Hezekiah's sickness and recovery, and the incident of the Babylonian ambassadors. The first two chapters face Part I. of the book, the last two Part III. These historical chapters are the bridge between the two great sections of the prophecy, binding thus into one the entire volume.

Part III. consists of chaps. xl-lxvi. The predictions contained in this section of Isaiah are surpassingly grand as to style, transcendently lofty as to conception, most precious in all the wealth of promise and assurance as to the future of God's people and the world itself. With consummate art the prophet has cast his inspired writing into three main divisions, each of which ends with a most solemn note of warning to the wicked. "No peace, saith Jehovah, to the wicked." (1) xl-xlviii. The antithesis of Jehovah and idols, Israel and the nations, ending with the knell of judgment, "There is no peace, saith the Lord, to the wicked." (2) xlix-lvii. The antithesis between the sufferings of the Servant of Jehovah and the glory which should follow, ending with a more emphatic note of warning than the former. "There is no peace, saith my God, to the wicked." (3) lviii-lxvi. The antithesis between the hypocrites and the faithful, between the immoral and the self-indulgent, and the mourners and the persecuted for righteousness' sake, between the world of sin and sorrow that now is, and the world of blessedness and holiness and purity which is to be, ending with the heaviest note of judgment of all, "For their worm shall not die, neither shall their fire be quenched, and they shall be an abhorring to all flesh."

The central theme of the first division of these magnificent predictions is *comfort*, the comfort of the Lord's people in prospect of their exile and suffering at Babylon, and the assurance of their deliverance and restoration through God's chosen instrument and servant, Cyrus the Persian. The central theme of the second division is the Servant of

Jehovah, the promised Messiah, who by His first advent in humiliation will bring in everlasting righteousness and salvation for God's people, and who by His second advent will introduce millennial and eternal glory. And the central theme of the third division is the realization of the promised glory.

Broadly, therefore, we say that the book of Isaiah is made up of seven grand divisions, three in Part I., one in the four historical chapters, and three in Part III., chaps. xl-lxvi.

About the question of the unity of Isaiah, controversy rages. Believers in the plenary, verbal inspiration of the Bible insist that the Prophet Isaiah, son of Amoz, is the author of the book that bears his name. This the higher critics strenuously deny. One of them (Ewald) imagines he can trace seven different hands in its composition. The majority, however, content themselves with asserting a twofold authorship, viz.: Proto-Isaiah, chaps. i-xxxix, probably written by the prophet; and Deutero-Isaiah, chaps. xl-lxvi, by the " Great Unknown," i. e., by some very remarkable prophet who lived during the time of the exile at Babylon and about the time of Cyrus. Difference of style used to be urged as a strong argument in support of this theory, but it is now almost entirely abandoned. The arguments now advanced are briefly these: (1) In Isaiah xl-lxvi, the writer speaks as if he were actually living in the times he describes. (2) It is not the ordinary method of prophecy to enter into detail, and minutely describe events, as is done in these chapters. (3) The captivity, the fall of Babylon, Cyrus, Messiah's suffering and Israel's restoration, are all given with such minuteness of detail as to preclude the belief that Isaiah, the son of Amoz, who lived some 170 years before could have been the author. Something of the true nature of the higher criticism is thus disclosed. It virtually denies that the prophets of God foretold anything future which was disconnected with their own times. That the prophet Isaiah, the son of Amoz, is the author of the whole book is firmly held by the present writer. The reasons for this belief are for him amply sufficient, amounting to a demonstration. Only some of them are here given.

(1) The novelty of the theory makes against it. For seventeen hundred years and more it was never heard of among the scholars of the church. One Jew, of the twelfth century, Aben Ezra, was the only writer, so far as is now known, that ever broached it. In fact, the theory is hardly a hundred years old. It would be well for us to bear in mind the old adage, " what is true is not new; and what is new is not true."

(2) The gross ignorance of the critics as to the 'Great Unknown" makes against the theory. Consider how forcible this argument becomes, had we the space and the time to draw it out in its full strength. Here is a writing the most transcendently eloquent, comforting, instructive, impressive, formative, and influential of the Old Testament prophetical Scriptures if we except Daniel; chaps. xlii, liii, lx, lxi, etc., have swayed the thought and animated the hope and encouraged the faith of God's people, both Israelitish and Christian, for centuries. It upheld the exiles at Babylon; it led Cyrus to issue his decree for the return of the captives; it kept bright

the expectation in pious Jewish hearts of the coming of Messiah; it has led many a sinner to the Saviour. And yet nobody knows who wrote it! It is the product of the "Great Unknown."

(3) The Septuagint version knows no other author of the book than Isaiah. Yet this ancient translation, B. C. 250, and earlier, does not hesitate to ascribe the various Psalms to different authors, as, e. g., David, Asaph, Jeremiah, Haggai, Ethan, etc.; but makes no hint of a composite composition of Isaiah.

(4) The son of Sirach, author of the apocryphal book of Ecclesiasticus, about B. C. 180, definitely ascribes this portion of the book (xl-lxvi) to Isaiah, the prophet, and speaks of him in such fashion as to preclude the idea that any other than he was ever conjectured to be the author of it.

(5) Cyrus' decree, Ez. i, 1, 2, is proof that the section of Isaiah under inspection was written before the captivity. In it the monarch refers to the wording of the prophecies concerning himself, Is. xliv, 27, 28; xlv, 1-3. The words of the edict are copied from these passages. Now is it credible that Cyrus would be influenced so powerfully as to issue his proclamation thus worded if the prophecy were uttered in his own day and by a contemporary? Josephus testifies that these prophecies concerning himself were shown Cyrus, and it was on account of them he published his decree for the Jews' return, and for the rebuilding of the temple.

(6) The historical chapters, xxxviii, xxxix, prepare the way for chaps. xl-lxvi, and in reality assert the connection of Hezekiah and Isaiah with them. "All that is in thine house shall be carried to Baby-

lon, and thy sons shall be eunuchs in the king's palace."

(7) The witness of the New Testament to the Isaian authorship of these disputed chapters is explicit and abundant. According to Westcott and Hort the whole book of Isaiah is quoted and referred to more than 210 times; chaps. xl-lxvi more than one hundred times. These references and quotations are varied, specific and inexplicable save on the supposition that the New Testament writers knew no author of the book except the son of Amoz. With them the book is no compilation; they recognize no "hand" in it but that of Isaiah. With them the book is the words of the prophet Isaiah, who spoke by the Holy Spirit. Matthew declares that the writer of chapter forty-two was Isaiah, Matt. xii, 17, 18. Luke testifies that chapter fifty-three was written by Isaiah, Acts viii, 28-35; that chapter sixty-one was written by Isaiah, Lu. iv, 17. Paul ascribes chapters fifty-three and sixty-five to the same prophet, Rom. x, 16, 20. Let it also be particularly noted that in every possible way the New Testament writers attribute the entire book to Isaiah. They speak of him again and again as "the prophet Isaiah," "Isaiah, the prophet," Matt. iii, 3; viii, 7, etc., i. e., when they would make prominent the *man* Isaiah they give first his name and second his official title; when the *office* of the man is to be emphasized the title precedes and his name follows. They mention, too, "the book of the prophet Isaiah," Lu. iv, 17; and "the book of the words of Isaiah the prophet," Lu. iii, 4, etc. That is, the inspired writers of the New Testament distinguish between the "book of Isaiah" and the "prophet Isaiah" who wrote the book.

Prophecy deals mainly with three subjects which are inseparably connected, viz.: Israel, Messiah, and the kingdom of God. That all three are conspicuously found in this book even the most cursory reader sees. It would be difficult to determine which has the larger place. Read from one point of view Isaiah appears to be wholly absorbed with the fortunes of Judah and Jerusalem; whatever else is introduced is subordinate or incidental. From another it is the promised Deliverer, the mighty Servant of Jehovah, who fills the entire horizon of the prophetic vision, in whom every promise and purpose of God shall have its ample accomplishment.

1. The prophet foretells the Messiah's incarnation, vii, 14. That this prediction relates to the Lord Jesus Christ is manifest from Matt. i, 18-25. No child of ordinary birth can be meant by the prophet, for He is to be the child of "the virgin," certainly of an unmarried female. He is to bear the great name Immanuel, "with us God." It should be borne in mind that from the very beginning the Messiah was to be the offspring in an extraordinary sense of the woman, Gen. iii, 25. Difficulties, it is freely acknowledged, envelop this prediction, nor can any attempt now be made to clear them away. The words of a profound student of the Bible (Prof. Cave) are worth quoting: "This Deliverer, the Branch of the Lord, is afterward announced as the Son of a virgin, before whose birth the two Hebrew kingdoms shall have ceased to be monarchies." Whatever interpretation be adopted, it must satisfy these conditions: (1) It must yield a sense worthy of the grandeur of verse eleven; (2) the Child must be of David's house, and the glory of it; (3) He must

be divine as His name Immanuel asserts; (4) His dignity must be superhuman.

2. The dignity of His person is announced by the sublime titles given Him, ix, 6. What a group of names is here found! He is identified with our race, for He is "a child born, a son given," the Son of man. But He is much more, He is God. He is wonderful—in His person, work, love and grace; the counsellor—the prophet, greater than Moses, Isaiah, Daniel, than any and all the prophets; the Revealer of the Father, Jno. i, 18; the mighty God, Himself God, co-equal and co-eternal with the Father; the Father of eternity, the Maker of heaven and earth, the Prince of Peace, the promised Shiloh, Gen. xlix, 10; Lu. ii, 10-14.

3. He is to be of the house of David and sit on David's throne, ix, 7; xi, 1; and He will be endowed with all the gifts and powers needed for the universal government which He is to sway, xi, 2-4.

4. His forerunner and harbinger is foretold, xl, 3-5; comp. Matt. iii, 1-3. John was only a voice, what every preacher of Christ should be.

5. The character of His ministry and His qualifications for its execution are described, xlii, 1-7. What wisdom and grace, what tenderness and power, courage and humility, lowliness and loftiness, stooping and conquering are here predicted of Him.

6. His prophetic office is announced, lxi, 1-3. In Luke iv, 18, 19, our Lord read these words in the synagogue at Nazareth; but it is very noteworthy that He stopped short in the second verse at a comma, "To preach the acceptable year of the Lord," He could not add, "And the day of vengeance of our God;" for that day was not come, nor is

it yet. Our whole dispensation of grace lies in that comma. How infinitely accurate is Scripture!

7. The priestly office is foretold, chap. liii. Let us note some things from this amazing chapter:

I. He is to be a suffering Messiah, vss. 1-3. "Dispised," "rejected," "man of sorrows," grief-smitten, "like one from whom men hide their faces."

II. Messiah's sufferings vicarious. There are at least twelve assertions of this truth: (1) "Borne our griefs;" (2) "carried our sorrows;" (3) "wounded for our trangessions;" (4) bruised for our iniquities;" (5) "chastisement of our peace;" (6) "His stripes;" (7) "Lord laid on Him the iniquity of us all;" (8) "For the transgression;" (9) "it pleased the Lord to bruise Him;" (10) "soul an offering for sin;" (11) "bear their iniquities;" (12) "bear the sin of many." How any one in the face of this Scripture can deny the substitutionary nature of Christ's atonement is almost incredible.

III. His sufferings propitiatory. This truth lies in the four expressions as to *bearing sin:*

1. Ver. 6, "The Lord hath laid on Him the iniquity of us all."

2. Ver 10, "Thou shalt make His soul an offering for sin."

3. Ver. 11, " He shall bear their iniquities."

4. Ver. 12, " He shall bear the sin of many," 2 Cor. v, 21.

Israel's Restoration, Isa. xi, 11, 12, 15, 16. The language of the prophet is precise. He announces, or rather the Spirit of the Lord by him, that the "Lord shall set His hand again the second time to recover the remnant of His people." "The second time" cannot be the first time. It is a future restoration that is meant; and it is still future, unless, as many think, it is already begun in the marvelous events of our own days touching this strange, indestructible people. How they are to be brought back again to their own land and to the favor and blessing of God; how the "land" (Palestine) is to become fertile beyond all antecedence; how the whole world is to share in Israel's blessing, is fully foretold by Isaiah, ii, 1-5; xi; xxxv; xlix, 22, 23; lxii, 4; xxvii, 6; lxvi, 19, 20, etc.

Promises respecting the Gentiles, xi, 1, 10; (cf. Rom. xv, 12); lxi, 1, 6; (cf. Matt. xii, 17-21); xlix, 6; lx, 3; (cf. Lu. ii, 32; Acts xiii, 47).

Millennial Blessedness. No prophet of the Old Testament is so full of this most attractive subject as Isaiah; none gives us so comprehensive a view of it. The vast cosmical changes which accompany its introduction; the revolution in all the ways and habits of men it involves, and its characteristic features, are the themes of this matchless pen. A meager outline of some of the more prominent things connected with it is here given.

1. Binding and imprisonment of Satan, the cause of the world's woe, xxiv, 21, 22; xxvii, 1; cf. Rev. xx, 1-3. We may be quite sure that no reign of peace and bliss is possible for the earth so long as this strong, fierce spirit is loose.

2. War shall cease, nor be learned or practiced more, ii, 4; ix, 5. Most graphic is the last sentence above quoted, "And every garment rolled in blood shall be for burning, even fuel for the fire." It is estimated that there are now under arms in Europe more than five millions of men, with ten millions of

reserves, all ready to fly at each other's throats at the bidding of their masters. The world-power, though Christian in name, is still a wild, ferocious "beast."

3. Antagonisms between man and man, and between man and the lower animals will be removed, and harmony, universal and unbroken, will prevail, xi, 6-9; lxv, 25. It will hardly do to say, as some do, that this explicit prediction as to the removal of hostility between animals means peace among nations and communities of men. For this is in addition to predictions of harmony among men. What is meant is, that man's supremacy over the lower creation will, in that day, be like what it was before the fall of Adam; creation will be restored to its original harmony as the final outcome of God's work of redemption, (cf. Rom. viii, 19-23).

4. The "outcast of Israel," and the "dispersed of Judah," gathered once more into their own land from all the countries whither they have been scattered, will be converted to God in a supernatural manner, and become a source of blessing to the whole world, xi, 10-16; xxvi, 13-16; xxvii, 12, 13; xlix, 12, 22, 23; lix, 20; lxvi, 7-12.

5. The resurrection of Israel's faithful dead, as likewise that of Gentile believers (1 Thess. iv, 13,18; 1 Cor. xv), to share the joy of the world's redemption will be another glad triumph of that day, xxvi, 19; cf. Dan. xii, 1-3; Ezek. xxxvii, 12; Hos. xiii, 14, etc.

6. Patriarchal years will return, lxv, 20. "Life will be protracted to its full measure, so that he who dies at the age of one hundred years will be regarded as having died young, and the sinner on whom the

curse or punishment of God falls will at least have his one hundred years of life." Sin and death will still exist in that blissful day, but according to the plain teaching of Isaiah they will be the exception and not the rule as now, xxv, 6-9; xxvi, 1-4; xxxv, 10.

7. There will be a seven-fold fullness and increase of light, solar and lunar, in that day, xxx, 26; lx, 19, 20.

Such are some of the glories God has promised for His ancient people, Israel, for the Gentiles who call on His name, and for the earth itself. It is the grand jubilee of the whole world we await. As certain as God has spoken it will be realized. How near it may be we cannot compute.

Isaiah's *admonitions to the nations* are most solemn. He reveals this great principle of the divine government, viz., that those nations which were employed to chastise the chosen people were held as guilty before Him. In every instance they exceeded their commission, they refused to show mercy to the captives; they executed their own cruel will on the helpless, and so in turn they were punished, xiii, xiv, xxi, xxxiii, xlvii, 6. Assyria's overthrow, Babylon's fall, and Egypt's humiliation are ascribed to their unmerciful treatment of Israel; and yet they were all used as His rods for the correction of his people.

Before we leave the book of Isaiah some of the predictions with which it abounds and their fulfillment may be adverted to.

1. The fall of Babylon and its subsequent desolation, xiii. So explicit is this event described by the spirit of prophecy that it might appropriately be called history written beforehand. The army which

is to accomplish this task is summoned from the mountains, from a distant land, vs. 4—Persia, no doubt, is meant. But Persia is not to act alone; other peoples join the mustering squadrons, Media more especially, vs. 17. The Lord of hosts calls them to execute His judgments on the guilty city, vss. 2, 3, 11, 19; and the earth trembles beneath the tread of marching men in response. It is declared that fear shall take possession of the doomed city; panic-stricken, it shall make no defence, vs. 8. How exactly this was fulfilled Daniel assures us, Dan. v. The consternation which seized the king on the night of Babylon's assault is read in the graphic words of Daniel, v, 6, "his knees smote one against another." "On that night was Belshazzar the king of the Chaldeans slain." Turn to the prediction of Babylon's desolations, Is. xiii. " It shall never be inhabited, neither shall it be dwelt in from generation to generation," vs. 20. Absolute loss of inhabitants is announced. Cities dwindle and decay; complete solitudes few of them ever become. A village crowns the hill formed by the ruins of Sennacherib's palace at Nineveh (Rawlinson); Arab huts are found clinging about the majestic ruins at Karnack and Luxor in Egypt; Tanis, the seat of government of Rameses II., the Pharaoh of the oppression and of his successor, lives in the mud hovels of San; Damascus, almost as old as Babylon; Athens, Rome, ancient likewise, remain to this day; but the great capital of the Chaldean Empire has no inhabitant Strabo, writing in the age of Augustus, could say, "the great city has become a great solitude." Benjamin of Tudela, writing in the twelfth, and Maundeville in the fourteenth centuries said the same, the latter testifying, "It is alle deserte, and fulle of dragons and grete serpentes." The accounts of modern explorers are similar. "The site of Babylon is a naked and a hideous waste" (Loftus).

"Neither shall the Arabian pitch his tent there; neither shall the shepherds make their folds there," vs. 20. On the actual ruins of Babylon the Arabian neither pitches his tent nor pastures his flocks, because the nitrous soil produces no pasture to tempt him (Rawlinson), and because he believes it is the "abode of evil spirits" (Rich).

"But wild beasts of the desert shall lie there, owls, satyrs (probably jackals; the word means *hairy ones*), dragons," vss. 21, 22. Every one of these particulars is fulfilled to this day, if the jackal is included in the enumeration. Lions, owls, serpents have been seen there, the only inhabitants of the once proud and splendid city. To the very letter has the prediction been accomplished.

2. The fall of Babylon, chap. xxi. This prediction differs widely from that of chapter thirteen. We are told that it is the Medo-Persian army that is to capture the Chaldean capital, vs. 2. It is to take place at the time of a feast, vs. 5 (cf. Dan. v). The steady advance of the hostile army with its battalions of horses, battalions of asses, and of camels is seen by the watchman, vs. 7. Herodotus tells us the Persian army had just such adjuncts as are here mentioned. Finally there is the sudden cry of the capture and overthrow, "Babylon is fallen, is fallen," vs. 9; and her chief gods, Bel, Nebo, and Merodach are forever discredited. The absolute accuracy of the prediction is fully attested by the history of Babylon's fall. It came about as here foretold.

3. **Prediction of Cyrus, xliv, 28; xlv, 1.** His name was given by the prophet, his special service designated, viz., rebuilding Jerusalem and the temple, long before he had existence. Josephus writes, "When, therefore, Cyrus had read this, and marveled at the divinity, a kind of impulse and ambition seized upon him to fulfill what was written." None but the Omniscient could have known the person and the name of him who was to conquer Babylon and deliver the chosen people.

4. **The gates of Babylon to be open for Cyrus' entrance, xlv, 1.** History relates that on the night of the capture this actually occurred. Marching into the heart of the city by the river channel, which he had drained, Cyrus found the gates open, and ingress unobstructed. Thus the accuracy of accomplishment attests the divine character of prophecy.

Note Isaiah's denunciation of idols, xl. He attacks them with argument, proves them to be mere things, futile, lifeless things. He pours contempt on them, scathes them with irony, blasts them with ridicule, explodes infinite laughter upon them. Nothing can exceed the exquisite sarcasm with which he describes the manufacture of idols, xl, 19, 20. The rich man employs a goldsmith to fashion for him a metal god. A poor man, unable to pay for so costly a divinity, selects a good hard stick of timber on which he sets to work a skilled mechanic; and presto! has, to his unspeakable delight, a wooden god. And then the blazing contrast he draws between these scornful things and the living God who bends the blue dome over our heads and suspends the world on His arm, and feeds the creatures thereof with His hands—how the miserable dumb idols shrivel into nothing in such a Presence.

Note also the power of prayer. Two instances are given: one, in the destruction of the Assyrian army, chap. xxxvii. "One night intervened between a mighty host and nothing," the fathers used to say.

The other relates to Hezekiah's sickness and recovery, xxxviii. Yet prayer for prolonged life may be a mistake. The king's most serious blunder, if not sin, took place after his miraculous restoration to health, xxxix, cf. 2 Chron. xxxii, 24-31. Prolonged life, health, prosperity, may not be the best things for us after all. For prosperity of soul we may always ask; for uninterrupted bodily health, we are incompetent to judge.

JEREMIAH.

The books of the prophets Isaiah and Jeremiah are as different as they can well be. The divergence between them is not simply one of style, but one of aim and contents. Isaiah clearly foresaw the defection and apostasy of the people of Judah, and their captivity; but he was removed from the final catastrophe by a hundred years or more. Jeremiah lived and prophesied at the time of the end. He saw the fall of the throne of David, the spoliation of the city and the temple by the strong and pitiless arms of the Babylonians, and the exile of the greater part of the chosen people. It seemed as if irreparable ruin had come, that God Himself had forsaken the children of the covenant, ignored His own promises, and given over His heritage to the "boar of the forest and to the beast of the field." This, mainly, constitutes the burden of Jeremiah's prophecies and distinguishes them. His ministry was exercised amid deepening apostasy, judgment and disaster.

Jeremiah was by birth a priest, and dwelt at the priestly town of Anathoth, 1 Chron. vi, 60, a few miles north of Jerusalem in the territory of Benjamin. His father's name was Hilkiah, who is not to be identified with the high priest of that name. It seems, however, that the prophet belonged to an influential family from the respect shown him by successive rulers, as Jehoiakim and Zedekiah, Ahikam and Gedaliah, the viceroys of the king of Babylon. His uncle Shallum was the husband of Huldah the prophetess. His friend and cousin, Hanameel, was their son. Baruch was his constant companion and scribe or amanuensis.

His call to the office of prophet was as distinct and as remarkable as that of Isaiah, i, 5. We learn from this striking verse that his designation to the office by the Lord antedated his birth. No event or exigency in the life of the individual and of the nation finds God unprepared. He had His chosen instruments ready to meet every emergency in the history of His people Israel. The fall was not a surprise to God, nor was redemption an afterthought. "He never is before His time, He never is too late."

Jeremiah's qualifications for the office of prophet like those of all the other prophets, were directly from God. He received both the message and the gift from Him, i, 5-10. By the touch of the divine hand there was imparted to him the revelation from the Lord and the power to deliver it to others. The action symbolized the communication of a message and the power of speech. Like Moses, like Isaiah, like all truly great and noble souls, Jeremiah was distinguished for his humility and native modesty. Very great ability, genius, is unaffected, is child-like. The highest attainment of Christianity is a glorified childhood (Tholuck). In simple, childlike ingenuousness Jeremiah made answer to God's call, "Ah! Lord God! behold, I cannot speak; for I am a child."

The time of his ministry is distinctly stated in chap, i, 1-3. These verses are not an introduction to the first chapter, but to the entire book, and they are also the authentication of all that follows. They are the great seal which the Spirit of God has set upon the words which He has given us through the mouth of His servant Jeremiah. His ministry began in the reign of Josiah, and continued for some time after the revolt of Zedekiah and the disasters which followed. The estimates as to its length vary by about ten years: Plumptre, B. C. 638-588; Horne, B. C. 628-586; Angus, B. C. 629-585. Something over forty years he exercised the office of prophet.

Three events of world-wide importance transpired during the life time of Jeremiah. The first was the battle between the armies of Judah and of Pharaoh-Necho at Carchemish at which Josiah lost his life, 2 Chron. xxxv, 20-25. Never perhaps has there been such profound and universal mourning for the death of a ruler. The sorrow of our country for the death of President Lincoln, the sorrow of England for the Prince Consort, or that of Germany for Frederick, was deep, but not so deep nor so lasting as that for Josiah. The penitential mourning of Israel at their conversion is compared to this sorrow, Zech xii, 11 One of the most pathetic elegies ever uttered was pronounced over the dead monarch by the most plaintive of prophets, Jeremiah. With the death of Josiah the noblest and most faithful spirit of the kings of Judah likewise expired. From that period the degeneracy of the kingdom was rapid. It was Jeremiah's lot to prophesy at a time when all things in Judah were rushing down to the final and mournful catastrophe; when political excitement was at its height; when the worst passions swayed the various parties and the most fatal counsels prevailed. It was his to stand in the way over which his nation was rushing headlong to destruction; to make a heroic effort to arrest it and to turn it back; and to fail, and be compelled to step to one side and see his own people whom he loved with the tenderness of a woman plunge over the precipice into the wide, weltering ruin.

The second event was a second battle at Carchemish between the Egyptian and Babylonian forces, the latter led by Nebuchadnezzar. In this engagement the Egyptians were totally defeated, and Syria and Palestine fell under the power of Babylon. The battle took place in the third year of Jehoiakim, according to Dan. i, 1, and was followed by the first deportation of Jews to Babylon. Jeremiah prophesied of the disastrous consequences of this battle to Egypt, xlvi, 1-12. In B. C. 609 Babylon had two powerful rivals, Assyria and Egypt. In 604 B. C. it had the undisputed mastery of the East.

The third event of Jeremiah's time was the capture of Jerusalem by the Chaldeans, the destruction of Jerusalem and the temple, and the exile of the major part of the people to Babylon. The fall of a great state is an epoch in the history of the world. The fall of Babylon and Egypt and Rome was of immense significance. But the fall of Jerusalem and the Jewish state, both the first and the second time— the one time by the Chaldeans, and the other by the Romans—affected the whole race of man as no other national disaster ever has. The ministry of Jeremiah is one of extraordinary interest from the fact that he was associated most intimately with the close of the kingdom of Judah. He is the connecting link and the bond between the old and the new, the monarchy and the dependency into which Judah sank after the captivity. What Jerome Savonarola was to the Roman Catholic church when sinking to the lowest point of infamy under Alexander VI., that, and much more, Jeremiah was to Judah in the closing years of the monarchy. His task was hard, thankless; his life one of contention and strife; but faithfully he finished his work and received his reward.

It happens always that when a state becomes involved in difficulties, when its affairs are entangled and ruin threatens, the people range themselves into contending and hostile parties. So it transpired in the closing days of the kingdom of Judah; much more so was it in the last years of Jerusalem in the first century of the Christian era. The nation split into fierce factions; each denounced the other as the chief cause of all their woes. Mutual distrust broke up families, divided friends, made a man's enemies those of his own household. Every one had to take heed to his neighbor and suspect his brother, Jer. ix. 4; xii. 6.

Amid such contending factions Jeremiah's life was spent. We do not know that he ever saw a day of true rest, of peaceful quiet. He knew not but that he should seal his testimony with his blood at any time. Yet he never quailed before the factions that clamored for his life, nor faltered in duty when to announce the tremendous judgments of God maddened his countrymen to desperation. It is strange that so many writers of modern times regard Jeremiah as weak, feeble-minded," almost cowardly. We have no sympathy with such unworthy and inadequate opinions of him. His ministry was one of admonition and antagonism, i, 17, 18. Against the whole land, against the kings of Judah, against the princes, against the priests, against the prophets he was to stand. He was to gird up his loins and arise and speak all that God commanded him. He was to be the solitary fortress, the column of iron, the wall of brass, fearless, undismayed in any presence; the one grand, immovable figure who pursued the apostatizing people and rulers, delivering his message in the temple court or the royal chamber or the street, whether they would hear or forbear. In consequence he was the prophet of unwelcome truths, hated of all, but feared as well by all. It was a mission requiring courage, faith, strength, will; a mission no weakling could fill, no coward would undertake. Jeremiah is one of the very great men of the world.

His prevailing tone is that of sadness. The song he sings is keyed in the minor. He is the dirge-poet of Israel. He composed the national requiem of his people, and his own also. His style is not so lofty as that of Isaiah; he does not rise so high, nor is his flight so sustained. Isaiah is the royal poet who sails aloft on powerful wing into the azure deeps above; Jeremiah wings a lower flight, with measured beat and slow, the very movement indicating the mournful nature of his theme.

Another thing to be noted is the personal character of his writing. No writer of the Old Testament enters so largely into his own composition as this prophet. His personal affairs are not meant. He never alludes to his private history except where the nature of a given narrative requires it. Nevertheless, his inner and outer life is woven into his prophecies. The man himself with his sorrows and woes, with his sensibilities always bleeding, with his disappointments and his blasted affections weeping out their life in silent injury, is ever before us as we read. The causes of his profound grief are not hard to find. His love for his people was one source. This is very striking; it reminds one of Moses and Paul. The prophet stands ready to make any sacrifice, to endure any pain, if thereby the people, *his* people, are reformed and restored. The lamentations are a proof of it. But then it is hopeless, as he well knows. Every effort to lead them back to God and to set them in the right place before Him, he saw was vain. They rejected the divine testimony, they would none of his counsel. God no longer hearkened to prayer for Judah. The end was drawing on apace. Jeremiah prophesies under this impression. A sorrowful task, a hopeless love. No wonder he longed for " a lodge in some vast wilderness " that he might leave his people and go from them, ix, 2. No wonder that he never married, that he would ask no woman to share the intolerable burden that weighed on his heart. Like Job he poured bitter imprecations on the day of his birth, xx, 14-18; was tortured with doubt as to the word of the Lord to himself, xxi, 7, 8. He is the "prophet of the broken heart." Who can forget the exquisite pathos with which he weeps over Judah, viii, 21, 22; ix, 1, 22. How much of genuine patriotism breathes in those tender words, " Weep ye not for the dead, neither bemoan him; but weep sore for him that goeth away: for he shall return no more, nor see his native country," xxii, 10. One cannot but see in Jeremiah something of the Spirit of Christ. Indeed, it is not too much to say that on a small scale that

Life which is above all other lives is reproduced in this prophet. Jeremiah's love for his people, his anxiety to do them good and naught but good, his tears at the defeat of his efforts to reclaim them, and the hopefulness with which he looks forward to their final recovery and blessing, are but a dim reflection of what was perfect in the heart of the Lord Jesus. Grace and the Spirit of God will make any one like Christ.

It is no easy task to give anything like a satisfactory analysis of these prophecies. It is well known that the order in the Septuagint version differs considerably from that found in the Hebrew Bible, chaps. xlvi-lii, being inserted after chap. xxv, 13, as also other changes. It is next to impossible to determine whether the Septuagint is translated from a different recension of the text from that of our Bible and an older arrangement of the prophecies, or whether they attempted to introduce an order according to their notions of the chronology of Jeremiah's utterances. At any rate in no other book is there so great variation. Two things should be borne in mind in reading Jeremiah: first, that the arrangement does not follow chronological order. This is evident from the introduction of the names of the kings (see xxxvii and xxxv, etc.). But this is not uncommon in Scripture. God often sets aside the natural sequence of events in favor of a moral sequence. Second, the arrangement seems to follow subjects. The prophecies are collated according to the themes and classed by thoughts rather than by time.

A very general division is the following: Part i, chaps. i-xxiv, prophecies with reference to Judah, with historical matter. Part 2, chaps. xxv-xlv, prophecies of judgment and of comfort. Part 3, prophecies respecting various nations, chaps xlvi-li. Chapter fifty-two is a historical appendix, added by another hand, cf. 2 Kings xxiv, 18-xxv.

A more particular analysis is submitted for the reader's aid:

I. Chaps. i-xxxviii: Prophecies and historical passages regarding Judah and its kings to the capture of Jerusalem. This section falls into two parts: (1) i-xxiv, wherein are pleadings with the people; sins rebuked, backsliding and apostasy exposed and denounced; repentance urged, with the sorrowful conviction on the part of the prophet that every appeal is vain; (2) xxv-xxxviii, announcements of approaching judgments and promises of assured blessing for the last days,—chaps. xxxi, xxxii.

II. Chaps. xxxix-xliv: Narrative, mingled with prophecies, after the fall of Jerusalem.

III. Chapter forty-five stands by itself, and is a special word of comfort from the Lord to Baruch, Jeremiah's friend and scribe. In the midst of Judah's ruin and the crashing down of Jewish hopes, God turns aside to assuage the sorrow and dry the tears of Baruch. That is very precious. The individual, no matter how obscure, is not forgotten by the great God of heaven and earth, even in the midst of stupendous providences and overwhelming judgments. A word of admonition is addressed to him to which all may well give earnest heed: "And seekest thou great things for thyself? seek them not," vs. 5. A mighty word which Mr. Spurgeon tells us kept him in the ambitions of his youth.

IV. Chaps. xlvi-li: Prophecies against certain

Gentile nations. The doom of the following is pronounced: Egypt, Philistia, Moab, Ammon, Edom, Damascus, Kedar, Elam, Babylon. All these predictions have been fulfilled. They were made when some of the nations against which they were spoken were at the zenith of their power. The majority of them were overrun and subjugated by Babylon, which in its turn was totally overthrown.

Under five different kings Jeremiah carried on his difficult ministry. (1) During eighteen years or more (i, 2) of Josiah's reign he bore his testimony often with tears, always with anxious forebodings. It was a time of distress and anguish for the prophet. For although Josiah was one of the best kings that ever sat on the throne of David, nevertheless the great reformation which he promoted was largely an outward one. Hardly was the king's sad funeral over when the people hastened to revive the abominations which he had so nobly suppressed, 2 Kings xxiii, 30-37. And so Jeremiah utters that despairing cry which reveals how hopeless was any reform, the sins were so inveterate: "Can the Ethiopian change his skin, or the leopard his spots?" xiii, 23. (2) During the reign of Jehoahaz, or Shallum as he is sometimes called (Jer. xxii, 11), which was very short. He was set up in opposition to Egypt, and was soon deposed by that power. (3) During the reign of Jehoiakim whom Pharoah substituted for Jehoahaz, 2 King xxiii, 34, for ten years the prophet pursued his difficult work. Opposed by false prophets who pretended to have a "word from Jehovah," with the court and the nobles following Egypt's policy, Jeremiah contended for the reforms inaugurated by Josiah; pleaded, warned, entreated, wept, but to no purpose. Judah was bent on having her own way, and nothing could turn her from it. (4) During the brief reign of Jehoiakim, called also Coniah, Jer. xxii, 24, he witnessed for God, but the danger so long foretold at length came nigh. First the king and queen-mother, then nobles, artisans, princes, the worth and strength of the nation, were carried away into captivity, 2 Kings xxiv, 15, 16. (5) During the eleven years of Zedekiah whom Nebuchadnezzar had placed upon the throne, and who rebelled against his master in spite of all the threats and predictions of the prophet, the final crushing blow fell, and Zedekiah lost his sons, his own eyes, the holy city and the state.

After the destruction of Jerusalem the party adverse to Babylon determined to cast in their fortunes with Egypt. Jeremiah, who had remained in Judea after the final catastrophe, protested against the movement, and predicted its calamitous issue. But the obstinate party, blind to everything save what appeared to them their only safety, would not hear. They fled to Egypt, and carried Jeremiah with them. Tradition has it that he died there; one form of it narrating that for his faithfulness in prophesying against the idolatry of his countrymen he was stoned to death; another, that he repaired finally to Babylon where he died. But all is uncertain.

The question may very properly be asked, Why did the prophet advocate submission to the Gentile king, and urge the opening of the city to him? xvii, 12, 13, 17; xxxviii, 17-23. Does it not look like treason, at least like disloyalty to Jewish interests? It is quite evident throughout the later prophecies of Jeremiah that God had conferred universal power on

Nebuchadnezzar, and he was to subdue all kingdoms to his rule. He is even called "God's servant," xxv, 9; xxvii, 6. To resist him was to resist God. It was in virtue of Israel's failure that power passed into the hand of the king of Babylon, and from this point in human history the "times of the Gentiles" begin their course. But of this we shall have occasion to speak more at length when we reach the book of Daniel. It was because a new order of things was now to be inaugurated that the prophet exhorted his people to submit to Nebuchadnezzar. According to Deu. xxxii, 8, the nations were originally distributed with reference to Israel as the center. All were grouped about the center, cf. Ezek. v, 5. Now this arrangement was to be broken up. Gentile supremacy, so long held in check, is to assert itself. It was God's doings. Hence submission to Nebuchadnezzar meant submission to the will of God.

The vast majority of the predictions in the book of Jeremiah related to his own times, to the kings and people of Judah and of Babylon, and to the captivity and its attendant scenes. But there are some that belong to the distant future—the future not only of Jeremiah, but also of us, for they are not yet fulfilled. Of some of these mention is now to be made.

1. The Messiah. Jeremiah has not so much to announce of Him as Isaiah has, but he is not deficient touching this great hope. What he does disclose concerning Him is of the deepest importance and very instructive. In chap. xxiii, 5, 6, we read, "Behold the days come, saith the Lord, that I will raise unto David a righteous Branch, and a king

shall reign and prosper and he shall be called 'The Lord our righteousness.'" In every way this is a very notable prediction. The King will be of the house of David, and prosperity shall attend His administration, judgment and justice He shall execute in the earth. Just at the time of this prophecy the throne of David was imperilled, justice and equity were almost unknown, and wickedness was in the ascendent. But a better day approaches. The name of the King is a wonderful one, *Jehovah Tsidkenu*—the Lord our righteousness. The name in this case, as in the similar instances, is in reality a sentence expressing a great truth: The Lord (is) our righteousness. Jehovah-Nissi (Ex. xvii, 15); Jehovah-Shammah (Ezek. xlviii, 35); Jehovah-Jireh (Gen. xii, 14), and this name in Jeremiah, are all promises and also revelations of the character and fidelity of God. Here we have the humanity of the Savior predicted as the descendent of David, and His Godhead likewise in the majestic name given Him. Christ our Righteousness is an all-sufficient answer to the claims of law and justice upon us, and to our deep need. Luther once said, "Your menaces and terrors, domine Satan, trouble me not; for there is one whose name is called the Lord our Righteousness on whom I believe. He it is who hath abrogated the law, condemned sin, abolished death, destroyed hell, and is a satan to thee, O satan." John Trapp thinks this sentence of Luther's is of so much worth that rather than be without it one should " fetch it on his knees from Rome to Jerusalem."

2. Restoration of Israel, xxxi. This is repeatedly promised in Jeremiah and secured by the most solemn asseverations which can be used, but it is

minutely described in this and the following chapter. The reason of their restoration is disclosed, vs. 3, viz., the unalterable love of God. The extent of the regathering is foretold, vss. 8, 31; from every quarter of the earth both the house of Israel and the house of Judah will be brought back again. With deep penitence and supplications for their sins will they come, the Lord Himself leading them, vs. 9. Scarcely anything can exceed the pathos, the exquisite tenderness with which the penitents and their Redeemer talk together, as it is foretold in vss. 18-20. Of course this is true of all genuine repentance, but it will most emphatically be true in restored Israel, Zech. xii, 11-14. A new covenant is made with them in the day they return to God, vss. 31-37. That we may be assured that the covenant was not fulfilled at the return from the Babylonian exile, it is quoted once and again in the New Testament and distinctly applied to the Jews of the future, Rom. xi, 26, 27; Heb. viii, 8-13; x, 16, 17. A still more convincing proof of the restoration is given in chap. xxxii, 6-15,—the account of the purchase of Hanameel's land by Jeremiah. The Chaldeans were laying siege to the city; and that they would capture it the prophet very well knew. And yet he is bidden buy his cousin's field, pay the money for it, for God gave him the assurance that in due time the people would be restored to their inheritance. Abraham bought a field for his dead; Jeremiah bought one for a nation yet unborn. God led him to commit himself openly to the faith of Israel's final restoration.

3. Symbolic acts. Jeremiah indulges in many such and each of them has a significant prophetic meaning. Ezekiel is fonder of them than Jeremiah. In-

struction by symbolic action is common in Oriental countries, however strange and even childish it may appear to the matter-of-fact dwellers in western lands. Southern Italians often will carry on a conversation by pantomime, not an audible word being spoken. Much more does such method of communication prevail in the Levant.

One of these striking acts of the prophet is recorded in chapter thirteen of our book. It is the account of his hiding by divine command a linen girdle in a cleft of a rock by the river Euphrates. The narrative tells us that the prophet did so, twice making the journey to the designated point. Considerable discussion has arisen among interpreters as to the reality of this transaction. From several considerations we believe that he actually performed what is here described. The only question of difficulty is as to the word rendered Euphrates (P'rath). Almost invariably it means the ancient river on which the Chaldean capital was situated. Some, however, contend that the word indicates some place near Jerusalem. It should be borne in mind that after Jehoiakim cut the prophetic roll into strips with his penknife and burnt the strips in the brazier at his feet, the prophet disappeared from Jerusalem, and for a period of nearly seven years his whereabouts is unknown. It is altogether probable that during that time he may have been once and again in the region of Babylon, at least of the Euphrates

Another most significant act of his was that of breaking the earthen bottle in the valley of Hinnom in the presence of the priest and elders, chap. xix. Most impressive must have been the lesson the prophet intended to enforce, when he dashed the jar to the ground in their sight, thereby intimating how the Lord would break "the people in the city," so that the ears of the hearer of such awful tidings should tingle. It was done in the valley of the Hinnom, the place, it would seem, which had witnessed the dreadful spectacle of human sacrifices to the brutal Moloch. His temptation of the Rechabites, chap. xxxv, must also have conveyed a very solemn lesson to the people, had they had ears to hear and hearts to feel. Jeremiah bade these ancient teetotalers to drink wine, offered them the cup; but they flatly refused. The prophet then pointed the moral and pressed home the application; but Israel would not heed nor repent nor obey. God, we may well say, exhausted all means, tried every agency, employed every kind of appeal, to move His people and to lead them back to their allegiance to Him. Obdurate, hard hearted, stiff of neck, rebellious, they were insensible to every effort and dumb to every entreaty. And so at length the judgment which could no longer be delayed, broke down upon them in all its appalling fury. Grace despised, mercy rejected, love spurned and goodness outraged, become at length whips in the hands of offended justice.

LAMENTATIONS

It is attested by an almost unbroken tradition that the author of this book was Jeremiah. The Septuagint Translation, the Targum, Talmud, Josephus, all unite in declaring Jeremiah, the prophet, to be the writer. Prefixed to the book we find in the Septuagint the following note: "And it came to pass after Israel had been carried away captive, and Jerusalem made desolate, Jeremiah sat weeping, and lamented this lament over Jerusalem, and said." It would require strong evidence indeed to set aside testimony so explicit and direct as this. Prof. Plumtre sums up the internal evidence in support of the common view as to the authorship thus: "The poems belong unmistakably to the last days of the kingdom, or the commencement of the exile, and are written by one who speaks with the vividness and intensity of an eye witness of the misery which he bewails." Local belief has placed "the Grotto of Jeremiah" in the face of a rocky hill on the western side of the city where these lamentations were uttered. The prophet may well be supposed to have taken his stand and poured out his grief over his fallen country at a point where the ruined city could be seen.

The main characteristic of the book is indicated by its title, "Lamentations." *Threnoi*, loud weepings, hot burning and choked with sobs, is the emphatic word the Septuagint uses. It is an elegy, a dirge, written over the desolation of Jerusalem by one whose love for it, guilty as he knew it to be, was like that of a father for a child, a wife for her husband. The prophet's grief for the smitten city reminds one of David's for Saul and Jonathan (2 Sam. i, 17-27), of Rachel's for her dead children (Jer. xxxi, 15). The cry of anguish at the fall of Constantinople; "the last sigh of the Moor," as he rode away an exile from beautiful Cordova; the wail of pity at the expulsion of the Huguenots from France and the Waldenses from the Piedmontese valleys, have not been forgotten, for they made a profound impression on the memory and the conscience of the world, and literature has recorded them in words of such tenderness as move even the coldest reader. But Jeremiah's lamentation for favored, sinful and ruined Jerusalem is a cry of sorrow so touching as to move the stoutest heart, and must have been read with streaming eyes and quivering lips by many a Jew. In all literature there is nothing more pathetic than this mournful dirge

1. The first lament, chap. i. There are two parts in this first chapter: (1) Zion, the widow, vss. 1-11. The description of the sorrow-smitten city is wonderfully graphic. Like a woman bereft of her husband and her children, seated on the ground with disheveled hair, stripped of all her ornaments, clad in weeds, weeping and wailing, is the prophet's vivid picture of the once proud and splendid city. It is *Judea capta* he describes. Of all her lovers not one is there to comfort her. The gates are gone, the priests sigh, the princes flee like the timid hart, and the children are gone into captivity. But the faithful servant of God fails not to make known the cause

of such unparalleled disaster, such fearful woe. It is the Lord who has afflicted Zion; it is because of her multiplied transgressions that He has turned against, and "left her naked to her foes." (2) Zion's confession, vss. 12-22. In this part Zion speaks, while in the first part it is the prophet who laments. She bewails her dreadful plight, challenges the world to furnish a parallel to her misery. Yet she acknowledges that her punishment is from the Lord and her sins have brought the accumulated woe upon her. "The Lord is righteous; I have rebelled" is Zion's confession.

2. The Second Lament, chap. ii, is spoken by the prophet. It is a very remarkable description of the siege of Jerusalem and the ruin which followed its capture, vss. 1-12. The walls and palaces of the city, the altar and the sanctuary are defiled, the elders sit covered with dust, the virgins walk with head bowed down to the ground, and the children swoon in the streets, and breathe out their young lives into their mothers' bosoms. Then again the prophet discloses the secret of these awful calamities; it is the sin of the people; the visions of the false prophets that have led astray. And now Jehovah has turned against His people and city like a mighty warrior, and doom has fallen upon them all.

3. The Third Lament, chap. iii, is likewise spoken by the prophet. But it differs from the preceding in that here he enters into the miseries of his people and makes them his own. In Zion's affliction he is afflicted. He shares to the uttermost the desolations of his people. We see the like spirit in Daniel, (ix). Love—love to God and man—is a marvelous thing. Paul could say, "Who is weak, and I am not

weak? grieved, and I not grieved? offended, and I burn not?" 2 Cor. xi, 29. The truest philanthropy and patriotism are found in the genuine servants of God.

4. The Fourth Lament, chap. iv, is uttered also by the prophet. The sense of the overwhelming overthrow that had come is intensified to the uttermost in this chapter. God's judgments on the guilty place have been pitiless, tremendous. Nothing is left but smouldering ruin, slain men, weeping women, orphan children.

But there is now a gleam of hope. Divine wrath has exhausted itself, and mercy can once more flow out to the stricken ones. Thus in verse twenty-two this glad announcement is made: "The punishment of thine iniquity is accomplished, O daughter of Zion; He will carry thee no more away into captivity."

5. The Fifth Lament, chap. v, spoken by the Jewish people, who make confession and appeal to God for help, deliverance and forgiveness. The ground of their appeal is their desolation and their utter helplessness.

The book of Lamentations teaches among others this great truth, that the affliction of God's people, even when they most deserve it, does not escape His eye. His Spirit enters into it through His servant the prophet, and shares it with them. "In all their affliction he was afflicted." The divine pity for the sufferings which love will not avert—how wonderful it is! Jesus weeping at the grave of Lazarus, over Jerusalem, is an amazing scene, and one which can not be fully comprehended.

EZEKIEL.

We should bear in mind that certain prophets were contemporary. Jeremiah should be studied in connection with Ezekiel and Daniel; in fact, the three, together with the minor prophets, Zephaniah and Habakkuk, might very profitably be taken together as a group that deal largely with the same period and to a great extent with the same events. Ezekiel is closely related to Jeremiah. He began his prophetic ministry in the fifth year of Jehoiakin's captivity, i, 5, and prosecuted it for twenty-two years at least, xxix, 17. Whether for a longer time or not we have no means of knowing. He was the prolongation of the voice of Jeremiah. He took up the theme of his fellow prophet touching the future of the chosen people and developed it more and more, until we get in him and in Daniel a full revelation of the divine purpose.

Like Jeremiah, Ezekiel was a priest as well as a prophet, and the priestly character in him is much more predominant than in the former. His call to the great office is recorded in i, 5, (cf. iii, 1-15). As Isaiah, Jeremiah and the other prophets, he was brought into immediate contact with God, whereby the gift was imparted. "The hand of the Lord was upon" him—the communication of a message and the power to declare it. The imposition of the hand was followed by a vision of the Lord, and the scroll written within and without with its awful burden, ii, 10.

The place where Ezekiel prophesied was at Tel-Abib on the "river Chebar," either a tributary of the Euphrates, or one of the great canals which Nebuchadnezzar constructed. He had been carried into captivity with many other Jews in the second deportation to Chaldea in the reign of Jehoiakin. A colony of exiles had located at Chebar, and to them was the prophet sent; among them he exercised his ministry. But there seems to be clear evidence that the word spoken by him was not intended exclusively for the captives who dwelt at Chebar. The expression, "the house of Israel," which occurs five times in chapter three, and once among these five is found "all the house of Israel," contemplates a wider circle of hearers, a larger audience than the exiles among whom Ezekiel dwelt. In fact, the message of this prophet is for all Israel of this day, and for all time down to their predicted restoration and blessing, as chaps. xl-xlviii abundantly attest.

Chap. i, 1, is the common formula for the authentication of the book, and not for the first chapter alone. The date "thirty years" of this verse is somewhat difficult to determine. The most satisfactory explanation is that it refers to Ezekiel's own age. According to Num. iv, 3, the sons of Kohath —the line of the priests, Ex. vi, 18, 20—were to enter on their duties as priests at this age. As a priest, it seems fitting that Ezekiel should begin his work at thirty. In chap. xi, 16, the Lord promises to be a little sanctuary to the exiles in Chaldea. Ezekiel was to be a sort of ministering priest to them at this sanctuary. Hence his prophetic office probably dates from his priestly age which was, of course, thirty years.

In this connection it may be well to record some other dates of real importance to the study of the books which historically belong to the time of the fall of the kingdom of Judah: Battle of Carchemish and death of Josiah, B. C. 611; first invasion of Judea by Nebuchadnezzar (third year of Jehoiakim), Dan. i, 1, B. C. 606; second invasion, Jehoiakin, king, B. C. 599; third invasion, Zedekiah, king, destruction of Jerusalem and fall of the kingdom, B. C. 589 or 588. About B. C. 594 Ezekiel entered on his prophetic mission in which he labored for at least twenty-two years, viz., to B. C. 572. For a considerable period he was Jeremiah's contemporary, though widely separated from the latter as to place.

The book may be divided into three parts: Part I, chaps. i-xxiv, testimonies from God against Israel in general and against Jerusalem in particular. Part II, chaps. xxv-xxxii, judgments denounced against surrounding nations. Part III, chaps. xxxiii-xlviii, the subject of Israel is resumed, and their restoration and blessing foretold.

A more minute classification is indicated by the prophet himself in the several dates which at intervals he places as the superscriptions to the messages he received. The groups with their time notes are the following: (1) Call and commission of the prophet, i-iii, 15; time note, i, 2. (2) Description of the wickedness of Israel, siege and destruction of Jerusalem and the subsequent calamities, iii, 16-vii; time note, iii, 16. (3) Profanation of the temple, corruption of the priesthood, God's determination to forsake His sanctuary, safety for the faithful remnant and punishment for the wicked, chaps. viii-xix; time note, viii, 1. (4) Terrific indictment against the guilty people, judgment no longer to be delayed, chaps. xx-xxiii; time note, xx, 1. (5) Announcement of the final end, chaps. xxiv-xxv; time note, xxiv, 1. The doom of the holy city and people is strangely represented by the sudden death of the prophet's wife, and by the stoniness of the grief that was too deep for tears and too terrible for a funeral dirge. But Judea would not be alone in the day of wrath; Ammon and Moab and Edom would share therein. (6) Predictions against Tyre, chaps. xxvi-xxviii; time note, xxvi, 1. (7) Predictions against Egypt, chaps. xxix-xxxi; time note, xxix, 1. (8) Overthrow of various nations and death wail for them, Israel not escaping, with appeals to repentance and promises, chaps. xxxii-xxxvi; time notes, xxxii, 1, 17; xxxiii, 21. (9) Israel's national resurrection and judgment on Gog, the end of God's judicial dealing with His people, chaps. xxxvii-xxxix; time note, xxxvii, 1. (10) Glowing picture of the latter-day glory, chaps. xl-xlviii; time note, xl, 1.

The main object of Ezekiel's prophecies appears to be to comfort the exiles in their desolation and loneliness, to fortify them against the idolatrous practices by which they were surrounded, and to turn their faces toward the land from which they had been expelled but to which God would restore them if with true hearts they should turn to Him again. His name is significant of his mission. Ezekiel, "God will strengthen." His whole ministry is characterized by strength. Like a giant he wrestled against Jewish degeneracy and Chaldean pride. He threw himself with all the force of his passionate soul against the evils of his people and of the times; but he was as strong in his tenderness and love as in his denunciations and reproofs.

Ezekiel is strictly the prophet. Unlike Jeremiah little of his feelings or his personal history enters into his prophecies; nor did he address himself to the guidance of public affairs; the circumstances of his ministry did not require he should. Isaiah, Jeremiah, Daniel, had to do with the kings of their times, with the people of Israel and with the first great Gentile empire. Ezekiel's mission was to the exiles in Chaldea; he was the prophet of the remnant, the seer of a glorious future for his people and for the earth.

1. His style is lofty and trenchant. Apart from his prophetic gift, which unquestionably was very great, he possessed profound erudition and genius.

2. In symbolic representations and prophetic action Ezekiel abounds. He has visions (viii-xi), symbolic action (iv, v, 1-4), similitudes (xii, xv), parables (xvii), proverbs (xviii), allegories (xxiii-xxiv), open prophecies (as vi, vii, xx, etc.). There is scarcely a form in which the divine communications were made to the men of God that is not employed by this prophet. This wealth of imagery imparts singular beauty and variety to his pages. They glow with life and action and brilliant colors. But this fact makes the book all the more difficult of interpretation. Jerome long ago called the book "an ocean and labyrinth of the mysteries of God" Yet if we keep in mind the distinction between symbols, and visions, and signs wrought in the prophet's own person, our under-

standing of the book will be greatly simplified. In chap. xxxvii, 16, 17, the prophet joins together two sticks to represent the reunion of the ten tribes with Judah and Benjamin. In v, 1-4, he cuts off his hair and burns it, smites and scatters it in the wind, to signify approaching judgment. At one time we see him stamping with his feet and clasping his hands, as if in the agony of grief, vi, 11; at another he portrays on a tile the holy city, lays siege to this pictured city, casts a mount against it, sets a camp and battering rams against it, in short, he enacts a mimic battle in the sight of the people, iv, 1, 2. Again, by divine direction the prophet collects his household stuff together for removal, and takes it upon his shoulders and sets forth, with covered face, as if he were bound on a long and tiresome journey, xii, 1-11. All these were acted parables with a deep significance for the house of Israel. And just as full of meaning was his allegory of the two eagles, xvii, 1-10. He showed by the one eagle (Nebuchadnezzar) who had cropped the highest twig in Judah (Jehoiakin), and by the other (Pharaoh) to whom the vine that was left (Zedekiah) was turning, the uprooting of the whole; and digressing from that he predicts the replanting of the whole under Messiah, the Branch (Leifchild).

How much of this symbolic action was really performed by the prophet it might be difficult to determine; yet there can be little doubt but that much of it, perhaps all of it, was literally done in the sight of his countrymen, that the divine message with which he was entrusted might impress the people all the more vividly and intensely. It is not too much to say that the prophets in some cases became actual signs, and what they did under the inspiration of the Holy Spirit was as certainly a revelation from God as what they spoke.

3. One symbolic transaction, however, deserves special mention, viz.: that recorded in iv, 4-17. The prophet was to lie, first on his left side, for a period of three hundred and ninety days; next, on his right side for forty days; the whole amounting to four hundred and thirty days. It is a question more curious than profitable, whether Ezekiel actually did this in the presence of his people, or whether it was a vision. That it is within the range of possibility no one will venture to deny. It is related that a nobleman of Louvain lay sixteen years in one posture, and many an invalid has maintained a like position for a much longer time than the prophet; for on the supposition that Ezekiel really did it he spent about thirteen months prostrate; nor are we required to believe that it was absolutely continuous. But this question is not essential to an understanding of the transaction. This prophetic action probably had reference to the future. Hosea had already predicted a repetition of the history of Israel in the afflictions which were about to come upon them for their sins; a repetition of bondage like that of Egypt, Hos. viii, 13; ix, 3. The forty years for Judah would be like that of the wilderness journey; years not only of punishment, but of discipline and preparation for the destiny that awaited them in the restoration. The northern kingdom would suffer for a much longer time than the southern, hence the significant 390 years, xx, 35-38. In this view, Israel is regarded as the greater transgessor, Judah the less guilty. And the facts appear to corroborate it.

Samaria was the leader in apostasy from God. Such is the opinion of Fairbairn, and one that commends itself to the reader. All Israel is for the time set aside, disowned of God as His peculiar people, and power passes over to the Gentiles in the person of Nebuchadnezzar. A second oppression, comparable in many ways to that endured so long before in Egypt, now awaits the people; longer, however, for the kingdom that originated the rebellion against the authority of God. In fact, Ezekiel resembles the Pentateuch in not a few particulars. But in this book a totally new order of things is announced, xl, xlviii.

4. The vision of the throne of glory, chap. i. Nothing can exceed the majesty of this description. It furnished the poet Milton the material for one of his finest paragraphs:

> Forth rushed with whirlwind sound
> The chariot of paternal Diety,
> Flashing thick flames, wheel within wheel undrawn,
> Itself instinct with Spirit, but conveyed
> By four cherubic shapes; four faces each
> Had wondrous; as with stars their bodies all
> And wings were set with eyes, with eyes the wheels
> Of Beryl, and careering fires between;
> Over their heads a crystal firmament,
> Whereon a sapphire throne.

It is the throne of the Eternal, the glory of the Lord of hosts that is the main object of the vision, vss. 26, 28. The "four living creatures" which are closely associated with the throne are identical with the cherubim of Scripture. Just what these were or symbolized, it is hard to determine. The term *cherub* has been defined to be one that guards and covers. In Gen. iii, 24, where the first mention of them is made, they guard the way of the tree of life. The prince of Tyrus is likened to the cherub that covereth, Ezek. xxviii, 14. Perhaps the reference in this last case is to the cherubim that overshadowed the mercy-seat of the ark in the tabernacle, Ex. xxv, 18-22. The ark of the covenant to some extent represented the throne of God. The cherubim formed the sides of the throne; their wings, which were projected over their heads and forward so as to cover the mercy-seat, made a sort of canopy; and the mercy-seat itself was the base or foundation of the throne. Between the cherubim and over the mercy-seat blazed the shekinah, the emblem of the divine presence. With the blood of atonement on the mercy-seat the ark became the throne of grace, and is no doubt the origin of that expression in Heb. iv, 16.

But the "living creatures" do more than guard and cover. Here in Ezek. i, and in x, they are intimately connected with the throne, are its supporters, and in some sense are the executors of the divine will. Instinct with the life of the throne, they "ran and returned as the appearance of a flash of lightning." Their activity and intelligence are figured by a system of complicated wheels, wheels within wheels, with high and dreadful rings, and filled with eyes. It was through them that the Spirit of the throne went forth, every way, whithersoever it would. Each of them in Ezekiel had four faces, the "face of a man and the face of a lion on the right side; the face of an ox on the left side; and each had the face of an eagle," vss. 6-10.

Moreover, each cherub in Ezekiel has four wings, i, 6; and each has the likeness of a man, vs. 5. The reference is doubtless to the bodily shape. They are composite, the four great heads of creation, the lion, the ox, the eagle and man being united in one complex symbolic figure. In Rev. iv, they have each six wings, and appear to be separate from each other. And in the Revelation they engage in acts of worship, v.

If now we gather together all that is told us of the nature and functions of the cherubim it will be seen that they not only guard and cover, but likewise execute the sovereign will of Him who occupies the glorious throne, and they render worship and homage to Almighty God. Besides, they are distinguished for intelligence and piercing insight, for they are " full of eyes before and behind "—they see into the future as into the past; they possess a kind of omniscience. And their action is of indescribable swiftness and irresistible power. Like the lightning burst they go and come.

What do the cherubim symbolize? Some say, the fullness of the deity; others, the manhood of Christ; others, angels; and others still, redeemed humanity. In determining the significance of them, it should be borne in mind that they are associated with the throne of God, and with the great work of redemption. On the throne as seen by Ezekiel, One whose likeness was "as the appearance of a man" sat. Those familiar with the language of the Bible need not be reminded that this is the Old Testament description of the Lord Jesus. Be it remembered that the throne of Ezekiel is one both of judgment and of grace. I believe the "living creatures" of Ezekiel are hieroglyphs of God's attributes, of the eternal forces and infinite powers of the throne of God.

Whatever they have or do, purpose or execute, is derived from Him and the result of His mighty energy. Intelligence, strength, stability, and swiftness in judgment, and, withal, the movement of the whole course of earthly events, depend on the throne. Majesty, government and providence unite to form the throne and execute His behests who sits on it. The execution of His will is through the powers and forces which He himself has created, angels, natural law, human beings, and the animal creation. Everything is subject to Him, does His bidding.

Let it be observed also, that the throne of the Supreme and Sovereign Lord is seen in Chaldea. In xi, 23, 24, "the glory of the Lord" departs from the city (Jerusalem) and is beheld by the prophet at Chebar. It never returns to the city or the land until the vision of the glorious temple and city (xlii, 1-7) has its ample fulfillment. It is noteworthy that when the glory of the Lord returns to Israel in the latter day, it comes "from the east." It had gone away to the east at its departure when the throne of David fell; power went forth to the Gentiles, and the "times of the Gentiles" began. When it comes back, it comes from the east whither it had gone, and Zion's time for favor has come again.

This affords the explanation of the title "son of man" given to Ezekiel and Daniel. Ninety and more times it is bestowed on Ezekiel, never by himself, but always by the Revealer; once to Daniel, Dan. viii, 17. It belongs to the two prophets in exile and to no others. The nation is rejected; God is outside of it, stands at a distance from it; and speaks to the prophets through whom He communicates

His will as if Jewish distinctions were gone, and God addresses them as men, only men. The title and the testimony are exactly adapted to each other.

5. Vision of the idolatry secretly practised at Jerusalem, viii. The chapter lets us into the real causes for the overthrow of the kingdom of Judah. In the subterranean passages beneath the temple area were fitted up chapels decorated after the fashion of Egypt with likenesses of sacred animals to which incense was offered. They had also a wailing-place where women wept and howled over the loss of the Syrian god Tammuz. Within the space of the sacred temple court between the porch and the altar there was a band of high dignitaries who turned their backs on the sanctuary and paid their devotions to the eastward, to the sun as he rose over the Mount of Olives. Although this was the most ancient form of idolatry it does not appear in Judah till the close of the monarchy.

We learn from Ezekiel's contemporary, Jeremiah, that the queen of heaven was worshipped, Astarte, (Jer. vii), and likewise the brutal Moloch (Jer. vii), a Phœnician idol. Children were sacrificed to it; the fruit of the body was given for the sin of the soul. The idol stood in the valley of the son of Hinnom, the scene of the unnatural rites was Tophet. Thence came the significant and dreadful word, Gehenna, hell.

6. Israel's restoration. In common with the other prophets Ezekiel announces repeatedly a glorious future for his people, the house of Israel—a future but partially realized in the return from the exile of Babylon. (See chaps. xi,17-20; xvi; xxxiv; xxxvi).

As if these predictions were not enough nor explicit enough, another more remarkable in various ways than any preceding it in the book is given; it is the famous thirty-seventh, viz., the vision of the Valley of Dry Bones. It is the graveyard of the Jewish nation the prophet sees, the helpless, dismembered, denationalized people, whose return and restoration to the favor of God and to national unity are as resurrection from the dead. It is common to apply this vision to the conversion of sinners, but while the process is the same in all cases, whether Jew or Gentile, the prime application is to Israel, as vs. 11 clearly shows, "Son of man, these bones are the whole house of Israel."

7. The judgment of Gog, xxxviii, xxxix. The revised version has made a change in the second verse of the first chapter named which is an improvement. The message is against "the prince of Rosh, Meshech and Tubal," names that are surprisingly akin to Rus, Moskovy and Tobolsk. It is a northern power that is meant, one north of Judea. He will invade the land with the suddenness and impetuosity of a storm; but he shall be destroyed by supernatural intervention. If Ezek. xxxix, 17-20, describes the same event as Rev. xix, 17, 18, then Gog's overthrow precedes the millennium. If John, in Rev. xx, 7-9, treats of the same power and invasion as Ezekiel, and the description seems to establish the identity, then Ezekiel's prediction refers to the very last outbreak of sin and rebellion in the history of the earth, viz., that which takes place after the millennium and in the little season during which Satan is loosed from the pit. Gog, then, is the end of all the dealings of God with Israel and the Gentile world, the last transaction before the setting of the great white throne.

8. The vision of the city and temple, xl-xlviii. This is the last vision of Ezekiel, and the most notable of all. The contents of these chapters may be distributed into three parts: The vision of the temple, xl-xliii; the vision of the worship, xliv-xlvi; the vision of the land, xlvii, xlviii. It should be remembered, however, that the vision is one, and glides easily from the temple to its worship, and then to the partition of the land among the restored tribes. The dimensions of Ezekiel's temple correspond with Solomon's; but the courts are enlarged considerably. Its services are very different from those of Mosaic times. The city of the vision is enormously enlarged. The circuit of Jerusalem in the time of Josephus was about four miles. The city of Ezekiel has a circuit of about thirty-seven miles. Ezekiel's land, likewise, is immensely larger than that of the olden time. Wilkinson's estimate is as follows: From north to south it extends about six hundred miles, and the average breadth about five hundred; which would give some three hundred thousand square miles for the whole country. Besides, the location of the tribes is very different from that of the past. If any measure of literality attaches to this wonderful description it belongs to the future; it cannot in any proper sense belong to the past. Just what the meaning of this vision is, it is by no means easy to determine.

(1) It is not a pattern for the second temple (Grotius), for it was never carried out. (2) Nor was it designed to furnish an idea of the magnificence and grandeur with which the second temple should be built (Hengstenberg); the whole description of this symbolic structure forbids it. In short,

Ezekiel's temple and the services connected with it cannot be identified with either the first or the second temple; it stands apart from Herod's also. (3) Note the *changes* in the dimensions of the sanctuary, the court, the gates, the walls, the locality, raised as it is on a high mountain. (4) There are *subtractions*. There is no ark of the covenant, no shew-bread, no candlestick, no veil, no mercy-seat, no cherubim, no tables of the law, no holy of holies, no high priest. The priesthood is confined to the sons of Zadock. The Levites have passed away as a sacred order. Of the three great festivals Pentecost is omitted; nor is there any mention of the day of atonement. (5) The *additions*, too, are wonderful. In this vision there is the return of the glory from the East, where it had gone when Judah failed and went into captivity (xliii, 1-5), to dwell in the temple forever; the living waters that flow from beneath the altar (xlvii, 1-5); the trees (xlvii, 7, 12); the new distribution of the land according to the twelve tribes, and the prince, and his portion, the suburbs; the new city and the immense temple area,—all combine to point to a future re-establishment of Israel and to the millennial glory. This whole prophecy is a symbolical representation, a typical foreshadowing of the bliss which awaits the chosen people of God and the entire earth. It has never yet had its appropriate fulfillment. To spiritualize it, as some do, exhausting all its splendors and hopes in the Christian dispensation, is to mistake its meaning and dwarf its magnificent proportions. For unmistakably the vision has to do with Israel in the last and glorious days when all God hath promised for that people shall have its accomplishment.

DANIEL.

The book of Daniel and the Revelation of John are companion prophecies, and must be studied together. They treat of the same great subjects, and use almost exactly the same symbols. Both deal in dates, both have what we may call a sacred arithmetic, and in both the stupendous scenes and events of the end of the age are the main features. Thanks to the patient toil and prayerful study of Daniel much of what was profound mystery to the fathers is now made plain. Our task is simply to gather up the results and set them forth as briefly as possible.

1. The prophet Daniel was of noble if not of royal birth, i, 3. He was made captive at the first invasion of Judah by Nebuchadnezzar in the third year of Jehoiakim's reign, i, 1. The entire period of his exile, which ended only with his life, was spent at Babylon and its vicinity. Under the reigns of Nebuchadnezzar, under his successors, Evil-Merodach, Neriglissar, Laborosoarchad, Nabonadius, Belshazzar; under that of Darius the Mede and of Cyrus down to his third year (x, 1), Daniel lived. He saw the mighty works inaugurated by the great Babylonian king who might be said to have rebuilt the city. He was a witness of the overthrow of the Chaldean Empire, and the establishment of the Persian rule. It was a momentous epoch in which

Daniel lived, one of the most notable in the annals of the world.

2. Fidelity of Daniel and his fellow exiles, i, 3-20. Nebuchadnezzar determined to extirpate the religion and patriotism of these four young men, first, by changing their names and imposing on them names which connected them with the gods of Babylon; second, by compelling them to live as the heathen. But heathenizing their names did not heathenize their hearts; changing their names did not change their creed or their character, and eat unclean food they would not nor did. Had Daniel and his companions done in Babylon as the Babylonians did, they would soon have sunk to the level of their heathen captors. But they knew truth has no latitude, and loyalty to God no longitude. Their steadfastness won the splendid attestation of the divine favor, i, 15-20. "The secret of the Lord is with them that fear Him, and He will show them His covenant," Ps. xxv, 14.

3. Authenticity of the book. Daniel has been furiously assailed. The attack began with Porphyry, a pagan, born in Syria, A. D. 233. And it rages still. Only the briefest outline of some of the arguments in support of its genuineness can be here given.

(1) The book claims to have been written by Daniel. In the last six chapters the author uses such phrases as, "I saw in the night visions;" "I, Daniel, alone saw the vision;" "I, Daniel, understood by books," etc. These chapters are inseparably bound up with the first six. The pertinent question is, Are these statements true? He would be reckless indeed who would impeach the author's veracity, or charge him with forgery.

(2) Josephus affirms that Alexander the Great was shown the prophecies in Daniel concerning himself by the high priest Jaddua, and the conqueror was so delighted that he offered to confer any favor on the Jews. Alexander antedated Antiochus more than 150 years.

(3) Daniel and his three companions are referred to in 1 Macc. ii, 49-60, in such a way as to lead us to believe the book was extant when this apocryphal writing was composed.

(4) Ezekiel testifies both to the existence and character of Daniel, xiv, 14, 20. In xxviii, 3, there is a manifest allusion to Daniel's wisdom as a revealer of secrets, "a resolver of doubts." It seems clear that Ezekiel knew of the prophet's interpretation of Nebuchadnezzar's dream, and of the handwriting on the wall of Belshazzar's palace. This witness is all the more important because the two prophets were cotemporaries, and no one doubts the authenticity of Ezekiel's book.

(5) Our Lord sets His seal to the reality of Daniel's official character and the truth of his predictions, Matt. xxiv, 15. Christ teaches that this prediction of Daniel still remained to be fulfilled when He uttered the memorable Olivet discourse, i. e., more than a century and a half after the time of Antiochus.

(6) The records of ancient Babylon as deciphered by archeologists harmonize with the statements of the prophet. In many minute particulars Daniel has been vindicated by modern research. The words of M. Lenormant deserve serious attention: "The more the knowledge of the cuneiform texts advances, the more is felt the necessity to revise (correct) the

too hasty condemnation of the book of Daniel by the German exegetical school," (La Magie, p. 14).

4. Division of the book. We may separate it into two parts: Part I. Chaps. i-vi. This section contains the following topics as marked by the chapters: Daniel and his companions in exile, i; Nebuchadnezzar's dream and its interpretation, ii; the fiery furnace, iii; Nebuchadnezzar's second dream, iv; Belshazzar's banquet and Babylon's fall, v; Daniel in the lion's den, vi.

Part II. Chaps. vii-xii. This section is prediction throughout and contains the main features and phases of Gentile rule, and its final overthrow by the Son of God, our Lord Jesus Christ.

A more suggestive analysis, due mainly to Dr. N. West, is the following:

I. Development of the world-kingdoms.

Chap. i, Introductory—Nebuchadnezzar the king, B. C. 606.

Chap. ii, The image dream; Nebuchadnezzar's second year, B. C. 604.

Chap. iii, The fiery furnace; Nebuchadnezzar's twentieth year, B. C. 580 (about).

Chap. iv, Nebuchadnezzar's mania; Nebuchadnezzar's thirtieth year, B. C. 570.

Chap. v, Fall of Babylon, B. C. 538; Belshazzar regent.

Chap. vi, Lion's den; Darius the Mede, B. C. 538.

Chap. vii, The four wild beasts, B. C. 555; Belshazzar regent.

II. Development of the conflict between Israel and the world-power.

Chap. viii, Vision of the ram and he-goat, B. C. 553; Belshazzar regent.

Chap. ix, The seventy weeks, B. C. 538; Darius the Mede.

Chaps. x-xii, Final vision—the apocalypse; B. C. 534, Cyrus king.

Under two empires, the Chaldean and Medo-Persian, Daniel's prophecies were made. They may be arranged thus:

I. Under Nebuchadnezzar.
  (a) The dream of the metallic image.
  (b) The idol image and fiery furnace.
  (c) The hewn tree.

II. Under Belshazzar.
  (a) The four beasts.
  (b) The ram and goat.
  (c) Belshazzar's feast.

III. Under Darius the Mede.
  (a) The lion's den.
  (b) The seventy weeks.

IV. Under Cyrus. The great apocalypse, chaps. x-xii.

5. Daniel's place in the general scheme of prophecy. It is a very remarkable one. The book differs from the other prophetic writings, not only in the design and objects of the messages, but also from the view-point of the messages themselves. The other prophets are concerned mainly with Israel. Other nations and people are the subjects of their predictions incidentally, as they come into contact with Israel; for the chosen people were still recognized as God's, and in covenant relationship with Him. As long as the house of Judah remained measurably faithful, the throne was secure, and Jerusalem enjoyed the divine protection. Gentile powers like Egypt, Assyria, Babylon, were ambitious to

gain the sovereignty of the world; but while Judah was owned of God, they were held in like fierce animals by an unseen leash. Providence would not suffer any one of them to obtain the mastery over the others. But Judah ere long followed in the footsteps of Samaria, and God gave the throne of David and the holy city into the power of the Chaldean king, Nebuchadnezzar. The supremacy passed into his hands: "The God of heaven hath given thee a kingdom, power, and strength, and glory. . . . Thou art the head of gold," Dan. ii, 37, 38. The remarkable words of the Savior, so full of significance and so pregnant of meaning, "The times of the Gentiles," (Luke xxi, 24), date from this gift of supremacy to king Nebuchadnezzar. Never since has Israel been a free and independent people. Subject to Babylon, Persia, Greece, Rome, they are still without a national existence, without a king, an altar, a temple, and a sacrifice. Their distinctive calling is in abeyance, their relation with God as the chosen people is suspended while "the times of the Gentiles" run on. It was in connection with this new order of things that Daniel prophesied. It was at the inauguration of the Gentile times he saw the visions recorded in this book. And it is this great fact which stamps the prophecies with the peculiar features here exhibited.

I. Nebuchadnezzar's dream — the Colossus; chap. ii.

The date is the second year of his reign, vs. 1, B. C. 604. The occasion of it was the king's anxiety as to the future of the kingdom which he had been instrumental in founding, vs. 29. The royal mandate to reproduce and interpret the dream baffled the sagacity and cunning of the professional fortune-tellers of Babylon. Daniel with the sublime confidence of faith in the living God offered to do both, vs. 16. He and his companions held a prayer meeting, and sought help from the source of all knowledge, the revealer of all secrets—God; and their prayer was heard, their faith rewarded, vs. 17-24.

1. The dream, vss. 31-35. It was a huge image or statue the king saw. Its form was that of a gigantic man, resplendent with brightness, imposing in attitude, and terrible in appearance. Unlike any other work of art with which the king was familiar this clossal man was composite. It was made up of five different materials; the head of gold; the breast and arms of silver; the belly and thighs of brass; the legs of iron; the feet and toes of iron and clay. As the king gazed on the lofty statue, suddenly and without premonition a stone, extra-human and superhuman in its origin, struck the image with crushing force on its feet, and crumpled the clay, iron, brass, silver and gold into powder which the wind carried away. If the size and splendor of the Colossus were impressive, how much more must have been its destruction.

2. The interpretation, vss. 36-45. It is certainly one which human ingenuity could not have hit upon. The wise men and flatterers of the Chaldean court never would have ventured to announce such a termination to Gentile supremacy. The interpretation bears on its face the proof of its divine authority. We gather the explanation into a few sentences.

(1) The Colossus symbolizes the World-kingdoms in their unity and historical succession, vss. 38-42. God makes known to Nebuchadnezzar "what shall come to pass" hereafter, vs. 29. Gentile dominion

is represented as a huge metallic man. Its whole history, from its rise, through its progress to its final demolition and disappearance from the earth forever, is summed up in this prophetic man. "Here we learn that every man contains in the very shape of his body, a history and a prophecy of the fate of the whole universe, from the commencement of the Babylonian captivity to the remote period of the future," (Deane).

(2) Four great empires, and only four, were to succeed each other in the government of the world from the Chaldean to the end. The first was the Babylonian with Nebuchadnezzar at its head. "Thou art this head of gold," vs. 38. The grant of empire was made to him, vss. 37, 38; Jer. xvii, 5-7.

The breast and arms of silver denote the Medo-Persian Empire which overthrew the Chaldean, and became its successor in the government of the world. The brass is the Greco-Macedonian, which overturned the Persian; and the iron is the Roman, which succeeded the Greek. It may be asked, How do you know that the various metals of the colossus symbolize the World-kingdoms above mentioned?—By the prophet Daniel himself. Dan. ii, 38, proves that the first was the Chaldean; chap. viii, 20, tells us that the successor of that empire was the Medo-Persian; and viii, 21, declares that "Grecia" follows Persia; while ix, 26, plainly intimates that Rome is the fourth, and Rev. xiii puts this beyond a doubt. Besides, the words, "king," "kings," "kingdoms," are used to designate empire or rule, throughout this second chapter of the book.

(3) Deterioration marks the course of Gentile rule, vss. 39, 40. There is decrease in the value of

the metals composing the image. Gold is better than silver; silver than brass; brass than iron; iron than clay. The distance between gold and mud is immense. Moreover, the first power is a unit, the second, dual; the third, quadruple (vii, 6; viii, 8); the fourth, in its final form, decimal-ten toes in the image, vss. 41, 42; ten horns in the beast, vii, 7; Rev. xiii.

Thus more and more does constitutional unity decline until it fades out into democratic license and communistic anarchy. Iron denotes the imperial, unyielding element; clay, the plastic and popular element. The two cannot blend. Imperial institutions and popular institutions war with each other. This is the state of things which marks the last stage in the history of the world-kingdoms—the strength of iron and the weakness of clay.

(4) The destruction of the image was accomplished by a "stone cut out without hands," vss. 34, 44, 45. Obviously it is divine power that is meant. Man has nothing to do with the appearing or fall of the stone. From first to last it is supernatural agency. Christ is the stone, Isa. viii, 14; Ps. cxviii, 22; Acts iv, 11, etc. He and His kingdom are identified in the prophecy.

(5) The time of the destruction is clearly indicated. It is "in the days of these kings," vs. 44. What kings?—Manifestly, the kings who belong to the world-power in its last, the ten-kingdom form—the time of the ten toes and the ten horns. The Stone smites the image, not in the head (Babylonian time), nor in the breast and arms (Persian period), nor in the body (Grecian times), nor in the legs (Roman times), but on the feet and toes, vss. 34, 44,

45. Not when Babylon fell, nor when Persia was overthrown, nor when the Greek Empire went down, nor at the birth of Jesus, nor at His death, nor when the Holy Spirit came on the church on the day of Pentecost, nor at the Reformation, was the colossus scattered to the winds. It still exists. Moreover, the Stone does not first fill the earth and crowd the colossus out, nor does it diffuse a transforming influence over it, and change it into a devout worshipper of God. No, it does nothing of the sort. It crushes it. Demolition is not conversion. A blind man ought to see that the action of the Stone is judgment, not grace; it is destruction, not salvation, that is here predicted. The times of the Gentiles end in wrath and ruin, and there succeeds them the establishment of the visible kingdom of God which shall be as wide as the world and as lasting as the eternal years of God.

II. The historical chapters, iii-vi. These chapters are intimately connected with the strictly predictive portions of the book. They are intended to exhibit the moral character of the World-power. And throughout the World-power is found to be idolatrous, self-willed, intolerant, defiant of authority, and blasphemous. Whether it be Babylonian or Persian, Greek or Roman, ancient or modern, it antagonizes Christ, repudiates His authority, flings His servants into the furnace or to the lions, and corrupts His truth whenever it touches it. A wonderfully searching light do these historical chapters of Daniel cast on the spirit and temper of the Gentile kingdoms.

III. The vision of the four predatory beasts, vii. The dream (ii) took place in the second year of

Nebuchadnezzar. The vision of the four beasts occurred in the first year of Belshazzar.

(1) Their origin. They rose out of "the great sea;" the Mediterranean, as the phrase invariably signifies. This is the territorial scene of the vision. Out of the sea torn by the four winds of heaven they emerge, i. e., out of the commotions and revolutions of the nations the beasts arise.

(2) The beasts are identical with the four universal kingdoms of the colossal image, (chap. ii), vss. 17, 23. " King " and " kingdom " are in the prophecy convertible terms. The Babylonian, Medo-Persian, Greco-Macedonian and Roman kingdoms are here likewise symbolized. The reason why these empires are twice represented in the prophecy—once by the metals of the colossus, and once by the beasts—is found in the difference between man's view of the World-kingdoms and God's. In man's view they are the concentration of all material wealth, majesty and power. In God's view they are a set of rapacious, wild beasts devouring one another by brute force.

(3) The fourth beast is the prominent object of the vision. That it is Rome that is meant is almost universally conceded. Because of the place of bad pre-eminence which that power has held, and is yet again to hold, in the affairs of the world, the Spirit of revelation dwells mainly on it, vss. 7-26. By Rome the Jews have been persecuted as by no other power; under it the Son of God was crucified; by it in its pagan state uncounted multitudes of Christians, and more under its papal form, were put to death. The world is not yet done with it, nor is God. But it is with its final form this prediction has to do. The Spirit looks rather at the *crisis* than the *course*

of its history. Here this fourth beast has its ten horns which correspond to the ten toes of the image. In Rev. xiii and xvii it also has the ten horns. It is the last stage in its existence that is meant.

(4) The little horn, vss. 8, 20, 21, 24, 25. It is an eleventh horn. It is to spring up from among the ten. A comparison of Daniel's fourth beast and its little horn with Paul's man of sin (2 Thess. ii), and John's beast with seven heads and ten horns (Rev. xiii) proves beyond any reasonable doubt that they are all one and the same power, the last enemy, the antichrist.

In Dan. ii the judgment stone falls on the feet and ten toes of the image. In vii the destruction of the fourth beast takes place when ten kings are ruling and dominated by an eleventh, the little horn. In Revelation the beast is seven-headed and ten-horned when the Son of God metes out to him his just doom. These prophecies co-ordinate and synchronize with each other, and they all deal with the scenes at the end-time.

These things being so, it follows that the world-power remains in some form down to the second coming of Christ. This is the clear teaching of Daniel, Paul and John. How it is possible to interpose a millennium this side of the advent, while Satan is loose and the beast has things much his own way, seems to us a difficult if not an impossible feat.

V. Vision of the ram and the he-goat, chap. viii.

These symbols are explained for us in the chapter itself. They relate to the second and third empires. The two-horned ram is Medo-Persia, vs. 20; the rough goat is Grecia, vs. 21; and the great horn between his eyes is the Macedonian conqueror, Alexander the Great. Most accurate and graphic is the description of the swift movements of the goat, and the " choler " with which he assaulted the ram. It is in exact accord with the historical facts in the case; for Persia had invaded Greece and aroused the national feeling of resentment in the highest degree; hence the " choler " with which the goat rushed upon the ram. In three battles Alexander made himself master of the world.

At his death, his empire was parcelled out among his four generals, and so "four kingdoms stood up " in the room of the one founded by Alexander. Out of one of these, the Syrian, there arose a " little horn" which is the prominent feature in the vision.

The little horn of the eighth chapter is not to be confounded with that of the seventh. The two are distinct. *That* is the last antichrist, the one who is yet to arise. *This* is the Syrian antichrist, Antiochus Epiphanes, who appeared about B. C. 175, and who was Israel's worst enemy, who harassed and slaughtered them without pity in his insane effort to impose the Greek civilization and heathen religion upon them; who profaned the temple by setting up in it an idol. It was this man whom the Maccabees so heroically combatted. At the same time it should be remembered that the antichrist of the Old Testament is also the type of the antichrist of the New. Antiochus will have his awful counterpart in the man of sin, the beast, who will be Israel's and the world's last scourge.

VI. Vision of the seventy weeks, ix. The prophet had learned from Jeremiah (xxv, 11, 12) that the captivity of Judah was to continue for seventy years, and he saw that the time had come when the restoration should be near at hand. Accordingly, he sought by prayer and supplication, with fasting and humiliation and confession, that God would forgive and restore His people. He received for answer a further and fuller revelation respecting Israel—one of the most comprehensive it has pleased the Spirit of God to give to men—ix, 24-27. The angel Gabriel tells Daniel that seventy weeks are determined or measured off upon his people and holy city, within which period of time God will perform His whole work, promised and predicted throughout all Scripture.

1. Within the compass of these mysterious weeks, six mighty events are to take place, vs. 24: viz., the termination of Israel's apostasy, arrest of their sins, the covering over of their iniquity, the in-bringing of abiding righteousness, the verification of what vision and prophet have predicted, and the consecration anew of the holy of holies. Such are the majestic promises that are to be fulfilled for Daniel's people and city, Israel and Jerusalem, within these seventy weeks. To such an end and outcome they are appointed or decreed.

2. Seventy weeks. The word week is retained by nearly all the writers on the book because there is no English word which exactly expresses the idea of the original. It is seventy times seven years that is meant, 490 years in all. It is not days that is mentioned, a day put for a year, but seventy weeks of years.

3. The seventy weeks are divided into three groups, vss. 25-27: viz., seven weeks; sixty-two

weeks; one week. Certain very definite events are specified as transpiring in each of these groups. The rebuilding of Jerusalem in the seven weeks; the cutting off of Messiah at the end of the sixty-two weeks and the appearing and doing of the prince of the people who destroy the holy city, in the last or seventieth week.

4. From what " commandment," or edict, are these seventy weeks to be dated and counted? If we could determine the exact starting point, we could know precisely when they will run out, when the great prediction of these verses will have its accomplishment. Many count from the twentieth year of Artaxerxes, when that monarch issued his decree to Nehemiah, Neh. ii, 1; and accordingly find that the second group of the weeks, viz., the sixty-two weeks, expired with the death of Messiah, Jesus of Nazareth. There is another reckoning by Dr. West which is worthy of the most serious attention on the part of all students of the Bible. Dr. West dates the seventy weeks from the issuance of the decree by Cyrus, Ezra i, B. C. 536. In the first group of seven weeks he finds an interval or gap of fifty-seven years; and the death of Messiah takes place at the close of the sixty-second in the series. (See his " Thousand Years in both Testaments.")

5. At the close of the sixty-ninth week, the angel declares that Messiah the Prince shall be cut off, and " there shall be nothing to Him." He announces also that the people of the prince that shall come shall destroy the city and the sanctuary. We know who the people were who fulfilled this prediction, the Roman people. In A. D. 70 the Roman eagles swooped down on the devoted city, and city and

temple went down amid the most frightful scenes of ruin and devastation. The prince is not with the people when they demolish city and temple; he is still to come when that event occurs.

6. This prince comes in connection with the course of the last or seventieth week, the last seven years of the whole series, vs. 27. It is clear as day that the last week is rent off from the other sixty-nine, and stands by itself. There is a mighty break between the sixty-ninth and the seventieth in the series. The death of Christ broke the chain of the weeks, for that event sundered the relation then existing between God and the chosen people. Jesus Himself plainly indicates the rejection of the people in His lamentation over Jerusalem, Matt. xxiii, 37-39: "Behold, your house is left unto you desolate. For I say unto you, Ye shall not see me henceforth, till ye shall say, blessed is He that cometh in the name of the Lord," (comp. Luke xix, 41-44). Nor are the other prophets silent as to the interval which should elapse between the death of Messiah and the end—His second coming. Hosea points to it when he says, "For the children of Israel shall abide many days without a king, and without a prince, and without a sacrifice," etc., Hos. iii, 4. Micah declares they shall be given up until "she which travaileth shall bring forth," Micah v, 3. Zechariah adds his testimony to the same fact of an interval between the rejection of Messiah and the final restoration of Israel, Zech. xi, 7-14. The same great fact of an interval between Christ's death and the rejection of the people for a long period of time appears in the parable of the nobleman, Lu. xix, and in the Olivet prophecy, Matt. xxiv. It is the firm

belief of the present writer that our whole Christian dispensation lies between the close of Daniel's sixty-ninth and the opening of his seventieth week—a gap which has run on for nearly nineteen hundred years.

In this remarkable prophecy, there are two peoples: Daniel's people, and the people who should destroy the city and sanctuary—the Roman people. There are two princes: Prince Messiah, who was to be cut off and have nothing; and the prince of the Roman people, the last antichrist, who is still future.

VII. The final vision—Daniel's apocalypse, x-xii.

These three chapters contain one vision, the last divine communications Daniel received, of which we have any record. At the time he must have been an aged man. He had been one of the first captives "in the third year of Jehoiakim;" had lived through the seventy years of the captivity, and this was now the third year of Cyrus. And yet there is no sign of declining power, or failing faculties. Indeed, he appears rather to have increased in strength, for he "understood" this vision, x, 1, a statement in marked contrast with what is told of other visions, vii, 28; viii, 27.

1. Chapter ten reveals the influence of supernatural beings in the affairs of earth. The heavenly messenger informs the prophet that he had been dispatched with the answer to his petitions on the first day of his supplication, but that he had been delayed by the prince of Persia for twenty-one days, vss. 12, 13.

2. Prophetic history of Persia, xi, 1-2. The Spirit now goes back and connects these fresh revelations

with the eighth chapter of the book. He takes up the power symbolized by the ram and adds some distinctive features to what is there given us. There was to be a succession of four kings from the date of the vision. These were Cambyses, the impostor Smerdis, Darius Hystaspes, and Xerxes.

3. Prophetic history of the third empire, xi, 3-20. The ram of Persia is now dropped, and the he-goat of Greece is taken up. The "mighty king" who founds the third empire, Alexander the Great, falls in the prime of life and in the plenitude of his conquests, and out of his kingdom four others are evolved. It is remarkable that the prophecy asserts that no one of Alexander's family should succeed him. Power passes from his family altogether, vs. 4. Then one of the four is dwelt upon at length—the Syrian kingdom—and its history is traced, in connection with Egypt, and their doings, with respect to the land of Israel. For as Judah lay right between the two rival powers, they made it their battle-field, and conquered it from each other repeatedly. They formed alliances with one another, inter-married, but it only proved the prelude to fiercer animosities, and more savage outbreaks; brothers, sons, and grandsons espoused the quarrels of their kindred. Such was the history of the rival kingdoms of Syria and Egypt; such has the Spirit of God depicted it in these verses, 5-20.

4. Prophetic history of Israel's enemy in Maccabean times, xi, 21-35. He is introduced as "a vile person." His character, animus and actions are fully described; much more so than any other of the various monarchs mentioned in the first part of the chapter. The reason is that this man was the worst

foe Israel had ever yet had, and he is also the truest type of the last ferocious foe who shall oppress them, the antichrist. For it is believed that the man painted in such lurid colors in these verses was Antiochus Epiphanes, who began his bloody and sacrilegious career about B. C. 175—a man who, because thwarted in his designs upon Greece by the Romans, and defeated in all his efforts to extend his kingdom into Europe and Africa by the same power, turned in his rage on prostrate Judah and wreaked his vengeance on its suffering population.

This is the man who set up the "abomination that maketh desolate," vs. 31. The allusion is to the idol which he erected in the temple. It was not from this verse our Lord quoted the expression in Matt. xxiv, 15; but from Dan. xii, 11. That of xi, 31, had already taken place when Jesus quoted the saying; but Dan. xii, 11, is yet unfulfilled. The account of Antiochus extends to verse thirty-five which verse prepares the way for a change of subject and of time in the prediction. It projects our thoughts forward "to the time appointed," to "the time of the end," and to the enemy who shall then appear.

5. Prophetic history of the last foe of God's people, the antichrist, xi, 36-45. He is abruptly introduced as "the king" in vs. 36. The prediction concerning Antiochus glides suddenly but naturally into that of his antitype who shall appear in the end, and be destroyed by the manifestation of the Son of God from heaven. By way of pre-eminence he is called "the king." In Isa. xxx, 33, we read of tophet prepared for "the king;" nor can it be doubted but that the same person is there ultimately referred to, as the connection evidently im-

plies. The description of "the king" in Daniel is strikingly analogous with what is told us of the little horn (vii, 20-25); with that of the man of sin (2 Thess. ii, 1-7); with that of the beast (Rev. xiii). Concerning him some things may be noted.

(1) He is still future. No one can read and study the prophecies relating to him without having this conviction forced upon him.

(2) He is a real person. It is not a system of evil nor an organized body under the delusion and leadership of the devil, like Mohammedanism or popery that is meant. It is freely admitted that Romanism bears an amazing likeness to "the king," and to the man of sin, in its origin, history, animus, idolatry, corruption of the truth, persecutions and blasphemies. All that popery is and far more. But bad as it is as an apostate church, still it has not yet reached the fearful height and towering eminence of wickedness which the Bible attributes to the antichrist. Something worse than anything yet seen is coming, viz., the man of sin, the king.

(3) His appearance is at the "end," the day of the Lord, Dan. ii, 44; vii, 13, 22, 26; ix, 26, 27; 2 Thess. ii, 1, 2; Rev. xix, 11-21.

(4) He will be the chief adversary and enemy of Daniel's people, the Jews, vii, 21, 25; xii, 1; Matt. xxiv.

(5) He will invent a new object of worship and compel all to do it homage on pain of death, xi, 38; Rev. xiii, 14, 15.

(6) He will perform miracles of some sort, 2, Thess. ii, 9, 10; Rev. xiii, 13.

(7) He will exalt himself above all, xi, 36; 2 Thess. ii, 4.

(8) He will be the antagonist of Christ, Rev. xiii, 6; xix, 19.

(9) He will be destroyed by the personal appearing of the Son of God from heaven, Dan. vii, 13; 2 Thess. ii, 8; Rev. xix, 11-21.

Thus these three men, Daniel, Paul, and John, prophesy of the mighty scenes and events of the time of the end, the day of the Lord. They solemnly assure us that, far from the Church "converting the world" evil will prevail to the end, wickedness intensify, culminating at length in the apostasy and revelation of the man of sin—the anti-christ. They jointly and severally declare that the great adversary will be destroyed by the coming of Jesus Christ Himself. Our Lord's own testimony is identical with theirs, Matt. xxiv, xxv; Mark xiii; Lu. xxi.

6. Three events of the end-time, Dan. xii, 1, 2. The first of these is, a time of unparalleled trouble, vs. 1. Our Lord in His Olivet prophecy speaks of the same unequaled tribulation, Matt. xxiv, 21; Mark xiii, 19. It is the great tribulation. The second event is, deliverance for an elect remnant of the Jews from the tribulation, vs. 1. Jeremiah refers to the same deliverance, xxx, 7: "It is even the time of Jacob's trouble; but he shall be saved out of it." (Comp. Zech. xiii, 8, 9.) The third event of the last time is, the resurrection of the righteous, vs. 2: "And many of them that sleep in the dust of the earth shall wake, some to everlasting life, and some to shame and everlasting contempt." This can only be an eclectic resurrection. Many does not mean all. Besides, the real force of the words is, "and many from among the dead shall awake," (so Tregelles, West, etc.). It is in exact accord with Rev.

xx, 4, 5, where the first and second resurrection are mentioned.

7. Dates in Dan. xii. Three particularly are mentioned. In verse seven the revealer solemnly swears with uplifted hands that the mighty events at the end-time shall be accomplished in a "time, times, and an half"—3½ years, or 1,260 days. It is the same number that occurs so often in Daniel and Revelation. It is the period of the tribulation, when wickedness and sin and crime will culminate, the antichrist having everything his own way. It is the last half of the last week of Dan. ix, 27, at the close of which the apocalypse of Christ will take place whereby the enemy will be forever overthrown. After that, thirty days more pass, and the sanctuary is cleansed, and all things made ready for the millennial glory; forty-five days more pass, and full blessing is enjoyed, Dan. xii, 11, 12.

A precious word is addressed the prophet for his comfort: "But go thy way till the end be, for thou shalt rest, and stand in thy lot at the end of the days"—a promise that might well have sent him singing to the grave. "Thou shalt rest." Toil and trouble have been thine; grief and disappointment, as well as splendid victories, glorious deliverances; much indeed has been mingled in thy cup, and thou hast drunk it all without a murmur or a sigh; thou hast been true and loyal; and now all is over; the long, strange journey is finished. Never more shall king or emperor honor or degrade thee; no more shalt thou be the target for the cruel shafts of jealous courtiers. Go, and rest, and wait; for resurrection is coming, and thou shalt shine above the splendor of the firmament's gleam.

THE MINOR PROPHETS.

The arrangement of the twelve minor prophets is in a sense chronological; that is, the earlier are put at the beginning, the later at the end of the collection. The order of time, however, is not observed with strict exactness; for Joel and Jonah are probably the oldest of the twelve. By whom the collection was made is somewhat difficult to determine, though the constant tradition that Ezra particularly, and probably also Nehemiah and Malachi, had very much to do in forming the canon, has never been successfully contradicted.

The great theme of these prophets is Israel primarily, then the nations that were either the foes of Israel, or were used of God for the punishment of His disobedient people. Nowhere do we find sin rebuked with more awful severity, the true meaning of the law more clearly expounded, or the future glory of Zion more confidently predicted. Israel's relation to God, the binding force of the Mosaic legislation, and the apostasy of the people from the Lord and their transgression of the law given at Sinai—these and the like fundamental truths afford the ground for the indictment against the chosen people, as also the ground of the appeals to them to repent and return to God. But while they denounced sin and announced judgment, they foretold the glory of the latter days, the re-gathering of scattered

Israel, the re-erection of David's fallen tabernacle, the coming of Messiah the second time, and the blessedness of the millennial age. Wrath is not the main topic of the minor prophets any more than it is of the major. God's love and pity, His yearning over the wayward people, His desire so often expressed to comfort and bless them, are prominent features of these books, as of the whole Bible. It is impossible to read it with any attention without perceiving this central truth.

It was a special function of the minor prophets to minister to the faith and hope of the few loyal souls who still clung to the truth of God, and who worshipped Him in sincerity. The faithful remnant is found in these books as likewise in the greater prophets. God never forgets those who are true to Him. He always has some special word, some sweet and tender promise and message of comfort for them. Hence we find in these prophecies the presence of the remnant and communications addressed particularly to them.

These twelve books may be classified into four groups, with three in each group.

1. Hosea, Amos, and Micah, who speak of the fall of Israel (Samaria), and of the overthrow that already threatened Judah. They pronounce judgment on the people, while unfolding with more or less fulness the dealings of God in grace at the end. With the exception of Amos, who prophesied in the early reign of Uzziah, they belong to the times of Uzziah, Jotham, Ahaz, and Hezekiah.

2. Obadiah, Jonah, and Nahum, who prophesy against certain Gentile nations; mainly Edom and Nineveh.

3. Haggai, Zechariah, and Malachi, who were post-captivity prophets, the first two dealing with the restored exiles, and the last bearing witness to the failure of the people and the coming of Messiah and His forerunner.

4. Joel, Habakkuk, and Zephaniah, who have a peculiar character such as marks them off from the rest. They chiefly speak of the end, the closing scenes, the great crisis toward which the world is fast hastening. They are *telesmatic*, i. e., they deal with the last days, the great day of the Lord.

HOSEA.

The prophet Hosea was contemporary with Isaiah i, 1. Under the reigns of the same kings of Judah he exercised his ministry as did Isaiah. At the time Jeroboam was king of Israel. Of course this was Jeroboam II., one of the most powerful monarchs that ruled over the ten tribes. In opening this first book of the minor prophets we must retrace our steps in Israel's history, and keep in mind that he antedates Jeremiah, Ezekiel and Daniel at least one hundred and fifty years.

Hosea gives us a vivid picture of the times in which he lived, and of the political and moral state of the people. His style is very concise, terse and abrupt, abounding in figures and metaphors that sometimes are intermingled. The transitions from one topic to another are frequent and sudden. In consequence the book is a difficult one to interpret, but patient study, relying on the guidance of the Spirit of God who alone is the competent interpreter of the Scriptures, will open rich mines of truth. One says he "exhibits the appearance of very remote antiquity." Another compares him to a bee flying from flower to flower, swift and restless, but always gathering and always laden. The title, i, 1, indicates the time of his prophecy, and is at the same time the authentication of the book. The second verse of the first chapter is somewhat peculiar both for its language and its aim. Mr. Deane translates it, "The beginning (of that which) Jehovah spoke by Hosea." The revision has, "When the Lord spake at the first by Hosea." But what is the beginning here mentioned? It cannot mean that Hosea was the first of the prophets by whom God made known His will to Israel, or the first of the minor prophets, for both Jonah and Joel, it is believed, preceded him. The meaning seems to be, the beginning of the prophecies which Hosea was commissioned to make known. The first verse is the heading for the whole book, and its authentication; the second verse is the special heading of the first section of the book which extends to the end of the third chapter. "By Hosea" is literally "in Hosea." It is identical with Heb. i, 1, where the revision has "in the prophets."

The book may be divided into two parts. Part I, chaps. i-iii. God's judgment as to the state of the people, with intimations of repudiation and restoration. Part II, chaps. iv-xiv, in which Israel's sins are described, warnings and threatenings are announced, expostulations and appeals are made, and promises of final recovery. Topically, the book may be summarized thus: 1. The relation which God formed between Himself and Israel originally; it was like that of marriage. 2. Israel's unfaithfulness in this relation. 3. Divorcement of the people from the Lord announced. 4. The people's guilt. 5. Punishment certain, captivity predicted. 6. Remonstrances with the guilty people, and entreaties to repent and reform. 7. Promise of a final and genuine repentance and restoration.

It is hardly needful to remind the reader that

Hosea addressed particularly the kingdom of Israel. He designates them in various ways, as Israel, Ephraim, Samaria, Jacob. Ephraim is specified because the largest of the ten tribes that separated from the house of David, and because it was the leader in rebellion and apostasy. The first king of the Northern Kingdom was Jeroboam, an Ephrathite, who organized apostasy, for he established for political reasons idolatrous sanctuaries at Dan and Bethel. It was one chief aim of the ministry of Hosea to recover Israel from idolatry and to restore them to obedience to God. To effect this end, he painted with no feeble or faltering hand the horrors of their sin, proclaimed the judgments of God against them, and appealed to them with the most passionate entreaties to repent. To what extent his ministry was successful we have no means of knowing. Some, no doubt, heard and heeded the warning voice; but on the nation as such no permanent impression was made. In God's economies, however, no waste is permitted. What appears often to us to be failure, what may have seemed to Hosea to be such, was with God success, for the prophet accomplished precisely what it was intended he should.

Some details of the book may be pointed out.

1. Hosea's marriage with Gomer, i, 3. Was it real, or only symbolic? This is the "vexed question" of the book. The ancient writers held quite generally that no literal union with her was formed by the prophet. Augustine's rule for such passages of the Bible as this is wise: If the language of Scripture taken literally would involve something incongruous or morally wrong, the figurative sense must be preferred.

There is something so unnatural and revolting in the thought that a prophet of God should be divinely ordered to marry an impure woman, and the whole transaction is so dishonoring to God, that it is not surprising that men should seek to relieve the record of all literality, and should interpret it as a vision. Yet the language is so explicit, the names of the parties being given, with the absence of any intimation of its being an allegory or a parable, that we seem to be shut up to the belief that some sort of transaction really took place whereby Hosea and Gomer were brought together as husband and wife. Pusey's words are worthy of serious consideration: "There is no ground to justify our taking as a parable what holy Scripture relates as a fact. There is no instance in which it can be shown that holy Scripture relates that a thing was done, and that with the names of persons, and yet that God did not intend it to be taken as literally true. There would then be left no test of what was real, what imaginary; and the histories of holy Scripture would be left to be a prey to individual caprice, to be explained away as parables when men misliked them."

The view which commends itself to us is this: Hosea really married Gomer. Her loose character is given her in the chapter by anticipation; she was not a fallen woman (or at least was conducting herself properly) when the prophet took her to wife, although God foresaw and announced what she would do after her marriage. Had she been a harlot at the time of her union with Hosea, she would not have served as a type or symbol of Israel at all. It was only as a wife who proved unfaithful to her marriage covenant that she became the living example of Israel's infidelity and apostasy from God.

To them were born three children and names were given them significant of the fate of the people. Afterward, Gomer like Israel became unfaithful and left the prophet's home, and became the paramour of another man. She seems to have sunk so low into vice and degradation that her position was that of a slave, for the prophet bought her back at one-half of the price of a female slave in money, and a portion of barley, iii. That the woman spoken of in chapter three is to be identified with Gomer appears from the following considerations: (1) The analogy requires it. It was Israel that stood in the relation of wife to Jehovah; no other nation was admitted to such relation. (2) The woman is the one already married, but unfaithful, which was precisely the case with Israel. (3) If she had not been the prophet's wife, and had gone away from him, there would be no point in comparing his love for her with that of the Lord for His erring people. (4) A command to love another man's wife to whom he was still attached would be repugnant to every idea of justice and propriety. Either the woman of chapter three was Gomer, or the whole scene is a vision. The word is, not "take," but "love," i. e., renew thy kindness to her, and receive her back into thy house (so Henderson). But she was to live apart from her husband (and he from her) for many days, iii, 3; so Israel was to remain for many days a spoiled and subject people. The prophetic action in this singular case indicated in a striking way the apostasy of the ten tribes, God's repudiation of them, their captivity and final recovery.

2. Israel's state morally in Hosea's time. It was as bad as it could well be. The idolatry inaugurated

by Jeroboam had now continued for more than 150 years, and had diffused every form of vice among the people. Chap. iv, 2, gives a summary of the crimes that filled the land; swearing, lying, murder, theft, adultery—an awful brood. The king and princes were drunken profligates, vii, 3-7. The idolatrous priests spread their shameful festivals and deceitful oracles over all the land, iv, 12-14; x, xii, xiii, 2; they even waylaid and murdered those who were passing on their way to Jerusalem, vi, 9. The people were ignorant, debased, dishonest and incorrigible, iv, 6, 10, 12-14, 17; xi, 7; xii, 7. The nation had forsaken the Lord and relied on human help. Sometimes it was Assyria, sometimes Egypt, they turned to, never really to God, v, 13; vii, 8-12; viii, 9, 10. A listless security blinded their minds, v, 4; xii, 8. Spasmodic repentance in a moment of danger was professed, vi, 4; vii, 16. The root of all the evil was, they had broken covenant with God, and He and His word were ignored and forgotten, vi, 7; iv, 1-6; viii, 12. It is a frightful indictment which God by the mouth of His servant Hosea brings against Ephraim.

3. God's compassion toward His unfaithful people. It is very remarkable; it is like Him. We see it in the strange narrative of Gomer; in the names Lo-ruhamah, unpitied, and Lo-ammi, not my people, changed into Ruhamah, pitied, and Ammi, my people, ii, 1. We see it in the touching expostulations and tender appeals as in xi, 8; xiv, 1-5. Nothing can exceed the earnestness and love with which the Lord entreats Ephraim to return to Him. Look at xi, 8, and see how Mercy interposes her four "hows," as if the great and good God could not possibly

give them up. Many an eye has filled at the nameless advertisement which sometimes appears in the public press: "Come home and all will be forgiven: we wait for you." But God names Ephraim and Himself, and writes it down in His book that all may read: "O, Ephraim, thou hast destroyed thyself; but come home again, come home." It is grace abounding, love exceeding.

4. Messianic predictions. These are not numerous in Hosea, but some there are. In iii, 5, Israel's return under a second David is announced (comp. Jer. xxx, 9; Ezek. xxxiv, 23, 25, etc.). That the David here mentioned is Messiah is evident from the other passages cited above. As Messiah is David's son and heir He is often called by David's name. Twice our Lord quotes vi, 6, "I will have mercy, and not sacrifice," Matt. ix, 13; xii, 17. In His use of the passage it is clear that He is the speaker in it. Hosea xi, 1, is quoted in Matt. ii, 15, and applied to the flight into Egypt. Israel was the Messianic nation, and its history presaged and adumbrated the earthly life of our Lord Jesus, xiii, 14, seems to be referred to in 1 Cor. xv, 55, and is applied to the resurrection of the saints when the Lord comes again.

5. Promises of Israel's restoration, i, 10, 11; ii, 16-20, 23; iii, 4, 5; xiv. It is the concurrent testimony of all the prophets. We may spiritualize these and similar texts if we will, and apply them to the revival of the Church, but beneath our uses of them there is still God's unchangeable promise to the chosen people. Delitzsch's fine word is worth remembering: "Interpretation is one; application is manifold."

BOOK OF JOEL.

Of the prophet Joel we know nothing beyond what is told us in i, 1. He was the son of Pethuel; but who Pethuel was, or where he dwelt, is unknown. Several persons of the name of Joel are mentioned in the Bible, but of few of them is less information given than of this prophet. From internal evidence mainly it is inferred that he was a native of Judah. His message is addressed to Judah. It is equally uncertain when he prophesied, or where he died. It is believed by some commentators that Amos i, 2 is a quotation from Joel iii, 16, and if so, then he must have preceded Amos. As this prophet lived during the reigns of Uzziah of Judah and Jeroboam II. of Israel, the ministry of Joel must have been anterior to that time. The absence of any reference to the Assyrians or Babylonians in the prophecy affords some corroberative proof. Altogether, the date B. C. 800 may approximately be fixed as that of Joel's ministry.

The first verse of the first chapter, as usual, is the inspired endorsement of the whole prophecy, the seal of its authenticity, "The word of the Lord that came to Joel, the son of Pethuel."

It is not easy to give a satisfactory analysis of this prophecy, for the book is a compact unit. The following is offered more as a suggestion than as an analysis. Part I., Devastation of the land by armies of locusts, and by drought, announced, chaps. i-ii, 11. Part II., Exhortation to repentance urged by many gracious promises, chap. ii, 12-32. Part III., Prediction of the day of the Lord, the judgment of the nations, and the glorious state of peace and prosperity to be enjoyed in the times of the Messiah, chap. iii. These parts, however, are very closely bound together in the prophecy. For out of the prediction of the impending scourge springs naturally the call to repentance, and penitence is urged by weighty motives and promises, such as the removal of the scourge and plentiful rainfall. Nor is it less natural for the prophet to pass from the material blessings, held, out to the spiritual, an abundant effusion of the Spirit upon the repentant people. And just as naturally he passes from these to the days of Messiah, the days of judgment, favor, blessing. Unity and progress characterize the book of Joel.

The occasion of the prophecy was the invasion of the land by successive swarms of locusts, and excessive drought, which threatened the country with destruction. But that Joel's message extends beyond his own times, and is not exhausted in them, we shall presently see.

1. Invasion and desolation of the land by locusts, i, 2-16. The plague is described in a very terse way in verse four. The four insects there mentioned are not so many species, as our English words would indicate, but locusts, either in their varieties, or more probably in the devastation they effect. Henderson translates the verse thus: "That which the gnawing locust hath left, the swarming locust hath devoured; and that which the swarming locust hath left, the

licking locust hath devoured; and that which the licking locust hath left, the consuming locust hath devoured." In Palestine the destructive work of these insects is often incalculable. Note, God does not need to summon the great forces of nature, as the earthquake, the lightning or the storm, to make effective His judgments against His rebellious creature, man; He can make the most insignificant instruments to fulfill His purposes.

The prophet then calls upon various classes to mourn—the drunkards, because their wine ceases, vss. 5-7;—the people, because their fields, crops and trees are destroyed, vss. 8-12;—the priests, because the meat-offering and the drink-offering "is withholden," vs. 13. The priests also are exhorted to proclaim a fast, vs. 14.

2. A drought succeeds the invasion of the locusts, or accompanies them, vss. 17-20.

3. The prophet urges the people to fasting and humiliation because of the terrible affliction which has befallen the land, chap. ii, 1-17. In the first part of the second chapter he returns to the invasion of the locusts, and describes it with imagery the most forcible and graphic. The warlike armies of the devouring insects, their battle-march, onset and victory, their spreading themselves with irresistible might over the land—is drawn with a masterly hand.

4. The call to repentance is enforced by promises, ii, 18-27. The pity of the Lord is one great motive held out to the people to secure their penitence, vs. 18. The promise of the removal of the scourge is another, vs. 20; of plentiful rain, and crops another, vs. 23; and the out-pouring of the Spirit is another, vss. 19-32.

Such is the "historical setting," as men name it, of the prophecy of Joel. But is this all there is in the book? Joel's prophecy is telesmatic. It relates to the end, the day of the Lord, the coming of the Lord, and the mighty events which are associated with it. The book deals in general terms with the characteristic features of that day, and with the blessedness that is to be brought to the earth at that time. The proof for these statements is found in the book itself.

1. The prediction of the out-pouring of the Spirit, ii, 28-32. By the words, "And it shall come to pass afterward," the prophet intimates that the promise of the Spirit was not to be expected nor fulfilled immediately. A period of time would elapse before its realization. The day of Pentecost witnessed its fulfillment, Acts ii. The apostle Peter interprets it as having reference to the times of the Messiah, "And it shall come to pass in the last days," Acts ii, 17, an expression which invariably designates Messiah's days, Isa. ii, 2; Heb. i, 2.

The accomplishment of the promise began on the day of Pentecost, Acts ii, 16-21. Peter does not say that Joel's prophecy was exhausted then, but, "This is that which was spoken by the prophet Joel." We have the earnest of the Spirit, 2 Cor. i, 22. Every believer is indwelt by the Spirit, and the Church has the Spirit, and He is in the world applying redemption to all those who are called and chosen of God unto salvation; but it can hardly be said that He is now poured out on all flesh, that He is given to all mankind. There will come a time when Messiah's "days" will be fully inaugurated, and then the Spirit will be poured out on all. So Isaiah predicts,

"And the glory of the Lord shall be revealed, and all flesh shall see it together; for the mouth of the Lord hath spoken it," xl, 5.

2. " The day of the Lord." Five times this expression is used in Joel, i, 15; ii, 1, 11, 31; iii, 14. " The day of the Lord " is a phrase of frequent occurrence in the Old Testament, and always refers, we think, to the execution of judgment on the earth. It sometimes means God's judicial interpositions when He is not actually present; but in its full sense it implies the judgment of the great day, the last day. This is its almost exclusive use in the New Testament. No doubt the judgments announced in Joel had partial fulfillment in the scourge of locusts, and much more in the destruction of Jerusalem and dispersion of the Jews, forty years after Pentecost. But his descriptions of the day of the Lord were not exhausted by those events, terrible as the second of these was. Take iii, 2, 14-16. Unquestionably the prophet here looks forward to the final day. The proof is at hand, and is conclusive. Zechariah, who prophesied some three centuries after Joel, announced the gathering of hostile armies at Jerusalem, the day of the Lord, the coming of the Lord, and the awful judgments that shall be visited upon the ungodly, Zech. xiv. 11-7. That the two prophets predict the same events, a comparison will show. Let any one confront Joel iii with Zech. xiv and any doubt about it will disappear. Both speak of the time of the end, the day of the Lord. Both announce the gathering of armies against Jerusalem, and of the miseries and suffering attending a siege. Both speak of the coming of the Lord, and of deliverance through His mighty intervention in the

behalf of His afflicted people; both, of the destruction of the enemies. And both predict the peace, prosperity, and blessedness that ensue.

3. "The harvest" in Joel iii, 13. The judgments predicted in this chapter do not run parallel with the history of the nations on whom they are visited, but are those which shall fall in the last days, when Judah's grievances are made Jehovah's own, and are treated as done against Himself. The nations are summoned to quit their peaceful occupations, to get ready their arms, and come to the valley of Jehoshaphat, the valley of decision. There the great question between them and God is settled; there the "harvest" is reaped. The harvest of Joel undoubtedly corresponds with the harvest of the parable of the wheat and tares, Matt. xiii, 37-42; and with the harvest of Rev. xiv, 18-20. The figures in all these passages are double; i. e., there is both a harvest of grain and of the vintage, exactly what is found in Joel; and the harvest is the end of the age.

4. Judah's restoration, iii, 1. It is most extraordinary that prophet after prophet announces it, as if the Spirit of God would make assurance doubly sure. It was fulfilled in the return from Babylon; it will be more abundantly realized when the chosen people, now dispersed among the nations of the earth, shall be brought back to their own land and to God.

From all this and much more, it appears that God had far more in mind than to address words of warning and of promise to His people in the days of His servant Joel. He spoke to His people through the prophet at Pentecost and at the destruction of Jerusalem; and will speak to them when the last restoration time comes, and when the last days arrive.

AMOS.

In the reign of Jeroboam I. a man of God came out of Judah by the word of the Lord unto Bethel (1 Kings xiii, 1), who confronted the king at his altar, and foretold its desecration by a prince yet unborn. While Jeroboam II. reigned over Israel, another man of God came out of Judah, and at Bethel (Amos vii, 13) cried against the sin of the people and prophesied the fall of Samaria. It was Amos, one of the most ancient of the prophets whose ministry, according to Horne, Angus, etc., lay between the years B. C. 810-785. He was the contemporary of Hosea, probably also of Isaiah, as verse one of chapter one would indicate. His native place was Tekoa, a few miles south of Bethlehem, a region adapted for grazing, and for no other purpose, we are told. His call to the prophetic office he thus describes: " I was no prophet, neither was I a prophet's son; but I was an herdman, and a gatherer of sycamore fruit; and the Lord took me as I followed the flock and the Lord said unto me, Go, prophesy unto my people Israel," vii, 14, 15. He was not a prophet by succession; he was not trained in any of the prophetic schools; he sat at the feet of no great teacher; he passed through no preliminary or preparatory study. He was only a shepherd on the wild uplands about Tekoa, and he combined with his pastoral life the care of the sycamore trees in the neighborhood. Little dreamed he while thus engaged amid the rugged scenery of his native place that he should stand in the presence of kings and people, and utter the sharp and threatening word of the Lord against the sinful practices of a nation. God called him from his humble walk as " cowherd," as one has named him, and sent him forth to be His mouth to a rebellious and idolatrous people, sent him forth to be tried, opposed, persecuted, discouraged, weary, but to finish his mission right manfully. God is never straightened for instruments. If priests and ministers fail in their testimony through indolence, perverseness and apostasy, He will raise up those who stand outside of the regular calling altogether, and filling them with His Spirit and grace send them forth on His errands.

We learn from i, 1, that the words Amos "saw" concerning Israel began " two years before the earthquake." This earthquake cannot have occurred after the seventeenth year of Uzziah, since Jeroboam II. died in the fifteenth year of that king's reign. Probably it was some years before Jeroboam's death that Amos was called to witness against the iniquity of Israel. The earthquake here mentioned made a lasting impression. It was remembered by Zechariah three hundred years afterward, Zech. xiv, 5. It is singular that the sole account of it should be found in the prophetic books; the historical having no trace of it. Josephus mentions it, and says it occurred at the time Uzziah was smitten with leprosy, 2 Chron. xxvi, 16-21. The king was bent on offering incense on the golden altar. The high priest forbade him. The monarch, angered at the resistance, boldly set forward toward the holy place, when lo!

the ground began to rock beneath his feet; the temple swayed back and forth as a leaf shaken in the wind; the Mount of Olives shook and reeled; the earth cleft asunder; and the dreadful leprosy mounted to the king's forehead.

1. The design of the book is quite apparent. The main object is to witness against the idolatry of Israel, against its concomitant evils, effeminacy, dissoluteness, and immoralities of every kind. His ministry was confined to the Northern Kingdom. Judah is mentioned, indeed, as an object of judgment, as also other nations, but only incidentally. Amos appeared on the hills of Samaria to denounce the nobles for their luxuriousness and despotism, iv, 1; at Bethel's sanctuary to predict the fall of the altar, and of the royal house and of the kingdom, iii, 14, 15; v, 4-6. It was this prophet who uttered that solemn, piercing cry which was addressed to the royal family and the ten tribes, "Prepare to meet thy God, O Israel," iv, 12.

2. The contents of the book may be arranged under three divisions: I. Burden of the nations, i, ii. II. Three addresses to Israel, iii-vi. III. A series of five visions, with explanations, warnings and promises, vii-ix.

(1) Burden of the nations, chaps. i, ii. They are those which were contiguous to Israel. He specifies the sins of each as it comes in review before him. The storm passses without pausing in its course, sweeping on irresistibly over Syria, Philistia, Tyre, Edom, Ammon, Moab, Judah; then stops to pour out its fullest woes on Israel. Here it rests, and gathers blackness, and thunders long and loud. There may be, as has been thought, an object in the

prophet's thus arraigning one nation after another before he begins to deal with the Northern Kingdom. Thus would he secure a hearing, win attention, and so gain a more favorable hearing for the awful tidings he had to deliver in the name of Jehovah. Like Paul, Amos would catch them with guile, 2 Cor. xii, 16.

(2) The three addresses to Israel follow, iii-vi. In the first address the prophet reminds the people of their obligations to the Lord; charges on their conscience their transgressions, and warns them of the penalty, chap. iii. The fact of their being God's people, redeemed out of Egypt, and chosen before all others, instead of being a palliation of their sin, was rather its aggravation, and would be the ground of more strict reckoning with them, vss. 1, 2. God hath revealed to His prophet what is soon to come to pass: An enemy shall press Israel on every side, invade the whole land, and a mere wreck and fragment of the nation will be left, no more than a courageous shepherd snatches from the jaws of a lion—the two shank-bones and a bit of ear, vss. 11, 12. The allusion, no doubt, is to Assyria.

The second address, chap. iv, is taken up with reproofs for prevailing sins, and with the chastisements with which they have already been visited. Oppression of the poor and weak, intemperance, wantonness, unauthorized worship at Bethel and Gilgal—these sins are charged upon them, and are shown to be the primal cause of the drought, famine and pestilence which they had suffered. But all these divine visitations were only harbingers and heralds of far worse woes to come. Since chastisement and paternal discipline fail to attain their object, exterminating judgments are on the way. Therefore, "Prepare to meet thy God, O Israel."

The third address, chaps. v, vi, contains a call to repentance, and predicts the overthrow of the kingdom and the subsequent captivity. With lamentations and profound grief the fall of the virgin daughter of Israel is announced. The helpless wail of the miserable people, the summons of professional mourners, the shouts of the conquerors and the cries of the vanquished, all is set before guilty Israel with unfaltering fidelity. Yet the Lord, the prophet tells them, is pitiful; His voice is lifted in mercy and entreaty: "Seek the Lord and ye shall live." Nevertheless, he warns them in the name of Jehovah, the great and dreadful God, that no mere outward service of feasts and offerings will avail to arrest the approaching doom. The reform that will serve to avert the judgments, must be one that is genuine, spiritual, and deep; one that affects the heart and conduct alike; one that will be a thorough conversion from sin to holiness, and from the service of idols to that of the living God.

(3) The visions, and denunciations of judgments which are connected with them, occupy the remaining chapters of the book, vii-ix. The first is a vision of locusts devouring the land. The second is a vision of fire, all-devouring. The third is a vision of the Lord with a plumb-line in His hand measuring a wall to cast it down. At the close of each of the first two visions Amos intercedes for Israel who of course is aimed at in all, and his intercession is heard and the threatening turned away for the time. But afterward there is no further intercession, and it is intimated to the prophet that God will cease to hear

any plea for them, their doom is sealed, vii, 8; viii, 2.

The three visions mentioned above are thought to symbolize three successive invasions of the land, each increasing over the preceding in severity. The first was that of Pul, king of Assyria, who exacted one thousand talents of silver from king Menahem, and retired, probably in consequence of Amos' intercession, 2 Kings xv, 19-21. The second invasion was that of Tiglath-pileser of Assyria, who took possession of the east and north of the territory of Israel, and carried many of the inhabitants into captivity, 2 Kings xvi, cf. 2 Kings xv, 29. Doubtless the judgment was again staid at the instance of Amos' prayer. The third was that of Shalmaneser who put an end to the kingdom of the ten tribes, and removed the people to Assyria, 2 Kings xvii. In connection with the third vision distinct reference is made to the sacrificial heights and shrines of Israel, as if to draw attention to the fact that the reason of the judgment is traced to the idolatry and other guilty practices of the people. Amaziah, the priest of Bethel, incensed against the repeated denunciations of this prophet of God, and perhaps also conscience smitten, brought against him before king Jeroboam the charge of treason, and openly sought to have him silenced, at the same time quietly advising him to flee to Judah, vii, 10-17. Amos' reply is a prediction against the priest and his family. We nowhere find in the historical books its fulfillment. None who observe how briefly the story of Israel's fall and Samaria's three years' siege is told in 2 Kings xvii will be surprised at the silence of Scripture about Amaziah. There much is said of the people's sins, nothing of their sufferings.

The fourth is a vision of ripe fruit, chap. viii. The basket of summer fruit which the prophet saw represented the guilty nation now ripe for judgment. Long time they had gone on in transgression, heedless of every warning, deaf to every entreaty. And the Lord, merciful and gracious, with whom judgment is His strange work, had suspended the penalty they had incurred. Now at length the cup of iniquity was full; punishment could no longer be delayed; and the Lord said, "The end is come upon my people of Israel; I will not again pass them by any more."

The fifth is a vision of the Lord standing beside, or upon the altar, commanding to smite, chap. ix. It is disputed what altar is meant—that of Bethel or that at Jerusalem. If we confront chap. iii, 14 with ix, 1, we will be helped to some right understanding of the point. But it is not very material to the apprehending of the prophecy which is meant. The altar itself is of subordinate importance. The prime thought is that Jehovah Himself is directing the judgment in such a manner that Israel shall in no wise escape. He is its executioner.

The book closes with a magnificent promise of resurrection and glory for the fallen tent of the house of David, ix, 11-12; and of the prosperity that shall attend it, vss. 13-15. It is quoted in Acts xv, 15-17 by James, and applied to the ingathering of Gentile believers into the Church, but an ingathering which is to be followed by divine favor shown to the house of David, and to the outcasts of Israel. The promise looks on to the period when the purposes of God touching both Jews and Gentiles shall be made good in the realization of universal blessing.

OBADIAH.

The name of Obadiah which stands at the head of this the shortest book of the Bible, is as common among the Jews, it is said, as Abdallah among the Arabs. Both mean the same thing. Obadiah signifies "worshipper, or servant of Jehovah." Four of the prophets are known to us only by name. Obadiah is one of them; the others are, Habakkuk, Haggai and Malachi. Of the first, as indeed of the other three, we have the briefest possible account, viz., that his name was Obadiah; there the record ends. Abarbanel alleges that he was a converted Idumean, and adds, it is an instance of "the hatchet returning (according to the Hebrew proverb) into the wood of which it was taken;" but this account is destitute of foundation. Jerome held with the Jews that he was the same person as the Obadiah who was governor of Ahab's house, and who hid and fed one hundred prophets whom Jezebel sought to slay with the other servants of God she murdered, 1 Kings xviii. If so, then he is the oldest prophet whose writings have come down to us, and must have lived some nine centuries before Christ. It is much more likely that he prophesied about the time of the capture of Jerusalem by Nebuchadnezzar, and that he was contemporary with Jeremiah, or immediately preceded that prophet.

It will be observed that there is a striking similarity between these two prophets, and that their predictions against Edom are closely akin, cf. Jer. xlix, 7-22, and Obadiah. Some dispute there is as to which copied from the other, or whether both copied from an earlier prediction. From internal evidence it is now believed by many that Obadiah is the original and that of Jeremiah is somewhat later; but whether the latter used the former or not cannot be determined, for there is difference enough to entitle us to the belief that neither saw or used the writing of the other.

Obadiah's design is to predict the overthrow of Edom. The Idumeans were the neighbors of the Jews, and their kinsmen, being the descendants of Esau, the brother of Jacob. But as they did not show any concern for the misfortunes of Israel, as they rather rejoiced thereat, the cordiality which might have been expected to exist between them gave place to intense and bitter hatred. The Edomites, according to Obadiah, are types of those who ought to be friends and are not, who ought to be helpers in the day of calamity, but who are found on the other side. The prophet touches on their pride and self-confidence, vs. 3; then denounces their violence against their brother Jacob in the day of his trouble, vss. 10-14. In the remainder of the verses he utters the most terrific predictions as to the final and complete destruction of Edom. The certainty of the future triumphs of Zion and the enlargement of Israel's borders is announced. Obadiah sees the house of Jacob and the house of Joseph, probably denoting all Israel, dispossessing Edom and occupying their land. Partially and typically the prophecy has been fulfilled, but no doubt it awaits a more complete accomplishment, when God will set His hand to recover His people, and make good to them the promises to the fathers.

The book of Obadiah is a favorite study of modern Jews. In it they read the future of their own people and of Christendom; for they hold that by Edomites are meant Christians who have treated them much as old Edom did their ancestors, and by Edom is specially meant Rome. Kimchi says, "All that the prophets have said about Edom and its destruction in the last times has reference to Rome."

The fifteenth verse of Obadiah is significant: "For the day of the Lord is near upon all the heathen; as thou hast done, it shall be done unto thee: thy reward shall return upon thine own head." It is *lex talionis*, the law of retaliation. Back on those who do evil against their fellows rebounds the like injury. A notable instance of it is seen in Judges viii, 18, 19, and i, 5, where we read of the cruelty of Adonibezek which returned on himself—"as I have done, so God hath requited me." Iniquity always recoils. Into the pit, the wicked dig for others, sooner or later they fall. The reprisals of sin are frightful.

JONAH.

The book of Jonah is unlike any other of the minor prophets or any other of the Bible. In its style and contents it is strictly a historical narrative. It is not so much an oracle or prediction as a type. The interest centers not so much in the message of the prophet as in the prophet himself. More than any other book of the Bible it has been assailed, ridiculed, tortured and wrested from its simple, straightforward record of facts, and pronounced a fiction, an allegory, a parable, or a vision. It needs scarcely to be said that the testimony of our Lord Jesus Christ forever settles the question of its authenticity and genuineness for every Christian.

1. Jonah was a native of Gath-hepher, a town of Lower Galilee, 2 Kings xiv, 25. He was of the tribe of Zebulon, and a subject of the Northern Kingdom. From the passage of 2 Kings xiv, 23-25, we learn that Jonah lived and testified during some portion of the reign of Jeroboam II., which, according to Neteler, extended from 789 to 749 B. C. But according to Horne, Angus, Usher, and others, his reign antedates this by some fifty years. Somewhere between B. C. 850-750 Jonah flourished, probably nearer the former than the latter date. More than eight centuries before the advent of the Savior he lived and prophesied and passed through his marvelous experience. He was a

child when Homer, old and blind, was singing his rhapsodies on the shores of the Aegean sea; a contemporary with Lycurgus the Spartan legislator; a hundred years older than Romulus, and four hundred years older than Herodotus the historian. Nothing of his early life, parentage (save that he was the son of Amittai) or personal history, except what is found in his book, is given us. Like Elijah the Tishbite, Amos of Tekoa, John the Baptist, he is abruptly introduced into the pages of revelation. God gathers out of the lives of His servants that which suits His purposes, and is precious in His sight, and records it in His book; over all the rest He draws His pen.

2. The book contains two well defined parts, viz. I. The historical narrative. II. The typical teaching of the narrative. Let us note some of the features of the history. (1) Jonah's mission. It was to denounce the wrath of God against the wicked city of Nineveh, i, 1, 2; iii, 1-3. The call of God took him out of his own land and beyond the sphere of the prophetic testimony as generally rendered. To the capital of Assyria he was sent. The reason for such an extraordinary mission of a Jew was, that the place was given over to sin, that its wickedness proceeded largely from ignorance, and that there was a multitude of persons, particularly children, who were not responsible for the state of the city, iv, 11, cf. i, 2. That Nineveh was as large and as densely populated as the book indicates is attested by trustworthy witnesses. Diodorus Siculus says it was sixty miles in circuit; Herodotus somewhat less. This would correspond to the statement that it was "three days' journey" in extent. Perhaps the view entertained

by many is well grounded, viz., that Nineveh consisted of a group or aggregation of cities, separated from one another by parks, gardens, walls and fortifications. If we take the parallelogram in Central Assyria covered with remains of buildings we shall have an extent equal to all that is affirmed as to its magnitude. Koyunjik is about eighteen miles from Nimroud; Khorsabad about the same from Karamless; Khorsabad about fourteen from Koyunjik; and Karamless about the same from Nimroud; so that the entire circuit would be about sixty miles. Jonah (iv, 11) mentions the children who were unable to discern between their right and left hands as 120,000, which would give the whole population as somewhere between 700,000 and 1,000,000. To this city, with its teeming population, its imposing temples and stupendous palaces, its idolatry and wickedness, Jonah was sent. (2) His flight, i, 15. The mission was very distasteful to the prophet; so much so that he determined not to obey the divine command; and he "rose up to flee to Tarshish, from the presence of the Lord." Of course it is not to be imagined that Jonah was ignorant of the divine omnipresence, for David had already set forth this truth in sublime language in Ps. cxxxix, 7-9. He fled that he might get away from his duty as Jehovah's prophet, cf. Ex. iii, iv.

No doubt a variety of motives combined to prompt a course at once wicked and foolish. Fear for his personal safety may have had something to do with his flight. The Assyrians were already recognized as the enemies of Israel and were feared as the most dangerous of their foes. How could Jonah go to that hostile race and preach to them?

The chief motive is given us by the prophet himself, chap. iv, 2: "I pray thee, O Lord, was not this my saying when I was yet in my country? Therefore I fled unto Tarshish; for I knew that thou art a gracious God, and merciful, slow to anger, and of great kindness, and repentest thee of the evil." Jonah thus seems to prefer judgment to mercy, fire to consume the Ninevites, rather than grace to lead them to repentance and forgiveness. Perhaps, likewise, he thought of the dishonor that might come to the Lord if He appeared to be changeful and inconsistent; perhaps, too, of the charge that might be laid against himself as a false prophet, who predicted an overthrow which never took place. Poor man! Yet not unlike the majority of God's servants in every age. How weak, pusillanimous, peevish and cowardly the most of them are. His flight was to Tarshish, either Tarassus in Spain or the Tarshish near Cilicia, a seaport of considerable commercial importance. Providence seemed actually to favor his disobedience; but facilities for doing wrong are not to be construed as indications of divine permission. If we flee from duty and go to the west when we are bidden go to the east, it will be found at length that the very easiness of the road only leads into more mischief and the terrors of death. "Jonah took his measures, but God took His also. He let the willful man have his way to a certain point, till quite committed to his folly; then He began to work and to restore His servant by terrible things in righteousness." A storm suddenly arose, and the ship was in great peril. The seamen threw the cargo overboard to lighten the laboring vessel. They rowed hard to bring her to the land. But all in vain. The angry sea grew more furious, and the helpless prophet, well knowing the cause of all suggested the only expedient to secure the safety of the ship. The hands of the sailors cast him forth. Jonah went down out of sight into the abyss, and the sea was calm.

(2) Jonah's miraculous preservation, i, 17; ii, 1-10. It is a marvelous account, but in no degree absurd or incredible. It is quite fashionable to sneer at it, and treat it as a fable, a myth, too gross and monstrous to be for a moment believed. Even some professing Christians smile incredulously when "Jonah and the whale" are mentioned: they cannot well conceal their contempt for the story. The early Christians believed it, for they painted the prophet and the fish in the rough frescoes they made in the catacombs at Rome. Our Lord Jesus Christ believed it, and has set the seal of His almighty approbation and confirmation on it once and again, Matt. xii, 39-41; xvi, 4; Luke xi, 29, 30, 32. Christ declares that Jonah was a type of His own death and resurrection, that as the prophet was a "sign" to Nineveh, so was He a "sign" to the people of Israel. The Lord prepared, or appointed (lxx), a fish which swallowed down the recreant prophet. It is not said He created it at the moment; He ordained that it should be in readiness to receive Jonah into its capacious maw. In Matthew the word is translated "whale;" but more properly, it was a sea-monster, as the revision has it in the margin, that is meant. In all likelihood, it was a species of shark (*pesce-cane*, the dog fish, Italian sailors call it), which is common in the Mediterranean, which has an enormous throat, and which sometimes attains a length of twenty-five feet or more, with space in its bulk ample enough to con-

tain the prophet's body. The miraculous element lies, not in his being swallowed alive, but in his being kept alive in his moving grave for three days. Great, indeed, too great for mere nature, but not too great for Him who is above nature, the Almighty.

(3) His preaching and its results, chap. iii. Jonah's message was appalling; his one piercing cry from street to street was, "Yet forty days, and Nineveh shall be overthrown." The probation was short, narrowed into one month and ten days. God sometimes speaks to a nation or to an individual but once. If His voice is not then heard, it is heard no more except in the thundertones of judgment. The results were wonderful. Nineveh heard and repented. One sermon did the work; one trumpet blast shook the city out of its sin and carnal security. The repentance was immediate, profound, universal and acceptable. Noah preached one hundred and twenty years in vain; two angels visited Sodom and announced its doom, in vain; three years Jesus with solemn voice cried to Israel, " Repent," but few heeded the call. Under one sermon by one prophet a vast heathen city repented in ashes and sackcloth. King and noble, with diadem and spangle laid by, down in the dust with the meanest subject and slave, the dumb brutes sharing the universal humiliation. It was a world spectacle worth seeing.

(4) What explanation are we to give as regards the remarkable success of Jonah's mission? It certainly seems strange and unusual that such an effect should follow the preaching of a solitary and unknown man. What credentials had he to show? What proofs that his message was from God? He wrought no miracle to attest his authority or the

truthfulness of his message. His own bare word as against the voice of a million was all he had. Yes, he had more. Though he wrought no miracle himself, a stupendous sign had been wrought in his own person. He was like a dead and risen man, and he came to the Ninevites as a messenger from the unseen world. The sailors had doubtless spread abroad the report of the storm, and how the sea had become calm. The people of Nineveh heard and believed the report; and when Jonah appeared in their streets, they virtually said: "Behold, here is the man who was entombed in the sea monster for three days and nights. He has been in the very region of death and of Hades; behold him. And he has returned to earth and to us with this frightful message." Hence their repentance.

3. Turn we now to the prophetic or typical features of the book. It is here that Jonah differs widely from all the other prophetical books of Scripture, viz., not the *prophecy*, but the *prophet*, is the main subject. There is nothing in the book that speaks of the future. The testimony Jonah rendered Nineveh was a present testimony, designed for the generation that then lived. Manifestly, the great aim of it is to present the prophet himself as a prediction or type of Christ. It is to this feature our Lord refers in the passages above cited; this it is which gives the book its supreme value, and makes it the book for all time. Some of the features of his typical character may be pointed out:

(1) Jonah in the body of the great fish was a type of Christ under the power of death. The prophet while in his strange sepulchre made use of certain Psalms with which no doubt he was familiar, and

which expressed exactly his experience and dark forebodings. He quotes more or less literally Ps. xviii, 4-6 (cf. ii, 2, 3, 4, 5, 7); Ps. xxxi, 6, 7, 22 (cf. ii, 4, 8); Ps. xlii, 7 (cf. ii, 3); etc. But there are allusions in the prayer of Jonah to the great Messianic Psalms, Ps. xxii; lxix; xvi. Some of the words our Lord employed to express His feelings when death was fast closing in upon Him were used also by Jonah, for he, too, seemed to be sinking into the depths of sheol and passing into the realm of the unseen world; the rivers of the ocean whirled him round in their vast eddies; the rocky roots of the mountains seemed closing in the gates of the world against his return; "the billows and waves" of God passed over him. A striking picture of what Jesus endured, Ps. lxix, 1, 2. Jonah calls the belly of the fish "the belly of hell," or sheol. To this entombment Jesus refers in Matt. xii, 39, 40; and He translates it, "the heart of the earth." Herein is Jonah a sign; as he was three days and nights in the fish, so Jesus was to be three days and nights in the heart of the earth—under the power of death. The sign had its fulfillment in those awful days when the body of the Son of God lay in Joseph's tomb, and His human soul entered the world of disembodied spirits.

(2) He is a type of Christ's resurrection. At the bidding of the Lord, the fish vomited out upon dry land the prophet alive. Jonah spake to the Lord; the Lord spake to the obedient fish. After God had spoken it was impossible he should longer be held in his prison. In ii, 6, Jonah says, "The earth with her bars was about me forever: yet hast thou brought up my life from corruption (or the pit), O Lord my God." It is almost the identical language of Ps.

xvi, 10; "For thou wilt not leave my soul in hell (sheol); neither wilt thou suffer thy Holy One to see corruption." Peter quotes the words, applying them to the resurrection of Christ, saying, "Whom God raised up, having loosed the pains of death; because it was impossible that he should be holden of it," Acts ii, 22-27. Matchless "sign," indeed, was this of the prophet Jonah. On the horizon of the Old Testament there always blazed this sign of the death and resurrection of the Lord Jesus—the sign of the prophet Jonah.

(3) The prophet was also a type after his recovery from the sea. It was after his figurative death and resurrection that Jonah was sent to the Gentiles. It is evident from 2 Kings xiv, 25 that Jonah prophesied in Israel and to Israel. But he is sent away from the chosen people to proclaim the word of the Lord to a great heathen city. God turned away from Israel to show mercy to the Gentiles. Now this was the sign which the Lord Jesus put before the Pharisees. Such was the moral state of the people that He would be rejected by them and be put to death. But raised from the dead, He would go forth in the power of resurrection life to proclaim salvation to the Gentiles. In obedience to His command the disciples went everywhere preaching repentance and remission of sins in His name. Thus, the Greater than Jonah was a sign to the Jews of His day, a Savior to every one who believes.

MICAH.

Micah was a native of Moresheth-gath, i, 14, hence he is called the Morasthite, i, 1. His name signifies "who is like Jehovah." Of course he is not to be confounded with Micaiah the son of Imlah who prophesied in the reign of Ahab (1 Kings xxii), for he was subsequent to him by more than a hundred years.

The time of his prophecy is stated in the first verse to be "in the days of Jotham, Ahaz, and Hezekiah, kings of Judah." The period of time during which these kings reigned was about sixty years. It is computed that Jotham reigned B. C. 758-742; Ahaz, B. C. 742-727; Hezekiah, B. C. 727-698. Micah's official service may have embraced fifty years, which is certainly not an extravagant estimate.

The design of the prophecy is stated in i, 1. "The word of the Lord which came to Micah . . . . concerning Samaria and Jerusalem." The sin and shame of both the Northern and Southern Kingdoms are exposed by the prophet, but the burden of his message is intended for Judah. The prophecy, however, is not confined to Israel. All nations are addressed likewise; the earth and its inhabitants. Like Hosea, like Amos, Micah enters into the moral condition of the people and connects their afflictions with their unfaithfulness. Judgment, the theme of so many prophets, is prominent in Micah, sin prevailing and inveterate, makes it a necessity. But grace also flows. The advent of the Messiah and the blessing of the people under His peaceful reign the prophet announces in glowing terms.

The book consists of seven chapters. But after the first verse which is the title and preface, it falls into three parts, each of which is introduced by the almost military challenge, or legal summons: "Hear ye." These three parts are the following: I. Chaps i, ii. II. Chaps. iii-v. III. Chaps. vi, vii.

1. The first division (i, ii) begins with a summons to all nations to hear God's testimony. The Almighty is coming forth out of His place on high to take His stand on the high places of the earth to witness against Samaria and to declare its doom. Nor shall Judah escape. The evil which shall overwhelm Samaria shall reach the gate of Jerusalem, for the sin of the former has come to Zion by way of Lachish, the near medium of the guilty communication. The prophet wails over the kingdoms as if the threatenings were already accomplished. He will strip himself and go naked, will roll himself in the dust, will utter shrieks and lamentations "like the long piteous cry of the jackal, like the fearful screech of the ostrich." His own immediate neighborhood in the maritime plains of Judah shall not escape; village after village shall be given to destruction. The moral evils that defiled the land and invoked the calamities are most graphically described. Idolatry, oppression of the weak by the strong, covetousness, and drunkenness are some of the sins for which the people are arraigned before the

great Judge. It was a time of weak government, and so of misrule and oppression. Through the reign of the wicked Ahaz, Micah lived, and we may well believe from what is told us of that apostate prince, that every species of vice flourished with rank exuberance. In the prophet's own striking imagery, it was a time when men did "evil with both hands earnestly," (vii, 3.) But like so many other prophets before and after him, Micah became the champion of the oppressed and the weak, and their stern and unfaltering advocate in the presence of an insolent and powerful oppressor.

2. The second division (iii-v) opens with a fierce denunciation of the nobles for the crimes of which they were guilty, iii, 1-4. With bitter satire the prophet describes the princes eating the poor and stripping the flesh from their bones as if in a cannibal feast; and foretells the cry of anguish with which they shall appeal to God in the day of their sore trouble, but He will not hear them. Next, he denounces the unholy alliance between the traitor prophets and mercenary priests and corrupt judges of Israel who prophesy for gain, and administer justice for reward, and teach for hire. By these combined parties Zion is built up with blood, and Jerusalem with iniquity, and Micah, filled with power by the Spirit of the Lord declares unto Jacob his transgression, and to Israel his sin. In iii, 12, he foretells the ruin of Jerusalem and the desolation of Zion. This prediction saved the life of Jeremiah, who would have been put to death for foretelling the destruction of the temple had it not appeared that Micah had foretold the same thing above a hundred years before, (Jer. xxvi, 18, 19).

With chap. iv, a notable change occurs in the current of the prophecy. The iniquities of the people and the punishment which these provoke give place to a magnificent vision of the establishment of Messiah's kingdom and the blessedness and glory that shall be connected with it. Verses 1-3 are with slight variation the same as Isa. ii, 2-4. In the judgment of many able and trustworthy interpreters the priority belongs to Micah; he is the original, and Isaiah probably copied from him. God's kingdom is to be exalted into an eminence in the world where it will have neither a rival nor a peer. Its sway shall be universal; its duration unending, its rule benignant and peaceful. War shall cease forever, wasting and desolation be known no more.

Chapter v contains a deeply interesting prediction of Messiah's birth (vs. 2). It was on this verse the scribes and priests laid their hands when Herod submitted to them the question as to Messiah's birth place. We learn from the whole passage that He is eternal (vs. 2). His appearing at Bethlehem was not His first; it was only one of many "goings forth." He will gather Israel at length into permanent occupancy of the land, and introduce them into new life and fellowship (vs. 3). His rule shall be over the whole world (vs. 4). He shall defend and deliver the people and exalt them over their adversaries (vss. 5-9). And He shall destroy all instruments of war, and remove every vestige of idolatry from the land, and punish the heathen for their sin (vss. 10-15).

3. The third division (vi, vii) exhibits the reasonableness, justice and purity of the divine requirements in contrast with the ingratitude, injustice and

superstition of the people, which caused their ruin.

Chapter vi begins with a most impressive scene, viz., the "controversy" which God had with the people. The mountains and hills are cited to hear the charges of the parties to the controversy—God and Israel. And in the presence of these stately, silent witnesses the people are asked to testify against their Deliverer and Creator, to show wherein He hath done them wrong or wearied them. At the same time He reminds them of the mercy and the goodness He hath showed them (vi, 1-5). What a revelation is this of the divine love and patience and also of the obduracy and ingratitude of the human heart. Then the prophet puts into the mouth of an inquirer the questions asked in vss. 6, 7. These are not to be taken as the words of Balaam, but of one who is anxious about his state before God, but uninstructed in the way of righteousness. Human sacrifice is certainly meant in the phrase "firstborn," "fruit of my body." The horrible rite was practised to some extent in the reign of Ahaz, 2 Kings xvi, 3; xvii, 17. No doubt the allusion is to the sacrifice of children to the brutal Moloch, the fire-god of the Ammonites. How much a man will do and suffer if thereby he can feel he has satisfied God as touching himself. Contrast with this costly outlay, the supreme devotion even to the slaughter of one's own child to obtain salvation, with the simplicity and freeness of the gift of eternal life in Jesus Christ. Why will men attempt the impossible, and refuse the gift? The answer to the inquiries is in vs. 8; and the assurance that the wise man will learn the way in vs. 9. In vss. 10-16 the prophet lays before them, in detail, the universal wickedness that reigned among them, and declares that judgment must surely come upon them.

In chapter vii, the prophet laments over the moral condition of his people (vss. 1-6), then intercedes in their behalf with God speaking in their name, and identifying Himself with them (vss. 7-10).

The prophecy closes with the assurance that God will make good to His people every promise and prediction, that He will pardon their iniquities and bury their sins in the depths of the sea. In spite of their rebellion He will never forget them in His matchless love, and in His faithfulness He will not forsake them forever.

We may summarize the predictions of Micah thus: (1) The fall of Samaria and the dispersion of Israel, i, 6-8, 9-16; v, 7, 8. (2) The cessation of prophecy, iii, 6, 7. (3) Destruction of Jerusalem, iii, 12. (4) Deliverance of Israel, iv, 10; v, 8. (5) Messiah's birth place, v, 2. (6) God's kingdom established over the whole world, iv, 1-7.

NAHUM.

Of the author of this prophecy we have no more knowledge than is afforded us by the scanty title, which leaves both his nativity and his age uncertain. He is called the Elkoshite, i, 1. But where Elkosh was situated is a disputed point. Jerome records that it was a village in Galilee, and says that its ruins were shown him as he traveled through that country. But Jerome lived nearly one thousand years after Nahum. Others locate it in Assyria where his tomb was declared to be. The internal evidences favor Palestine rather than Assyria as the scene of the prophet's ministry (i, 4, 5). Henderson is of opinion that Capernaum, which he translates "the village of Nahum," may have been the home of the prophet. But no certainty as to his birth place can be had. The date of the book can be determined with as little precision. Some think he was contemporary with Habakkuk, others with Manasseh, but the majority that he prophesied during the reign of Hezekiah. Horne assigns it to 720-698 B. C.; Knoble 713-711 B. C. Others bring it down to a later time, B. C. 700-636. But in all cases the book is placed at a time prior to the fulfillment of the event it predicts. Nineveh was destroyed B. C. 606 or 612. The probability is that the "vision" was seen by Nahum one hundred years before the event took place.

The subject of the prophecy is announced in the superscription, i, 1: "The burden of Nineveh." Organic unity is maintained throughout, the three chapters into which the book is divided form a consecutive whole. The style is elevated and graphic, its imagery majestic and bold, and its tone solemn and terrible in the highest degree. The entire prophecy is aimed against Ninevch, the metropolis of Assyria. It sounds the death-knell of the proud, luxurious and wealthy city. It denounces God's heaviest judgments against the guilty place and predicts its final and complete overthrow and extinction. We note some of the causes that provoked the divine wrath against it.

1. Impenitence of the people. More than a hundred years before Nahum, Jonah preached to Nineveh, and the whole city gave itself up to repentance. From the sovereign on the throne to the humblest subject, all united in confession, humiliation, and earnest appeal to God for mercy. But great as was the result of Jonah's preaching at the time, it was not permanent. A brief period served to blot out the memory of the doom which that prophet announced, and which was averted by their contrition and humiliation. They turned again with redoubled zest to their old brutal customs. The repentance was not followed by any lasting amendment of life. Hence, as always happens in the like cases, their last end was worse than the first.

2. Assyrian pride. It was proverbial. The insolent message of Sennacherib to Hezekiah (2 Kings xviii, 13) was but a specimen of it. Nahum lived and prophesied, probably, at the time when the arrogance of Assyria reached its climax. God and His laws were despised, and the rights of men and nations trampled on by the haughty power.

3. Assyrian cruelty was also proverbial, iii, 1-3. Nineveh is called "the bloody city." In it the hiss of the whip and heavy sound of the scourge were constantly heard. Rarely did the Assyrians show mercy to the conquered and the captive. It was their custom to stamp out their foes, leaving no vestige of city or hamlet behind. In the excavations made at Nineveh the evidences of cruelty are abundant, cruelty of the most barbarous sort. A common method of torture was to flay their victims alive. Nahum represents their ferocity as that of the lion, ii, 11, 12.

4. Idolatry. It was of the most degrading kind, and as is always the case, witchcraft, sorcery, necromancy and demon worship were associated with it. There were found those strange, hideous composite figures which were the principal idols of Assyria, viz., the huge winged monsters which the antiquarians have exhumed and exhibited to the civilized world. The body of the idol is that of a bull or a lion, generally the former; the head and face are human; two immense wings are attached to the shoulders. They seem to have been designed to represent the divine principle by the various forms of animal life, beast, bird and man.

5. Oppression of God's people, Israel. While God used Assyria as His rod to punish the stubborn and rebellious ten tribes, He nevertheless held that power responsible for all its abuse of the ascendency He had permitted it to gain over His people. And Assyria, like Babylon and Persia in aftertimes, did exceed all just bounds in its dealings with its captives; therefore, judgment visited it in turn.

The destruction and utter desolation of Nineveh

is described by Nahum with magnificent eloquence, and with marvelous detail.

1. It was predicted that "with an overrunning flood he will make an utter end of the place," i, 8. The allusion is to an invading army, no doubt that of the Medes and Babylonians who attacked Nineveh and completely demolished it.

2. The Tigris was to assist in its overthrow, ii, 6. This was fulfilled. The ancient historian, Diodorus Siculus, mentions an old prophecy that Nineveh should not be taken until the river (Tigris) should become its enemy. He adds that when the assailants attacked it the river burst its banks and washed away the wall for twenty stadia.

3. It was to be destroyed partly by fire, iii, 13, 15. This, too, was literally fulfilled. In the excavations which have been made on the site it is discovered that one of the gates, and most of the buildings had been burnt.

4. The population was to be surprised when unprepared, "while they are drunk as drunkards they shall be devoured as stubble fully dry," i, 10. Diodorus states that the last and fatal assault was made when they were overcome with wine. In the remains that have been exhumed carousing scenes are represented, in which the king, his courtiers, and even the queen, reclining on couches or seated on thrones, and attended by musicians, appear to be pledging each other in bowls of wine.

5. It was to be despoiled of its idols, i, 14; and of its silver and gold, ii, 9. This prediction likewise was amply fulfilled. The images of Nineveh were swept away, either destroyed or carried off by the conquerors. Enormous amounts of gold and silver

were conveyed to Ecbatana by the victorious Medes. Very little of the precious metals have been found in the excavations of recent times. The city was spoiled of all its treasures.

6. The captivity of the inhabitants and their removal to distant provinces were announced, ii, 7; iii, 18. The place was depopulated and the proud city sank into a mass of ruins and rubbish.

7. It was to disappear and become a perpetual desolation, i, 14; iii, 19. For centuries its site has been an arid waste of yellow sand. Every trace of its existence disappeared for ages. Two hundred years after its capture Xenophon, in the retreat of the ten thousand, passed near it, saw the ruins, but knew not what they were, and did not so much as learn the name of Nineveh. Even "garrulous Herodotus," who visited the spot, had no more to say of it than this: "The Tigris was the river upon which Nineveh formerly stood." For centuries the only sound heard in its vicinity was the lonely cry of the jackal, and hoarse growl of the hyena. God had said by the mouth of His servant the prophet, "I will make thy grave." He did. Wide and deep He did dig it; low and deep He buried Nineveh, never more to rise again, save to be gazed at with curious eyes amid dim torchlight by the archæologist, whose pick and spade have confirmed the Lord's predictions.

HABAKKUK.

Habakkuk is one of the four prophets who are known to us only by name. Of his parentage or his nativity nothing whatever is told us. There are traditions concerning him but they are entitled to little or no credit. One is found in the apocryphal story of Bel and the Dragon, and is to the effect that an angel caught up Habakkuk by the hair of his head and carried him to Daniel while in the lion's den, whom he fed with the food he was conveying to his laborers in the field. It has been inferred from the inscription in iii, 19, that he was a Levite, but this also is very problematical.

As to the date of the book the authorities vary, as usual. But the discrepancy is not very great in this instance. Some place it in the reign of Josiah, B.C. 630; others in that of Jehoiakim, or the latter part of Josiah's rule, B. C. 612-598.

1. The subject of the prophecy is two-fold: First, the overthrow of Judah by the Chaldeans. Second, the overthrow, in turn, of the Chaldean monarchy—each power for its sins.

2. Characteristics of the book. It is distinguished for its magnificent poetry. Habakkuk is unsurpassed for the splendors of his style. Bold as Isaiah, he is his equal in sublimity; for pathos he is even more remarkable than Jeremiah; for loyalty he resembles David; and for confidence in God, Paul. The grandeur of his description of Almighty God in chapter three is unparalleled even in the

Bible itself. Nothing is more majestic, nothing more sublime and awful.

3. The contents may be divided into two parts: I. A dialogue concerning judgment for iniquity. This is the "burden." (1) The prophet's complaint, i, 2-4. (2) The Lord's reply, i, 5-11. (3) The prophet's appeal that the Holy One should not suffer His people to perish, i, 12; ii, 1. (4) The Lord's answer, with direction that it should be plainly written down for the guidance and consolation of the godly, ii, 2-20.

The Chaldeans are denounced (1) for rapacity, ii, 6-8; (2) for trust in unhallowed gain, ii, 9-11; (3) building cities and towns with the blood and treasure of strangers, ii, 12-14; (4) degrading and outraging the peoples whom they subdued, ii, 15-17; (5) confidence in idols, ii, 18-20.

II. The prayer-song of Habakkuk, chap. ii. It is called a prayer, like Ps. lxxxix, xc. etc., not merely because it begins with prayer, but because the whole ode is an expansion of the opening petition. It is likewise a song. If the word *selah*, which occurs in it three times, is to be understood as a musical term, then it follows that it was intended to be rendered musically on some occasion or in some place of which we have no information. The inscription at the close, "To the chief singer on my stringed instruments," appears to furnish some evidence in the same direction, (comp. Ps. iv, title).

The great sentence of the prophet, "But the just shall live by his faith," ii, 4, is quoted three times in the New Testament, Rom. i, 17; Gal. iii, 11; Heb. x, 38. Chap. ii, 3, seems to be referred to in Heb. x, 37.

ZEPHANIAH.

This prophet is remarkable for giving us his genealogy to the fourth generation—a rare occurrence with the prophets. In no other case does the record of lineage extend beyond the grandfather of the prophet, Zech. i, 1. Zephaniah wished to distinguish himself from others of the same name, but mainly to point out his relationship to the great monarch Hezekiah, for the Hizkiah of i, 1, the fourth in the prophet's line, is identical with that king. He was, therefore, of royal descent.

He prophesied during the reign of Josiah, i, 1. Tregelles dates B. C. 625-610; Angus somewhat earlier. The internal evidence evinces the fact that Nineveh was in a state of peace and prosperity, while the notices of Jerusalem touch upon the same tendencies to idolatry and crime which are condemned by Jeremiah.

1. The design of Zephaniah is two-fold: First, to announce God's judgment; second, to disclose the moral condition which necessitated it. As to the first, it is to be remarked that the revelation of judgment is very full and explicit. The prophet's name seems to indicate the character of his mission "the watchman of Jehovah." He is on the outlook for wrath and indignation to be poured out on the guilty and impenitent. This appears in the description of the great and terrible day of the Lord, i. This is

the prediction which formed the basis of the Latin hymn of the Middle Ages, the *Dies Irae*. The desolation of Israel is made the image of a far wider judgment still to come, viz., the judgment of the whole earth. The sins that provoke the judgment are idolatry, i, 4-6; oppression, rapacity, cruelty and treachery, iii, 1-5.

2. Contents. (1) Denunciation of judgment, i. (2) The nations that are its objects, Judah, Philistines, Moabites, Ammonites, Ethiopians and Assyrians, ii-iii, 1-6. (3) Prediction of future restoration and blessing for Israel, iii, 7-20.

3. The future according to Zephaniah. This brief prophecy is full of it, as are all the other prophets. After the frightful picture of wrath which he so vividly draws, he changes to a sweet and triumphant theme, a song of gladness and of victory in which the glory of Zion, favor to the Lord's people, God's delight in His redeemed, the holiness and devotedness of the restored Israel are set forth in rapturous strains. He closes with a vision of hope and joy and peace. And so Zephaniah is apocalyptic and telesmatic.

"The Lord thy God in the midst of thee is mighty; He will save, He will rejoice over thee with joy; He will rest in His love; He will joy over thee with singing," iii, 17.

Redeemer and Redeemed.
I. The Redeemer.
   1. He is mighty to save.
   2. He exults over His redeemed.
   3. He is silent in His love—finds no fault with them.
II. The Redeemed.

1. They are finally and forever delivered.
2. They are exalted.
3. They are forgiven.
4. They are made perfect.
5. They are happy for ever.

HAGGAI.

Haggai, Zechariah and Malachi are the post captivity prophets. They exercised their office after the return from the exile at Babylon. The great majority of the Old Testament prophets bore their testimony prior to that epoch-making event. Jeremiah's ministry extended into the period, but he was not an exile. Only two, Ezekiel and Daniel, prophesied during the captivity.

1. The three ministered to the restored remnant. The circumstances of the returned Jews made it needful for such beneficent work as these prophets could render. We learn from the books of Ezra and Nehemiah under what difficulties and obstructions the Jews labored in rebuilding the temple, and reorganizing the commonwealth and the services of Judaism. Opposition and discouragement beset them on every side. To every achievement they had to fight their way. They built the house of God and the city "in troublous times," in very truth. And these prophets, particularly Haggai and Zechariah were raised up to strengthen the heroic but feeble remnant.

2. The throne of God was not again set up at Jerusalem on the restoration of Judah. Power still remained with the Gentiles. The first great empire, Babylon, upon which God conferred supremacy, had proved itself unworthy of the mighty trust imposed

and had been set aside. Another, the Medo-Persian, had succeeded, and it was the governing power even over the Jews in their own land. They were never again independent. And the prophets served to instruct and to comfort them amid the trials incident to their subject life.

3. Their main effort was to maintain fidelity and obedience in the new position. As the center of faithfulness was the temple and the service connected with it, these prophets labored to keep the people attached to the place and its rites of worship and to all therein implied. As failure in the remnant became apparent the prophets turned away from the present and fixed their eyes on the advent of the Messiah whom they describe minutely and for whom they yearned with an intensity of desire that challenges our admiration, in whom they well knew there would be no failure.

Haggai prophesied in the sixth month of the second year of Darius the king, i, 1. It was probably Darius Hystaspes. His ministry covered a period of about four months, B. C. 520.

I. The design of his testimony was to encourage the restored captives in the arduous labors in which they were engaged. The decree of Cyrus (Ezra i) induced a large number of Jews to set out for the Holy Land, some 50,000 in all. But on the death of Cyrus the emigration ceased. Under the reign of some of his successors, particularly Cambyses and the Pseudo-Smerdis, the work on the temple and the city was suspended, nor was it resumed until the second year of Darius, Ezra iv, 24. The arrest of the good work of restoration and rebuilding was accomplished through the determined hostility of the adversaries of Judah and Benjamin, Ezra iv, 1-23. It was by means of the ministry of Haggai and Zechariah that it was recommenced, Ezra v.

II. The contents of Haggai. The prophecy consists of only two chapters, but it contains four addresses, each marked off from the other by clear lines of separation.

(1) The first address, with a notice of its effect, is found in chapter one. It was spoken to Zerubbabel and to the high priest Joshua. The former was a prince of the house of David, and the head of the government; the latter was at the head of the priesthood. Its object was to rouse these leaders and the people under them from the apathy into which they had sunk. Haggai sharply reproves them in that, while they lived in ceiled (paneled) houses, the house of the Lord was neglected. Their own were comfortable and well furnished, whilst the temple had only its foundation and bare walls with no protecting roof, with no pavement, door, furniture, altar, form or beauty. The address achieved its aim, as i, 12-15, Ezra v, vi, show.

(2) Chap. ii, 1-9: The design of the second address is to correct a tendency to discouragement and depreciation which had begun to appear. It is to the same officers and through them to the people. They were peculiarly disposed to discouragement. When the foundations were laid old persons who had seen the first temple wept at the contrast. After the first burst of enthusiasm in the work of rebuilding, there came, as almost always comes in human enterprises, the reaction, the time of flagging interest and waning energy. Haggai set himself to reanimate their drooping spirits and rekindle their

fainting ardor. In the latter part of this address, vss. 6, 7, the prophet grounds his appeal on the great fact that God will ere long shake heaven, earth, sea, and all nations—a passage quoted in Heb. xii, 26,27; and adds, " and the desire of all nations shall come," or " the things desired of all nations shall come." It is a difficult phrase, but in view of what is said of it Heb. xii, 25-29, it must in some way be connected with the kingdom of God and the Messiah.

(3) Chap. ii, 10-19. Instruction, reproof, appeal and promise.

(4) Chap. ii, 20-23. This last address was delivered on the same day as the preceding. It was spoken to Zerubbabel alone and was designed to stimulate that officer to zealous efforts in the good work undertaken. The prophet again refers to the supernatural shaking of earth and sky and kingdoms, but amid it all the prince shall be as a signet, firm and immovable, because chosen of the Lord. This can be no other than the day of the Lord, the day of the Prince Messiah.

ZECHARIAH.

This prophet was the son of Berechiah and grandson of Iddo, i, 1. In Ezra v, 1, he is called the son of Iddo. The word son, like brother, is often used in a wide sense, and here no doubt is equivalent to grandson. He was a priest as well as prophet. His name signifies "whom Jehovah remembers." He was contemporary with Haggai, and began his ministry in the second year of Darius Hystaspes, B. C. 520. How long he continued it is difficult to determine; but in the fourth year of Darius, Zechariah received a message from the Lord, vii, 1. Probably for five years he continued to prophesy.

1. Is this prophet to be identified with Zechariah the son of Barachiah mentioned by our Lord in Matt, xxiii, 23? The majority of expositors think not; but that the reference in Matthew is to the priest Zechariah, son of Jehoiada, who was slain at the temple, 2 Chron. xxiv, 20-22. There is no record of the death of the prophet; yet it should be borne in mind that the book of Chronicles does not extend to a date so late as his death. The Jewish Targum states, we are told, that Zechariah, the son of Iddo, prophet and priest, was slain in the sanctuary. Neh. xii, 4, identifies Iddo with the priests; Zech. i, 1, with the prophets. Josephus likewise says that Zechariah the son of Baruchus was slain at the temple. Baruchus is closely akin to Berechiah.

2. Is Matt. xxvii, 9, 10, quoted from Zechariah or Jeremiah? In the gospel it is ascribed to Jeremiah, but is so nearly identical with Zech. xi, 12, 13, that it was taken from the latter. Some think Matthew quoted from memory and wrote Jeremiah when he meant Zechariah—by no means a satisfactory explanation. Others, that the quotation was originally made from Zechariah and that Jeremiah's name was inserted by the oversight of some copyist. Still another explanation is, that Matthew quoted Jeremiah xviii, xix, which prophecy lies at the foundation of Zechariah's. As there is some variation in a few of the oldest versions of the New Testament, and also in the Greek copies, it is not unlikely that an error has crept into the text, e. g., Matthew either wrote "prophet," and the name Jeremiah was introduced into his text, or (if he used an abbreviation) he wrote *Zriou*, which might be easily mistaken for *Iriou*.

3. The book may be divided into two parts: Part I. Chaps. i-viii. The contents of this portion of the book may be distributed as follows: (1) Introduction, i, 1-6; a warning voice from the past. (2) A series of visions, some of which were soon to come to pass, while others lose themselves in the distant future, i, 7; vi, 8. The visions appear to be intended to strengthen the feeble Hebrew colony in Judea. The first is that of horses and riders in the valley of myrtles, i, 7-17, representing a time of peace, opportune for the building of the city and temple. The second is, the four horns and four carpenters, or artisans, i, 18-21. It symbolizes the comparative safety of Israel in the midst of the contending world-powers. If the horns are understood as the

emblem of the kingdoms which overthrew Israel, then their demolition by the smiths signifies their powerlessness toward the Jews. The third is that of the man with a measuring line, ii. The meaning seems evidently to be that Jerusalem should have a wider extent than ever before; it should be too large to be encompassed by walls—evidently, still future. The fourth relates to Joshua the high priest, clad in filthy garments, the angel and the adversary Satan, iii. Typical of the removal of the remnant's guilt and acceptance before God. The fifth is, the candlestick and the two olive trees, iv. All obstacles should be removed, and the chosen people at length shine in God's light, anointed with His Spirit. The sixth is the flying roll, v, 1-4. It is a solemn warning of the swift curse of God upon thieves and perjurers—the land should be purified. The seventh is the woman and the ephah, v, 5-11. It is wickedness personified; it should be caught, shut in a cage as a savage beast, and held in by a weight as of lead, and transported to the land of Shinar, i. e., Babylon. Two interpretations are given of this difficult vision: first, that it means idolatry and that the action signifies the removal of the abominable practice from Israel and the transfer of it to Babylon where it belonged. As a matter of history, it is well known that idolatry ceased in Israel with the return from the exile. Second, that it means the unbelieving and impenitent Jews who shall be thrust out of the land, and be identified with Babylon where they really belong. If the visions pertain to the times of Zechariah, then the first is preferable; if to the times of Jerusalem's destruction, then the latter is its meaning. The eighth vision is, the four chariots, vi, 1-8. It seems to refer to the time of the end, and is to be interpreted by the four horses and their riders of Rev. vi.

(3) Symbolic act, vi, 9-15. It is the crowning of the high priest Joshua. By this act the two great offices of priest and king are united in his person, type of the person and work of the man whose name is the Branch, vs. 12, and who shall sit on His throne of glory as a priest.

(4) Chaps. vii, viii, contain prophecies of later date than the preceding (vii, 1). They are partly didactic—obedience to God's word, justice, mercy, truth, a tender heart and sensitive conscience are more pleasing to Him than fasts and ceremonial observances. Partly, they are predictions of near and remote blessing: near, Jerusalem visited with divine favor; remote, many nations visiting the holy city and clinging to Israel and sharing in their blessings.

Part II. Chaps. ix-xiv. This section of the book does not bear the name of Zechariah, nor of any author, and much dispute has arisen as to its authenticity. That there is a difference of style traceable in these chapters is freely admitted, but that this difference is so great as to be accounted for only on the supposition of a difference of authorship is not admitted. The quotation in Matt. xxvii, 9, seems to favor the idea that the latter part of Zechariah was not written by him, but by an earlier one, viz., Jeremiah. So Joseph Mede thought, the first to call the integrity of this section in question. The all-sufficient reply is this, that the author of these chapters must have written at a later date than Jeremiah, for he refers not only to Joel, Amos and Isaiah, but also to Jeremiah, Ezekiel and Zephaniah. (See Zech.

ix, 2, and Ezek. xxviii, 3; Zech. ix, 5, and Zeph. ii, 4; Zech. xi, 4, and Ezek. xxxiv, 4; Zech. xi, 3, and Jer. xii, 5; Zech. xiv, 10, 11, and Jer. xxxi, 38-40, etc.). The proof seems overwhelming that these chapters were written after the exile, and although they are anonymous save as found in this book, yet the presumption is very decidedly in favor of the view that Zechariah was the author.

The second part of the book is divided into two sections, each of which begins with the expression, "The burden of the word of the Lord."

(1) Chaps. ix, x, xi, "The burden of Hadrach and Damascus." The name of the land of Hadrach is somewhat obscure, but that it is connected with Syria in some way can hardly be doubted. The Persian empire, or Gentileism in general, cannot be meant, as some have imagined. There is nothing to intimate that it is a symbolic name. Its association with Damascus and Hamath is fatal to that suggestion. The view of Canon Drake in the Bible Commentary is probably correct, that it signifies Syria "from the name of its king, Hadrach." Tyre and Sidon and Philistia share in the awful judgments threatened against the former places. The reference may be to the invasion of Alexander the Great, for these very countries were overwhelmed by his army. Yet it is promised that the house of the Lord, and by implication, Jerusalem, shall be preserved by the intervention of God Himself, ix, 8. From ix, 9, to the close of xi, we have a series of predictions, some of which relate to the appearing and rejection of Messiah, the destruction of Jerusalem, and the powerlessness and ignorance of the Jewish rulers, and the final establishment and glory

of the kingdom of God and some of them to the distant time when Jerusalem shall be encompassed with armies for the last time, and when a mighty deliverance shall be wrought for the chosen people, such as never was experienced before.

(2) Chaps. xii-xiv. "The burden of Israel." The old comprehensive name *Israel* returns, and the entire twelve tribes appear in the predictions in this section. Judgment, repentance, forgiveness and cleansing are all secured to Israel through the gracious work of Messiah. It is of Israel's restoration, redemption and re-establishment as God's center for earthly and universal blessing of which these chapters treat. The last chapter introduces the universal peace and blessing and glory by the personal return of the Messiah, Jesus Christ.

4. Messianic predictions. Zechariah is remarkable for the fullness with which he treats this great subject. He is but too well aware that the people who had returned from captivity were not maintaining fidelity toward God. Declensions and apostasy were but too manifest among them. Even Ezra and Nehemiah recognize the fact that only a remnant exhibit any genuine faithfulness. But in Haggai, Zechariah and Malachi it becomes quite manifest that "all were not Israel who were of Israel." It is in but a few that they find the true spirit and character of the people of God; and ere the voice of prophecy is hushed, Malachi distinguished in the most solemn way between the godly remnant and the mass of the nation, whether people or priests. Accordingly, these prophets, and more especially the last two of the Old Testament, turn away from any further hope in the restored captives, and gaze

with eager joy and swelling hope on the coming of the Messiah in whom every promise and prophecy will be made good.

Chap. iii, 8, 9. "For behold, I will bring forth my servant, the Branch. For behold, the stone that I have laid before Joshua; upon one stone shall be seven eyes," etc. That Christ is meant by the name Branch is evident from Isa. iv, 2; xi, 1; Jer. xxiii, 5, 6; Zech. vi, 12. By this title is denoted among other things the great fact that Messiah is to be identified with our race, and incorporated with our kind. He is to be born of a woman. He is to spring from the stock of Abraham, but especially from the root of Jesse, the family of David. He is, therefore, to be of royal lineage and princely descent. Moreover, He is Jehovah's Servant (cf. Isa. xlii, 1), one who perfectly fulfills the will of God, and the neglected duty of His people. And further, He is to be supremely intelligent—as Zechariah expresses it, He possesses seven eyes" (cf. Rev. v, 6). He is to have the power to know and to execute the will of God, as it has never been performed by man nor by all men.

Chap. iv, 12, 13. "Behold the man whose name is the Branch; and He shall grow up out of His place, and He shall build the temple of the Lord: even He shall build the temple of the Lord; and He shall bear the glory, and shall sit and rule upon His throne; and He shall be a priest upon His throne: and the counsel of peace shall be between them both." Messiah shall unite in His own person the priestly and the kingly dignities. The two characters, so long distinct in Israel, will be blended in Him. Nor will there be divergence or disagreement between them, or pre-eminence of the one over he other, as so often happened in the past. The regal office will not overshadow the sacerdotal, nor the sacerdotal the regal.

Chap. ix, 8. This great prediction was literally fulfilled when Jesus made His memorable entry into Jerusalem, John xii, 14, 15.

Chap. xi, 12, 13, contains the announcement of Messiah's betrayal and rejection, cf. Matt. xxvii, 3-10.

Chap. xii, 10-14, is the account of Israel's conversion, at least of the remnant, " in that day," which seems to mean the beginning of the day of the Lord. Their conversion is attributed to the Spirit of God, vs. 10. Their repentance is stated very distinctly to be universal, individual and profound, and its occasion is the sight of Him whom they had pierced, vss. 11-14.

Chap. xiii, 1. The sin of the nation thus bemoaned is washed away. The "fountain opened" denotes Messiah's death, and the application of the benefits of His death to the house of David and the inhabitants of Jerusalem.

Chap. xiii, 7. Messiah's death is in fulfillment of the will and plan of God for the redemption of His people.

Chap. xiv, records the tremendous crisis through which Israel is yet to pass, their sufferings from the nations which gather against Jerusalem "in that day," their ultimate deliverance by the direct and personal interposition of the Lord, and the cosmical revolutions, and the sway of the kingdom of God over the renewed earth. That this majestic prophecy cannot have been fulfilled in the past every right principle of interpretation must lead us to conclude. It was not fulfilled when Christ ascended from the Mount of Olives; much less when the Roman army besieged and destroyed Jerusalem, for then no deliverance was had, and no earthly blessing ensued. It evidently looks onward to the day when the Lord will once more interfere in behalf of His repentant and mourning people, and when His feet shall stand on Olivet, and when He will accomplish every promise He has made, and every word He has spoken touching Israel and the whole world.

MALACHI.

Nehemiah is the last of the Old Testament historians; Malachi the last of the prophets. He is called "the seal" of the prophets, because his book closes the Old Testament canon. His name is thought to be significant—a contraction of Malachijah. The Septuagint translates "by Malachi" (i, 1), "by the hand of his angel," as if it were an appellative and not a proper name. Some, accordingly, think that Malachi, "my messenger," is the official title of the prophet, and not his real name. Some of the fathers went so far as to assert that he was a supernatural being, an angel, for which of course there is no ground.

Malachi lived between B. C. 436 and 397; he prophesied probably B. C. 433-430. The first company of exiles returned to Judea, B. C. 536. The second, under the leadership of Ezra, took place fifty-seven years after the completion of the second temple, B. C. 458 (Ezra vii, 6, 7). About B. C. 444, Nehemiah went up to Jerusalem from the court of the Persian king, Artaxerxes Longimanus, and began his work of reformation, and after twelve years of arduous toil he returned to Babylon, and thence again to Judea. There are clear intimations in the prophecy of Malachi that he was engaged in a like work with Nehemiah. The same abuses, unhallowed alliances, and flagging zeal are encountered in the prophecy as in the history. What Haggai and Zechariah were to Zerubbabel and Joshua the high priest, Malachi was to the reformer Nehemiah. But it can scarcely be doubted that the evidences of decline and apostasy are much more visible in these later books than in the former. Priest and people alike are here turning away from God, and the prophet separates the remnant from the mass of the returned exiles, and addresses them, and holds out to them the hope of the speedy coming of the Deliverer, Messiah.

The contents of Malachi may be distributed thus:

1. Chaps. i-ii, 9. The sins of the priests sternly reproved.

2. Chap. ii, 10-17. Condemnation of marriage with heathen.

3. Chaps. iii, iv. Predictions of the appearing of Messiah's forerunner and the advent of Messiah Himself.

Interspersed among the denunciations and warnings against the wicked are found gracious promises and assurances addressed to the faithful few who still adhered to the name and worship of Jehovah; as the precious word in iii, 16-18, where the little company who fear the Lord and who speak often one to another, are assured that God will remember them, has written down in His book of remembrance their sayings and doings, and will one day own and reward them; as in iv, 2, where the sun of righteousness is promised to rise upon those who fear His name.

Chap. iii, 1, announces the coming of Jehovah's messenger and of Jehovah Himself. In Mark i, 2, according to the revised version, these words which are quoted from Malachi, as also words from Isa. xl, 3, are all ascribed to Isaiah the prophet. There is in reality no contradiction here; for the prediction of Isaiah is unquestionably the foundation of that in Malachi, and accordingly the inspired evangelist goes back to the fountain of the prophecy, viz.. Isaiah.

There is a striking contrast between the close of the Old and the New Testaments. The Old ends with the awful threat of the divine curse on the earth; the New, with the gracious words, "Even so, come, Lord Jesus. The grace of the Lord Jesus Christ be with the saints" (Wescott and Hort).

Thus closes the Old Testament canon. With hopes and promises of a better day and better things, the rising of the sun of righteousness, the book of remembrance, the appearing of Elijah to restore all things—with such splendid assurances it closes. It was in the night time of our race and of partial revelation that it closed; but a night thickly set with blazing stars and the roseate glimmer of the coming dawn. It closed with the sound of many voices along the shore, all uttering a cheerful and hopeful good night. The night passes round, and the shore of the New Testament becomes visible; evangelists and apostles cry, Hail to the morning. And their good morning is in blessed harmony with, and in full realization of, the cheerful and hopeful good night of the prophets from that other shore.

www.ingramcontent.com/pod-product-compliance
Lightning Source LLC
Chambersburg PA
CBHW031424230426
43668CB00007B/426